Wealth Creation

A new approach to rural development is emerging. Instead of being about attracting companies that might create jobs over which communities have no control, the emerging paradigm is about connecting the unique underutilized assets of place with market opportunity to grow assets that are owned and controlled by and for the benefit of low-wealth people and places. But asset development is about more than bricks and mortar or narrowly defined financial assets. There are many kinds of assets that communities require to thrive – such as social capital, natural capital, political capital, and intellectual capital. The emerging new approach to rural development is, then, about broadening the definition of "wealth," engaging underutilized assets, and a key third element: harnessing the power of the market – rather than relying solely on philanthropy and government. *Wealth Creation* provides a conceptual guide with practical examples for policymakers, practitioners of economic and community development, community organizers, environmentalists, funders, investors, and corporations seeking a values-based framework for identifying self-interests across sectors that can lead to opportunities to transform existing systems for the collective good.

Shanna E. Ratner is the founder and principal of Yellow Wood Associates, a firm specializing in rural economic and community development since 1985, and a member of the Aspen Institute's Learning Cluster on Rural Community Capacity Building. She was selected by the Ford Foundation to conceptualize and support implementation of a new approach to rural economic development that became WealthWorks. Ms. Ratner was trained in systems thinking as a member of the first class of Donella Meadows Fellows and has been a Mel King Fellow at MIT. She holds a MS degree in Agricultural Economics from Cornell University and a BA in Value Systems from New College in Sarasota, Florida, and lives in rural Vermont.

Wealth Creation
A New Framework for Rural Economic and Community Development

Shanna E. Ratner

NEW YORK AND LONDON

First published 2020
by Routledge
52 Vanderbilt Avenue, New York, NY 10017

and by Routledge
2 Park Square, Milton Park, Abingdon, Oxon OX14 4RN

Routledge is an imprint of the Taylor & Francis Group, an informa business

© 2020 Taylor & Francis

The right of Shanna E. Ratner to be identified as author of this work has been asserted by her in accordance with sections 77 and 78 of the Copyright, Designs and Patents Act 1988.

All rights reserved. No part of this book may be reprinted or reproduced or utilised in any form or by any electronic, mechanical, or other means, now known or hereafter invented, including photocopying and recording, or in any information storage or retrieval system, without permission in writing from the publishers.

Trademark notice: Product or corporate names may be trademarks or registered trademarks, and are used only for identification and explanation without intent to infringe.

Library of Congress Cataloging-in-Publication Data
Names: Ratner, Shanna E., author.
Title: Wealth creation : a new framework for rural economic and community development / Shanna Ratner.
Description: 1st Edition. | New York : Routledge, 2019. | Includes bibliographical references and index.
Identifiers: LCCN 2019034957 (print) | LCCN 2019034958 (ebook) | ISBN 9780367257392 (hardcover) | ISBN 9780367257422 (paperback) | ISBN 9780429289620 (ebook)
Subjects: LCSH: Rural development. | Investments. | Infrastructure (Economics) | Business planning. | Community development.
Classification: LCC HN49.C6 R38 2019 (print) | LCC HN49.C6 (ebook) | DDC 307.1/412–dc23
LC record available at https://lccn.loc.gov/2019034957
LC ebook record available at https://lccn.loc.gov/2019034958

ISBN: 978-0-367-25739-2 (hbk)
ISBN: 978-0-367-25742-2 (pbk)
ISBN: 978-0-429-28962-0 (ebk)

Typeset in Sabon
by Taylor & Francis Books

To Samuel Gaelen Ratner
And to all the smart and courageous wealth creation value chain coordinators and partners, past, present and future that venture into unchartered waters to try something different. May you continue to reshape our world for the better.

Contents

Preface		viii
Acknowledgments		x
1	Introduction	1
2	What is Wealth?	9
3	What is a Wealth Creation Value Chain?	28
4	How Do Ownership and Control Change the Game?	48
5	What Does It Mean to Be Demand-Driven?	64
6	How Do We Connect with Investors?	84
7	Where Does Technology Fit into Wealth Creation Value Chains?	102
8	Rethinking Measures of Economic Impact	113
9	The Critical Roles of Wealth Creation Value Chain Coordinators and Coaches	138
10	Taking a Wealth Creation Approach to Scale	150
	Index	159

Preface

What if we could harness the power of the market to create shared wealth and reduce external costs of development instead of enforcing inequality and exploiting individuals, communities, and natural and built resources? What would happen if we could re-invent capitalism so that the invisible hand becomes visible, self-interests are transparent, shared interests can emerge, and common interests can be served? Is it really possible to develop in ways that improve the quality of life for all people in present and future generations, or is this just empty rhetoric? Is robbing Peter to pay Paul inevitable in a market driven economy?

In 2008, the Ford Foundation began an experiment in defining and implementing a framework for economic development based on concepts of wealth creation. The experiment was focused in three of the poorest regions in rural America: Central Appalachia, the Deep South, and the Lower Rio Grande Valley. The first few years of the experiment were spent in research and defining the framework; the application of the framework on the ground began in 2010 in Central Appalachia and 2011 in the Deep South and the Lower Rio Grande Valley. Results of this experiment suggest that it is possible to re-invent the connection between producers and consumers in ways that change the nature of what we produce and how we produce it, reduce externalities, and benefit heretofore excluded or marginalized people and places.

Though the work supported by the Ford Foundation was focused on rural areas of the United States, the vision behind a wealth-based approach to economic development has always been one of integrating rural areas into larger regional economies and identifying the self-interests of urban areas in investing in rural economies to meet their own needs. The principles and practices of this approach are equally relevant in urban and rural settings in the United States as well as to development practitioners seeking a framework to improve market access and make multiple wealths stick in economically marginalized places in other countries, including developing countries. WealthWorks is an alternative economic development framework that has been tested and proven on the ground in the United States and shown to have applicability internationally.

This book is intended for policymakers, practitioners in economic and community development, teachers, students, financers, and funders looking for a way to make a difference at scale by changing whole systems. Scale is a fluid concept that looks different depending on context; however, it has certain characteristics that include moving beyond dependence on one or a handful of individuals who are champions of change to sustainable, market-driven solutions that are integrated into private, public, and nonprofit institutions as a new normal. This book will explain the theory behind the wealth creation approach to development and tell the stories of some of the early adopters that are using it to re-invent capitalism by connecting with markets in new ways that benefit those typically left out.

If you are looking for a framework that will help you articulate and actualize your drive to reshape our world toward a more sustainable future you have come to the right place. WealthWorks is more than a theory about the future of capitalism; it is a framework and set of practices that reshape the economy from the ground up and bring about many of the changes those of us who long for a more equitable and sustainable economy wish to see. We still have much to learn, but we will only learn by rolling up our sleeves and creating the new economy as we go.

On a personal note, I am now semi-retired and, like so many other aging baby boomers, I want to offer what I have experienced for the benefit of those coming up behind me and the ones coming up behind them. WealthWorks is not a silver bullet, but is a good place to begin to understand the possibilities for reconfiguring the systems that have led to exploitation into systems that lead to shared prosperity and sustainable livelihoods. If you are challenged, motivated, or moved by this work and have skills or connections that would help engage a wider audience, please feel free to reach out to me at wealthcreationframework@gmail.com. Perhaps together we can help move these ideas and related practices to scale and start to undo the systems of exploitation we have come to rely on that are fundamentally unsustainable.

Acknowledgments

My thanks go out to all the community and economic development practitioners willing to take risks to try something as different as the wealth creation approach to economic development. Their efforts continue to prove, at least to my satisfaction, that with clear intent and sufficient perseverance we can satisfy self-interests while changing systems to achieve more inclusive and sustainable results. It isn't easy, but it is possible.

I would especially like to thank the first cohort of wealth creation value chain coordinators including Jim King, Justin Maxson, Michelle Decker, and all the other members of the Central Appalachian Network, and the second cohort including John Littles, Cheryl Petersen, Ines Polonius, Jessica Norwood, Amadou Diop, John Squires, Marilyn Hoke, Nick Mitchell-Bennett. Thank you for everything you do. I would especially like to thank Deborah Markley for her help in shaping and framing this work in its early days and to Janet Topolsky and her staff in the Community Strategies Group at the Aspen Institute for their work and for continuing to maintain the WealthWorks website at www.wealthworks.org. Thanks also to the many other wealth creation value chain coordinators, past, present, and future; my hat's off to you. To the many others too numerous to list individually that have been and continue to be involved in supporting a wealth creation approach to development in all its dimensions, I am grateful to each and every one of you; even those with whom I did not always see eye to eye. I received encouragement to write this book from participants in the WealthWorks Training for Coordinators and Coaches, several of whom continue to allow me to coach them. Thank you for that. I would especially like to thank Melissa Levy and Barbara Wyckoff for their ongoing contributions to this work and their personal support.

I would also like to acknowledge Wayne Fawbush, former Program Officer of The Ford Foundation who selected me as the "thought leader" for an initiative that began as Wealth Creation in Rural Communities and later became WealthWorks. Though my work on a wealth creation approach to economic development began before my involvement with the Ford Foundation, without the opportunity thus afforded me to gain a bird's eye view of the development and implementation of this work over an eight year period, this book would not have been possible. I received great support during the implementation of WealthWorks from the staff at Yellow Wood Associates including Ginger Weil, Melissa Levy, Jacqueline LaBlanc, and Samantha Dunn.

WealthWorks is continuing through the good work of regional hubs, including Rural Development Initiatives in Oregon, Community Roots in Vermont, Communities Unlimited in Arkansas, and the Region Five Development Commission in Minnesota, with the support of the National Association of Development Organizations and The Aspen Institute Community Strategies Group, among others. May you all continue to flourish and share what you are learning.

Many thanks as well to Mark Lapping and Elaine McCrate for reviewing and commenting on the entire manuscript in draft form, and to Jim King, Michelle Decker, Ines Polonius, Tami Hornbeck, Cheryl Petersen, John Littles, Ryan Coffey Hoag, Justin Maxson, Heidi Khokar, Amy Hause, Michael Held, Sulynn Creswell, and Jessica Norwood for reviewing and commenting on sections of the manuscript pertaining to their work. All opinions expressed are mine alone, except where otherwise noted. I take full responsibility for any errors of fact or interpretation.

1 Introduction

Epigraph

Pete Kelly, former economic developer for the City of Ansonia, wrote:

> I work as the economic development director for a small community in south central Connecticut. The community, in my opinion, suffers from an identity crisis: it was once a thriving mill town, part of the nation's industrial heartland many years ago, and is looking to reclaim this vitality through reconstituting industry or serving as a bedroom community to the Gold Coast, which has reached a critical mass of sorts. Unfortunately, in my estimation neither of these approaches holds much potential for revitalizing the community at the current time. A great deal of foundation building, e.g., brownfield remediation and elimination of slum and blight, would need to occur before Ansonia could effectively pursue these strategies. Ansonia can improve its condition, but likely not through the conventional (i.e., chasing smokestacks) methods of economic development. The community has not made a conscious effort to integrate as part of a broader regional economy, and so has many of the characteristics of an isolated rural community, despite being only 20–30 minutes from Bridgeport, the state's largest city, or New Haven, the state's most successful example of economic development based on "Eds and Meds." So I'm struggling mightily to determine how best to approach my job as economic development director and what model(s) to apply.

We hope this book will begin to provide that alternative model by introducing a way of thinking about community and economic development that is fundamentally different from the conventional wisdom.

Building a Bridge between Community Development and Economic Development

The wealth creation approach provides a bridge between community development, which is generally focused on single communities and their issues

2 Introduction

and emphasizes community organizing, vision and "voice," and economic development, which has become too narrowly focused on "creating" jobs, usually by offering tax breaks and other incentives to attract businesses from one location to another.

The focus on business attraction is actually a symptom of the way we have come to think about development. In America, development equals jobs. It is a lot easier to "create" jobs by attracting a large company that brings jobs with it than by nurturing the underlying assets required to sustain a vibrant local economy. Of course, the jobs that come with attraction are not really "created;" they simply leave one place and arrive at another. The net job change from domestic relocation is negligible. Nationally, the range of net job change from gains and losses due to business relocation from 1999 to 2008 was +3% to −1.4%. For 38 states, the net change was less than plus or minus 1%. [1]

Even so, the incentive system we have created is such that an economic developer who can claim to have "created" a lot of jobs at one time through business attraction and re-location is rewarded, regardless of the cost associated with attracting them. The tools used to attract businesses generally amount to some combination of tax, wage, or real estate subsidy, and/or regulatory relief that generates externalities. Yet, the data suggests there is no correlation between wages and domestic job relocation.[2] Nor is there a correlation between state taxes and decisions to relocate overseas. States without income taxes were just as likely to lose jobs overseas between 1994 and 2008 as those with income taxes.[3] Businesses that relocate simply to take advantage of subsidies often leave once those subsidies have run out.

By focusing on development as jobs many important societal considerations are overlooked. Little or no attention is paid to who gets those jobs, what the working conditions and wages are, and whether or not the business offering the jobs is likely to increase the failure rates of locally-owned businesses or reduce locally driven entrepreneurial activity. One negative consequence of jobs that pay unliveable wages is an increase in worker dependency on public assistance for food, shelter, transportation, health care, and more. Other potential negative impacts that are often overlooked might include, but are not necessarily limited to, a rise in crime rates during construction or operation, increases in property values that push out longtime residents including business owners, increased pollution and natural resource degradation, increased traffic congestion and reduced traffic safety, and loss of neighborhood cohesion. Similarly, little or no attention is given to how long the jobs last, and whether the people who get the jobs are able to save and invest enough to make themselves more secure over the long term.

The narrow belief that development equals jobs has not served us well. The percentage of the US working-age population, 16 and over, that is in the labor force was just 63% as of January 1, 2014, and is virutally unchanged in 2019 at the height of an economic expansion. The labor force is the actual number of people available for work. The percentage of the US working-age population that was actually employed was even lower—only 58.8% (down from nearly 65% in 2000) and only around 60% in January, 2019.[4] Not only are we not providing

Introduction 3

employment for those in the labor force, but more and more of the population is being excluded from the mainstream economy. The result is increasing inequality of income and financial wealth.

As Angela Glover Blackwell, founder and president of PolicyLink, a national research and action institute that works to develop and implement policies at the local, state, and federal level to achieve economic and social equity says, "Having a job doesn't get you out of poverty or keep you out of poverty."

Income is the flow of dollars earned over a period of time. Wealth is the stock of assets owned and controlled by households. Income may be invested in assets that become wealth, such as education, health care, social activities that build trusted networks, and financial savings. Wealth may generate income and increase a family's capacity to survive economic shocks such as sudden illness or unemployment.

According to the Pew Research Center, income inequality has been increasing steadily since the 1970s and has now reached levels not seen since 1928 when the top 1% of families received 23.9% of all income and the bottom 90% received 50.7%. Income is defined as pre-tax cash market income and does not include government subsidies. As of the end of 2012, the top 1% received nearly 22.5% (during a period of economic recession) and the bottom 90% fell below 50% for the first time ever.[5] Interestingly, there are almost as many households in the top 1% in the poorest places in rural America as in the highest amenity rural communities.[6]

Defining wealth as "marketable wealth (or net worth), equal to the current value of all marketable or fungible assets less the current value of debts," Edward Wolff finds that the top 1% saw their average wealth (in 2007 dollars) rise by over $9 million or by 103% between 1983 and 2007. The remaining part of the top quintile experienced increases from 81% to 142% and the fourth quintile by 71%. While the middle quintile gained 50%, the poorest 40% lost 63%! By 2007, their average wealth had fallen to $2,200.[7]

The problem of inequality is not getting better; it is getting worse. In fact, it is so scary to a number of Silicon Valley tycoons that they are becoming survivalists, investing in their own security rather than the institutions that require rebuilding to serve us all.[8]

In contrast to trickle-down theory, recent research has discovered that, when we look at economic growth across countries over time, "equality appears to be an important ingredient in promoting and sustaining growth."[9] So, how do we begin to reverse course? What if the equation were broadened from development equals jobs to development equals sustainable livelihoods and widely shared prosperity for current and future generations? How can we get from here to there?

One place to begin is by recognizing the underlying causes of poverty. The root of poverty is isolation. In some regions, like the American South, that isolation is chronic and interwoven with the legacy and continuation of racism; in others, like the Rust Belt, regions that were once productive contributors to the larger economy became isolated as the market for what they had to offer changed and they failed to adjust. There are many

4 *Introduction*

dimensions to the isolation that results in poverty, including isolation from economic opportunity, from new ways of thinking, from access to resources to make a change, from the corridors of power, from people whose life experiences are different than one's own.[10]

A number of forces have come together that exacerbate this isolation, including policies like redlining that forced poorer minority families into certain neighborhoods that were cut off from surrounding, more prosperous areas by lack of transportation and other services; underinvestment in education that allowed the quality of teaching and learning to deteriorate unevenly across the country; underinvestment in health care, wellness, and prevention nationwide; underinvestment in physical infrastructure including broadband, and more.

The liberal "solution," which has been to throw money into programs targeted at poor people (defined by income level) has not worked. One reason for this is that people fundamentally do not want to be treated as "needy." We do not want to be the objects of charity. It makes us feel less than. It also contributes to social and economic isolation. In order to feel better, recipients of what amounts to societal charity begin to see this as an entitlement. Seeing it as an entitlement makes it feel more acceptable. If they are entitled, then everyone is entitled and there is no need to feel less than. Now we have come to a point where many blame the victims (those who feel entitled) for their sense of entitlement, failing to recognize that the systems we have developed through the patterns of our disinvestments have left too many with no other alternative. It is more and more difficult for people born into circumstances of limited resources to become productive contributors to society. *Transformation can come from connecting people and places that have been economically marginalized with a larger economy by building the relationships that allow larger economic forces to combine with local ownership in ways that produce lasting and profound change.* This is the goal of WealthWorks—to rebuild our economic system one value chain at a time to include economically marginalized people and places as productive contributors to our economy and society.

This requires a radically different approach to "job creation" from the traditional one in which economic developers attempt to use local incentives to attract new businesses into what are essentially isolated and economically depressed areas. Incentives, such as tax breaks and related concessions, are weak ties that decline and expire over time. They are offered in return for economic performance (i.e. job creation) that often fails to materialize and is expensive and difficult for any locality to enforce, especially after the incentives have been used. What happens if, instead of asking how we can pull economic activity into a local vortex, we turn that paradigm on its head and ask how the assets of a local place can contribute to a larger economy? How does a market-based approach to development provide place-based practitioners with the perspectives they need to transform entire systems for the benefit of poor people and places?

The WealthWorks approach recognizes that jobs are not "created" in a vacuum. Jobs result from investments in innovation, infrastructure, skills, human and environmental health, and the capacity to change regulations and resource allocation to respond to a changing world. Jobs result from new relationships that create new economic opportunities. WealthWorks aims for inclusive, sustainable development based on the following assumptions:

- Wealth, not just income, is the foundation of prosperity.
- Economically marginalized places and people will stay poor unless they are connected to larger economies.
- Economically marginalized people and places have assets, which, if properly developed, can contribute to larger regional economies.
- The economy does better as a whole when more of us are doing better.

We assume that the root cause of poverty is isolation from all or many of the forms of wealth required to be able to contribute productively to the mainstream economy. As Angela Glover Blackwell, founder and president of PolicyLink, a national research and action institute that works collaboratively to develop and implement local, state, and federal policies to achieve economic and social equity, says:

> If we solve problems for the most vulnerable, if we solve problems of poverty, we solve problems for everybody ... We need to help people be able to contribute. What sense does it make if we lock people out of the resources they need to be able to contribute? [11]

Lack of income is a consequence, not a cause, of poverty. If we fail to invest in the forms of wealth required to enable productive contributions to the mainstream economy, no amount of subsidy or income redistribution will, in and of itself, reduce poverty in the long run. Similarly, "jobs" are not the answer without the targeted investments required to connect jobs and workers and ensure that production processes themselves are life-affirming. We offer the concept of a wealth creation value chain as one mechanism to connect underutilized resources to the mainstream economy for the benefit of both.

The difference between a job creation approach and a wealth creation approach is evident in the experience of the Deep South Community Agriculture Network (DSCAN). One of the many underutilized resources in the Deep South is its unemployed and underemployed youth. A typical approach to this issue is to establish training and employment opportunities that depend on government grants or private subsidies and are all too often not tied to real market opportunities.

Using the wealth creation framework, the Deep South Community Agriculture Network identified youth as one of, but not the only, significant underutilized resource in the region. Another significant underutilized resource was minority-owned agriculture land lying fallow. Most significantly, the

6   Introduction

farmers who owned the land lacked strong connections with potential demand partners that would find value in what they could be producing. McIntosh SEED, facilitators of DSCAN, helped its members research the demand for products they could grow, not by conducting surveys or researching secondary data on market trends, but by reaching out and talking with specific buyers and learning what products they were looking for and why.

Concrete and personal connections with demand began to bring the land back into production and jobs for youth emerged where there had been none. Once market-driven opportunities were identified, DSCAN was able to help farmers hire young people to bring more acres into production. Youth earned income while receiving training in agricultural production and leadership. These jobs are based on market-driven demand; not on subsidies.[12] As the capacity of DSCAN's farmer members to produce in accordance with market requirements grows, sustainable employment opportunities will follow. Entrepreneurial opportunities will also open up for youth and others that wish to become producers, processors, distributors, chefs, nutritionists, etc. in response to growing demand for regional food. Without a connection to demand, any jobs created through subsidies are vulnerable to fluctuations in funding. With a market orientation, new opportunities are continuously emerging along with the information required to adapt in a timely way to changes in market conditions.

The equation development equals jobs represents a linear way of thinking that assumes that the world proceeds in a sequential manner, the shortest distance between two points is a straight line, and a one-dimensional outcome—jobs—solves the equation. The example above demonstrates what can happen when we broaden our thinking to consider whole systems and look for complex patterns that are not linear. This is what happens when our thinking is intentionally inclusive of people and places that have been economically marginalized.

The wealth creation approach is a framework; it is not a cookie cutter. It will look different in different places. And, as the example above suggests, it is not entirely proven. However, the evidence accumulated over the last ten years spent developing, introducing, and testing this framework in Central Appalachia, the Lower Rio Grande Valley, and the Deep South, which are among the poorest parts of rural America, strongly suggests that the wealth creation framework and the approach to development that stems from it can change systems and create new opportunities for wealth building, even in the places that and with the people who have been most economically marginalized for long periods of time.

The wealth creation framework is built around a set of key assumptions and guiding principles.

Guiding Principles for a Wealth Creation Approach to Economic Development

1   **Demand-oriented. Leads with demand** and incorporates the power of market relationships for social change.

2 Inclusive. Intentionally connects people who and places that have been economically marginalized with mainstream economic opportunity.
3 Multi-solving.[13]Designs for the present and the future by building and maintaining multiple forms of wealth while doing no harm.
4 Place-based. Ties regional wealth to place through place-based ownership and control.
5 Focuses on systems change. Achieves scale through retooling systems of consumption, production, investment, regulation, and incentives using innovative and responsive approaches and technologies to achieve scale.
6 Iterative and adaptable. Is strategically flexible in application, adapts to unique place-based opportunities, and requires measurement to support continuous learning and ongoing adaptation.

The purpose of these principles is to guide us toward connecting community assets to market opportunities for sustainable livelihoods. The concept of sustainable livelihoods is broader than having a job or earning income. Having sustainable livelihoods means that individuals, households, and communities can contribute formally and informally to the world around them and receive equitable benefits in return and, through engagement, can build the assets that allow them to rebound from setbacks in everyday life and respond to ever-changing market conditions. The path to sustainable livelihoods is through ownership, control and/or influence over assets, and demand-oriented, mutually beneficial relationships with other producers and the market. Assets include not only financial assets but the skills acquired through education and experience, the relationships and trust that allow problems to be solved by bringing resources together from many different parties, and the unique assets of place such as the natural and built environment. In our evolving economy, where personal data is increasingly used as an asset, we have an opportunity to rethink systems of ownership and control of personal and business data as well.[14]

Wealth creation is neither liberal nor conservative. It is based on respect for all people regardless of their circumstances and the belief that it is only through combining the talents and resources of all sectors—private, public, and non-profit—that we will be successful in creating an inclusive and sustainable economy. By working from the ground up with an eye toward the larger system we can learn what has to change from the top down to support shared prosperity.

We will examine each of these principles in detail in the following chapters and show how a wealth-based approach to development can create new opportunities for economic transformation that forms the basis for a truly sustainable economy, while reversing the dangerous trend toward increased economic inequality.

Notes

1 Hoffer, D. (2012) Internal Contracted Research Report prepared for Yellow Wood Associates, Inc. Data from National Establishment Time Series (NETS).

8 *Introduction*

2 Ibid. Data from Bureau of Labor Statistics, Occupational Employment Survey and NETS, comparing median annual wage, 2010 by state with net domestic job relocation 1994–2008.

3 Ibid. Data from US Department of Labor, Employment and Trade Administration, Trade Adjustment Assistance Act.

4 Bureau of Labor Statistics. (2019). Labor Force Statistics from the Current Population Survey [Time series]. Retrieved from https://data.bls.gov/timeseries/LNS12300000

5 Desilver, D. (2013, December 5). U.S. Income Inequality, on Rise for Decades, is Now Highest Since 1928. Retrieved from: http://www.pewresearch.org/fact-tank/2013/12/05/u-s-income-inequality-on-rise-for-decades-is-now-highest-since-1928/

6 Hamilton, L. C., Hamilton, L. R., Duncan, C. M., and Colocousis, C. R. (2008). Place Matters Challenges and Opportunities in Four Rural Americas. University of New Hampshire. Retrieved from: https://scholars.unh.edu/cgi/viewcontent.cgi?referer=&httpsredir=1&article=1040&context=carsey

7 Wolff, E. N. (2010). *Recent Trends in Household Wealth in the United States: Rising Debt and the Middle-Class Squeeze—an Update to 2007* (Working Paper No. 589). Levy Economics Institute. Retrieved from: http://www.levyinstitute.org/pubs/wp_589.pdf

8 Why Some Silicon Valley Tech Executives are Bunkering Down for Doomsday (2017, January 25). Retrieved from http://www.npr.org/2017/01/25/511507434/why-some-silicon-valley-tech-executives-are-bunkering-down-for-doomsday

9 Berg, A. G. and Ostry, J. D. (2011). Equality and efficiency. *Finance & Development*, 48(3). Retrieved from: http://www.imf.org/external/pubs/ft/fandd/2011/09/berg.htm; Berg, A. G. and Ostry, J. D. (2011). *Inequality and Unsustainable Growth: Two Sides of the Same Coin?* (SDN/11/08). International Monetary Fund. Retrieved from: http://www.imf.org/external/pubs/ft/sdn/2011/sdn1108.pdf

10 As one reviewer pointed out, the very rich are also among the most isolated in our society and this framework offers them opportunities to connect beyond their own siloes as well.

11 Blackwell, A. G. (2016). The Role of Public Policy in Alleviating Poverty (audio podcast, May 27). Retrieved from: http://ssir.org/podcasts/entry/the_role_of_public_policy_in_alleviating_poverty?utm_source=Enews&utm_medium=Email&utm_campaign=SSIR_Now&utm_content=Title

12 Though some philanthropic money has been raised to support youth employment with DSCAN farmers in the proof-of-concept phase, as the scale of production grows such subsidies should no longer be necessary.

13 I am indebted to Beth Sawin, Co-Director of Climate Interactive for the term "multi-solving."

14 *The World's Most Valuable Resource is no Longer Oil, but Data* (2017). *The Economist*, May 6. Retrieved from: http://www.economist.com/news/leaders/21721656-data-economy-demands-new-approach-antitrust-rules-worlds-most-valuable-resource

2   What is Wealth?

When we hear the world "wealth" in the United States, most of us think of financial assets. But wealth is a lot more than financial assets, and financial assets alone cannot sustain us. After all, money isn't tasty or nutritious and research has established that money alone can't make you happy. Financial assets become productive when they are invested in other forms of wealth that together create resilient households and communities and a truly sustainable economy with widely shared benefits.

If money alone isn't the answer, what is? What are the other forms of wealth that create the foundation for a truly sustainable economy? We include *eight forms of wealth* in the WealthWorks framework. They are only "wealth" to the extent that they are fully productive and can contribute to meeting current needs while remaining capable of meeting future needs as well. If they are degraded and not fully functional and they require investment to restore functionality, they are not "wealth," they either are or are on the way to becoming liabilities.

The concepts behind these forms of wealth are not original to WealthWorks; in fact each form of wealth has its own origin story briefly described below. Economists have been attempting to redefine wealth as more than financial capital since at least the turn of the 21st century, using terms like "inclusive wealth,"[1] "genuine wealth,"[2] and "intangible capital".[3] The community capitals framework, familiar to many community developers, is comprised of seven forms of capital and was first introduced by Cornelia and Jan Flora in 2004 as a means to focus on rural community assets rather than deficits.[4] The Floras' work has been instrumental in taking these concepts beyond academia and into communities. In general, there is no widely shared cross-disciplinary agreement on the precise definitions of many non-financial forms of wealth. What follows are the definitions we found most workable within the WealthWorks framework.

Eight Forms of Wealth

Intellectual capital is the collective stock of creativity and inventiveness that allows us to see and understand the world in new ways and to imagine new possibilities. We invest in intellectual capital when we invest in research and development, the arts, and any creative endeavor. Individuals may be

10 *What is Wealth?*

creative; it is the sharing of ideas and inventiveness that creates community wealth. Investments in intellectual capital can provide solutions to pressing problems while simultaneously creating new opportunities and challenges and the means to address them. As the challenges of climate change and environmental degradation collide with income and wealth inequality and the restructuring of livelihood opportunities, we need to foster creative solutions that allow us to solve multiple problems with the same solutions instead of creating new problems with every action we take. At a minimum, we need improve our ability for early detection of deleterious unanticipated consequences. According to William J. Hudson, the term "intellectual capital" was first proposed by John Kenneth Galbraith in 1969.[5]

Individual capital is the stock of skills and mental and physical health of individuals. Without skills and the requisite health to apply them, people cannot be productive contributors to our economy. Right now, the gap between skills needed and skills available to fulfill market demand is quite high. [6] In addition, as a society, we are bearing a substantial economic and social burden related to poor health,[7] some of which is directly tied to our degraded environment.[8] We have created a vicious cycle in which some of our "productive" activities actually degrade our health. This suggests that we need to change *the way we produce* if we are serious about having a truly sustainable economy. The concept of human capital, which often includes elements of individual capital, has been traced back to at least the 17th century.[9] We chose the term "individual capital" to emphasize the need for investment in the health and skills development of individuals so that they can, in turn be productive contributors to the economy.

Social capital is the stock of trust, relationships, and networks that support civil society. There are two forms of social capital: bridging and bonding. Investments in bridging social capital are those that lead to unprecedented conversations, shared experiences, and connections between otherwise unconnected individuals and groups. For example, organizations like Better Angels are working to bridge the political divide by bringing "Reds" (people who lean conservative in their political views) together with "Blues" (people who lean liberal in their political views) face to face in facilitated civil dialogue.[10]

Investments in bonding social capital are those that strengthen relationships within groups. For example, organizing a town-wide festival could be seen as an investment in bonding social capital for town residents. It is a place where residents can come together and get to know each other in new ways. Today's concern about living in "bubbles" suggests that we spend more time developing bonding social capital than we do with bridging social capital. This work is an invitation to move beyond our comfort zones and bring curiosity to bear in unfamiliar circumstances.

Earnings from investment in social capital include improved health outcomes, educational outcomes, and reduced time and energy spent on things like finding employment and social support, among others.[11] The lack of social capital creates

What is Wealth? 11

real barriers to sustainable livelihoods. For example, when the majority of parents with children in Head Start do not know anyone with a job, as was the case in South Wood County in Central Wisconsin in 2010, how much more difficult is it for them to become productive contributors? This illustration from Wisconsin is, unfortunately, hardly unique. Many studies trace the first use of the term "social capital" to a 1916 academic study by Lyda Judson Hanifan, a school supervisor concerned with the deterioration of civic culture in rural West Virginia. Jane Jacobs' work also emphasized social capital in her study of the decline of American cities in 1961.[12] Robert Putnam re-popularized the concept in his book *Bowling Alone*, published in 2000.

Investing in these three forms of wealth—**intellectual, individual, and social capital**—has proven to be the starting point for wealth creation in the poorest areas of rural America. For example, before wealth could be created in relation to residential energy efficiency retrofits for low-income households in Kentucky, utilities companies had to be introduced to a new way of thinking called on-bill financing that allows utility customers to pay for retrofits out of savings accrued over time, rather than requiring a capital investment up front. Intellectual capital in the form of on-bill financing was introduced by the Mountain Association for Community Economic Development (MACED), the WealthWorks value chain coordinator organization, after research to identify new ways of achieving energy efficiency for low-income homeowners. MACED is a 42-year-old nonprofit based in Berea, Kentucky, that works with businesses and communities and was one of the first to implement the WealthWorks framework on the ground. Once MACED introduced intellectual capital to utility companies and others, the relationships (social capital) and skills (individual capital) to implement the value chain had to be developed. Prior to WealthWorks, MACED had only an arm's-length adversarial relationship with the utility companies. Through their work together, sufficient social capital has been built to impact policy decisions of the Kentucky Public Service Commission. Social capital has laid the foundation for political capital.

Political capital is the stock of connections, power, and voice that result in influence over resource allocation decisions of any group or organization whether in the public, private, or nonprofit sectors. Investments in political capital begin with investments in social capital. Coalitions are built through relationships. Within the context of WealthWorks, political capital is targeted to those decisions that affect the functioning of WealthWorks value chains (see Chapter 3). For example, forest certification is expensive for small and minority forestland owners in the South and the lack of certification prevents entry into markets that would contribute to sustainable livelihoods. The National Wildlife Federation, working as a WealthWorks coordinator, was able to use its relationships with the Natural Resources Conservation Service (NRCS) and forest landowners to convince NRCS to provide the resources required to get basic management plans written for underserved forest landowners through its Cooperative Conservation Partnership Initiative program. This is an essential first step without which small and

12 *What is Wealth?*

minority forestland owners would not be able to participate in group certification that opens up new market opportunities. Forest certification requires improved forest management practices that increase forest health, and grow the stock of natural capital. The concept of "political capital" was first introduced by Edward C. Banfield, an American political scientist, in 1961.[13] Pierre Bourdieu elaborated on the concepts of both political and social capital in 1991.[14]

Natural capital is the stock of all renewable and non-renewable natural resources, and ecosystem services provided by those resources. When we use non-renewable resources wisely and set aside profits from their use for investments in other forms of wealth, we are transforming the stock of natural capital into stocks of other forms of wealth. However, when we exploit natural capital in ways that deplete or degrade it (or deplete or degrade other types of capital such as human health), we are not creating wealth; we are creating liabilities for ourselves and for future generations. We invest in natural capital whenever we increase the health and function-ing of the ecosystem. For example, when we restore wetlands or mines or brownfields, we are investing in natural capital. When we protect wilderness areas in an effort to sustain healthy, functioning ecosystems or when we remove toxins from the environment, we are investing in natural capital. The first use of the term "natural capital" is credited to E. F. Schumacher in his book *Small is Beautiful*, published in 1973.[15]

Built capital is the stock of physical infrastructure, including everything from buildings, roads, and bridges, to computers, greenhouses, and laboratory equip-ment. The vast majority of our built capital, however, undermines other forms of wealth because it was built in periods with different standards that allowed the use of toxic materials, poor placement in flood zones and other sensitive areas, energy inefficiency, lack of safe public spaces, and shoddy construction that leads to degradation of natural, social, intellectual, and/or individual capital.

Sometimes our efforts to improve built capital have significant negative con-sequences. For example, advocates for the poor hoped that the federal urban renewal program created by Title 1 of the Housing Act of 1949 and implemented over the next two decades would replace subpar housing in urban centers with decent affordable housing. However competing interests often resulted in the destruction of poor neighborhoods, displacement of poor people, and the intro-duction of commercial interests that did not serve poor residents but instead changed the character and rent structure of neighborhoods. At the same time, federally subsidized public housing, built to accommodate those displaced from "renewed" neighborhoods, had the effect of concentrating poverty in high rise buildings and segregating residential from commercial activity.

Built capital can be a contributor to other forms of wealth through, for example, design and construction that produces zero emissions, cleanses stormwater, reduces the need for artificial lighting, conserves/recycles water, includes sites that contribute to social capital through attention to safe public spaces, or produces renewable energy. A wealth creation approach can help counter our tendency to consider built capital as an end in itself without taking into account it impacts on all the other forms of wealth.

The term "physical capital" has long been used to refer to tangible assets created by humans and used in production, but may also be used to refer to natural capital. We chose the term "built capital" to clearly differentiate between assets created by humans and our natural endowment of resources and ecosystem services.

Cultural capital is the stock of practices that reflect values and identity rooted in place, class, and/or ethnicity.[16] Cultural capital influences the ways in which individuals and groups define and access other forms of capital. Cultural capital includes the dynamics of who we know and feel comfortable with, what heritages are valued, collaboration across races, ethnicities, and generations, etc. Investments in cultural capital create or sustain the values, traditions, beliefs, and/or language that become the currency to leverage other types of capital. Investments in cultural capital could include support for venues to showcase cultural achievements, programs to preserve and pass on cultural knowledge and skills, and support for cultural transformations, among other things. "Income" from investments in cultural capital may include increased "buy in" to institutional rules and shared norms of behavior, strengthened social capital and increased access to other capitals through increased visibility and appreciation of cultural attributes and through cultural transformation, e.g. acquisition of language skills.

Culture is expressed through the values, behaviors, and ownership patterns associated with the other seven forms of wealth. Where specific aspects of culture are critical to wealth creation, they can be defined and measured in relation to other aspects of wealth. For example, if a language or a craft is a critical form of wealth for a community, it can be defined and measured as a form of individual, intellectual and/or social capital. If shared savings is an existing or desired cultural norm, it can be measured as part of financial capital. In a context where cultural capital is considered distinct enough from the other forms of capital to be measurable, it could certainly be added. The concept of "cultural capital" was first introduced by Pierre Bourdieu and Jean-Claude Passeron in 1973 in *Cultural Reproduction and Social Reproduction.* [17] They defined cultural capital from the perspective of individuals; we define it as the social context within which individuals and groups develop and value knowledge, behavior, competencies, status, and the other forms of wealth.

Financial capital is the stock of financial or near financial assets that are available to invest in other forms of wealth. Some financial wealth is controlled by individuals and corporations who may see their own self-interest in investing in collective wellbeing, both in the way they do business and through charitable contributions. Bill Gates, for example, has famously used much of his accumulated wealth to address global concerns. However our country, states, cities, and towns also have financial assets derived from tax dollars.

14   *What is Wealth?*

These are our collective financial assets that can be used to directly improve our collective wellbeing rather than simply to subsidize private sector activity.

Income is not a stock and does not, by itself, constitute financial capital or wealth. Financial capital derives from saving. There are plenty of examples of individuals and households with substantial incomes and no savings. A stock of savings can generate additional income that can be consumed or reinvested to grow the stock. In the wealth creation framework, we emphasize savings, not debt, as financial capital, while recognizing that productive debt can be an effective tool for wealth creation.

Part of the problem we have in our economy today has to do with the increasing inequality of distribution of financial wealth, but even more significant is the failure to reinvest the financial wealth we have into other forms of wealth. Cash stockpiles among non-financial US corporations held abroad amounted to $2.4 trillion at the end of 2016, up from $1.2 trillion in 2009.[18] This is a giant sucking sound that has contributed to wealth inequality and lack of capacity for reinvestment in basic goods and services in the United States. These stockpiles of cash have accumulated due to increases in profitability at the expense of consumers and workers. Real wages, meaning the actual purchasing power of wages once inflation is factored out, have remained virtually constant since 1960 for private-sector employees who are not managers.[19]

According to *The Economist*, hardly a radical publication,

> Profits have risen in most rich countries over the past ten years but the increase has been biggest for American firms. Coupled with an increasing concentration of ownership, this means the fruits of economic growth are being hoarded. This is probably part of the reason that two-thirds of Americans, including a majority of Republicans, have come to believe that the economy "unfairly favours powerful interests", according to polling by Pew, a research outfit.[20]

The money stockpiled by US corporations is conservatively invested to maintain its value, but it is not being invested strategically in other forms of wealth that would contribute to a sustainable economy and reduced inequality in the United States. If it were, we would see more private investment in new systems of production that reduce and reuse waste and eliminate toxins and more investment in research and development, energy efficiency, education, childcare, training, health, infrastructure, natural resource protection and restoration, and more.

The problem is replicated at the local level. Interviews with wealthy individuals in West Virginia conducted to assess the feasibility of creating a locally funded angel investor network found that those with wealth were uncomfortable investing locally because, among other things, the emerging opportunities were in sectors, like high technology, that were different from those, like retail stores or real estate, in which they made their fortunes.

What is Wealth? 15

Groups like Slow Money are in the very early stages of creating pathways to connect some local investors with local place-based investment opportunities. In addition, the advent of crowdfunding is allowing individuals to invest in businesses and projects all over the world. Some states, like Vermont, have taken steps to make it easier for state residents to invest in in-state businesses[21]. But, by and large, the infrastructure to create personal connections between people with the means to invest and viable investment opportunities in their towns and regions remains weak.

Rates of public investment have also declined significantly since 1980.[22] The gap between what we are investing in the foundations of our economy and what we need to be investing for sustainable livelihoods is large and growing. For example, the estimated needs beyond current spending for investment in transportation infrastructure alone (roads, bridges rail, aviation, mass transit, inland waterways) is \$26.4 billion.[23]

As a result of the lack of both public and private reinvestment in all the forms of wealth critical to a resilient and sustainable civilization, we have crumbling infrastructure, millions of unemployed and seemingly unemployable, a nationwide epidemic of chronic disease, obesity, and addiction, environmental degradation, and a dysfunctional political system that is no longer able to even debate matters of public good in good faith. These are some of the depreciated capitals we have to work with to build the economy of the future. Before we can expect to turn things around, we will need to invest in bringing the many depreciated and underutilized forms of capital we have back into productive use; in other words we need to build our stocks of wealth so they can produce the flows of "income" we need to sustain ourselves collectively and individually.

Stocks versus Flows

You will notice that we have defined each type of wealth as a stock, not a flow. What is the difference between a stock and a flow?

A stock is a supply of something that is available at any given point in time. A flow is the movement of resources into and out of stocks over time. In a conventional approach to economic development we focus on flows, not stocks. For example, development professionals are encouraged to count the number of jobs they "create" but not the number of jobs available in a given locality at a specific point in time. Jobs could be "created" at, for example, the rate of 1 new job per day, but if jobs are being lost at the rate of 5 jobs per day, the stock of jobs will still go down. Failing to account for both the quantity and quality of our stocks gives a false reading of the health, or lack thereof, of our economy. Further, without measuring the stock of jobs, there is no way to know whether (and the ways in which) the stock is sufficient to meet the needs of residents of a given locality. Critical information such as the types of jobs that are being created and the types of jobs that are being lost is missing. The question of what it would take to retrain job losers for emerging opportunities is impossible to answer without this information.

16 *What is Wealth?*

Without information about what is happening to the overall stock of jobs, it becomes impossible to manage resources to reach the goal where everyone who wants a job has one. [24]

All forms of wealth are stocks but not all stocks are forms of wealth. Note that "jobs" is not a form of wealth; jobs come about as a result of investments in multiple forms of wealth. The tunnel vision of conventional economic developers is only the tip of the iceberg. Many lack any coherent vision of how jobs emerge from investments in the stocks of wealth. The vulnerability created by this tunnel vision is analogous to the vulnerability of the Titanic as it attempted to navigate through fields of ice floes without seeing what was under the water.

Community Wealth

Community wealth refers to wealth that is shared by two or more individuals. *In a sense, all forms of wealth are actually "community wealth" if you consider that it is ultimately the behavior of others as well as one's own behavior that determines the value of any stock of wealth be it natural capital, social capital, built capital, intellectual capital, and even financial capital.* The value of, for example, a share of corporate stock as a store of financial capital depends completely on the behavior of a community much larger than any single investor. Some forms of wealth, like individual capital (skills and mental and physical health) reside within individuals, but are strongly influenced by the larger community. How skills are transferred and taught and by whom has a significant impact on how they are received and the extent to which they are developed. Mental health may be influenced by the nature of interactions one has with others, as well as by other factors. Part of the shift in thinking we are searching for involves increasing our awareness of the relationships between what we most often think of as individual wealth and community wealth.

A recent study by the University of Michigan Health System found that the poorer the *community* in which children live, the more likely individual children are to become overweight and, once they become overweight, the more likely they are to remain overweight as adults. The lack of investment in community wealth in the form of recreation programs and parks combined with lack of access to full-service grocery stores has a direct impact on the health of individuals. No amount of investment in nutritional education will by itself create a system in which children are likely to attain and maintain healthy weight. Lack of systemic investment in the stocks of community wealth and specifically built capital directly affect individual capital; and making a difference requires investment in multiple forms of wealth at the same time.[25]

Visualizing Stocks and Flows

Think about the water in a bathtub as a stock of capital. (Actually it *is* a stock of natural capital—water!) Water flows into a bathtub through the faucet and goes out through the drain (see Figure 2.1).

What is Wealth? 17

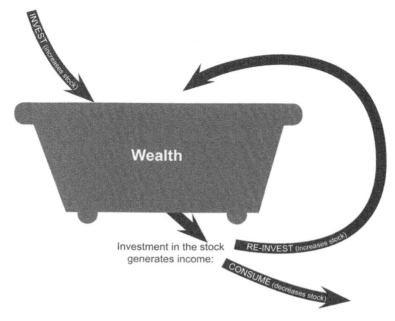

Figure 2.1 Bathtub Diagram of Stocks and Flows
Source: Yellow Wood Associates, Inc.

If you fill a tub with water and let it sit there, what happens? It evaporates. Over time, the water level goes down. It may also get yucky and start to grow things you wouldn't want in your water. All of the capitals, left alone and untended, depreciate over time. Quantity decreases and their quality tends to degrade.

Stocks of capital that are not in good shape and capable of producing "income" on a sustained basis are not wealth as we define it. Depreciated stocks of capital can create lots of problems and even undermine other forms of capital. For example, polluted water undermines human health. Polluted water isn't productive capital; it's a depreciated resource that requires investment to become productive capital. Without this investment, it cannot contribute to some forms of wealth without undermining others.

If you want to maintain or increase the quantity and quality of water in the bathtub over time, you need to turn on the tap. The water flowing into the tub represents a flow of investment. Keeping any stock of capital healthy and growing requires ongoing investment. In order for clean water to flow when you turn on the tap, someone had to invest in pumps, pipes, filters, power, and enough water quality protection to keep the water clean enough to use.

But if all you ever did was add water to the tub, the bathtub would overflow and you'd have a mess to clean up! Fortunately, bathtubs have faucets and drains. In addition to adding water to the bathtub, you can

18   *What is Wealth?*

intentionally let water out of the bathtub in a controlled way through the drain. As long as the investment (clean water) coming into the bathtub comes in faster than the water that drains out of the bathtub, the stock of clean, productive water will increase.

We are not trying to fill the tub for its own sake; we fill the tub so that we can use the water as we need it. To live sustainably, we need to balance our consumption of healthy water with reinvestment in the capacity of our infrastructure to maintain a stock of healthy water. If we consume too much and forget to reinvest, the bathtub runs dry; if we consume too little, we are foregoing the potential benefits gained from using healthy, clean water. If we consume it in a way that pollutes the water, our stock of water depreciates in value over time and it can't do all the good things for us that we need. The water we use represents a portion of the return on investment in a stock of clean water; the return that is created as the stock of water is put to use. For example, the return to society and to individuals from a stock of healthy water includes healthy people, habitats, food, and more. The water we reinvest in the stock is the other part of our return on investment.

One of the ways in which we frequently "miss the boat" is by focusing on one end of the bathtub and not the other without taking into account the impact on the stock in the tub. For example, when we seek to address chronic health issues like diabetes, our goal should be to increase the stock of people without diabetes. If we invest all our resources in treating people that already have diabetes and no resources in preventing the onset of diabetes, we will never achieve this goal. Focusing on stocks helps identify the *full* range of investments we need to make to achieve our goals and create sustainable and resilient communities and economies.

When we focus all our attention on one end of the bathtub or the other, we may end up with too much or too little water or a degraded stock of water that no longer contributes to wealth. For example:

- If we only focus on our need to consume water and don't invest in conservation and infrastructure to maintain the stock of clean water over time, the tub will run dry.
- If we only focus on increasing the supply of healthy water without paying attention to how it is being polluted through use, it will become harder and harder (and more and more expensive) to maintain a healthy stock over time.
- And if we only add to the stock of water, and don't use it to build the other capitals, like healthy people, we will lose the benefits from healthy water.

Building wealth means focusing on both ends of the bathtub—what goes in as well as what goes out—and what happens to the quantity and quality of each stock of capital as a result. It's a balancing act.

At a very basic level, if we are going to build our stocks of all capitals, or wealth, we need to pay attention to three things:

1 The level and quality of the stock in the tub;
2 The rate of investment and reinvestment; and
3 The rate of consumption.

The level of the stock in the bathtub will increase over time if, instead of over-consuming, we reinvest a portion of every unit produced to maintain and grow the stock. This means consuming where we need to and reinvesting where we can. If we can figure out how to do this across all capitals, we can have a sustainable economy that meets current consumption needs while preserving the basis for future consumption.

How do we begin to build our stocks of multiple forms of wealth? First, we need a way to communicate with each other and with familiar and unfamiliar partners about what we're doing. The wealth creation approach provides a vocabulary related to the forms of wealth and wealth creation value chains that can facilitate better communication. Next, we have to refocus our attention away from income (a flow) and back to the foundation of an equitable economy: stocks of wealth that support us individually and collectively. Creating jobs is a flow; the jobs that are available at any given time are a stock. When we focus only on creating jobs, we fail to measure changes in the overall stock of jobs. If jobs are draining out of the tub more quickly than they are being created, the stock is going down. Jobs are not a form of wealth; they are the result of investments in multiple forms of wealth including intellectual, individual, social, built, political, natural, and cultural capital. A wealth creation approach to development asks, what are the investments in multiple stocks of wealth that are required to create and maintain sustainable livelihoods in particular places?

The Wealth Matrix

The wealth creation approach uses a Wealth Matrix as a tool for assessment, planning, implementation, and evaluation to focus our attention on how the things we do in the name of community and economic development can actually improve stocks of multiple forms of wealth (see Table 2.1).

At the assessment stage, the wealth matrix can be used to identify the stocks of wealth that are available in a given place with respect to a given wealth creation opportunity. Specifically, it can be used to identify underutilized assets.

In the planning stage, the wealth matrix allows practitioners to think about how they can use the stocks of wealth available to them and stimulate market-driven investment in depreciated forms of capital (those, like polluted water, that are not healthy and not able to produce sustainable streams of "income"). Many groups are striving to plan for more sustainable outcomes without a common framework that would allow them to become more intentional about the impacts they consider. If a version of the wealth matrix were used in "vetting" new laws, for example, it would help us pay attention to the full range of wealth-related impacts, positive and negative, instead of privileging financial returns and/or "job creation" exclusively. For

20   *What is Wealth?*

Table 2.1 Wealth Matrix

Type of wealth	Outcomes tied to interventions
Individual	How will your activities impact the stock of skills and physical and mental health of people in a region?
Social	How will your activities impact the stock of trust, relationships, and networks that support civil society?
Intellectual	How will your activities impact the stock of knowledge, innovation, and creativity?
Natural	How will your activities impact the stock of unimpaired environmental assets in a region?
Built	How will your activities impact the stock of fully functioning constructed infrastructure?
Political	How will your activities impact the stock of power and goodwill held by individuals, groups, and/or organizations and the capacity to influence resource allocation decisions?
Cultural	How will your activities impact the stock of practices that reflect values and identity rooted in place, class, and/or ethnicity?
Financial	How will your activities impact the stock of unencumbered monetary assets at the individual and collective level?

Source: Yellow Wood Associates, Inc.

example, the Union of Concerned Scientists, in writing about the future of renewable energy in the United States, says:

> The bottom line is that as long as fossil fuel price forecasts are low, there will be very little development of new renewable energy. What is needed is a new law that accounts for the full range of benefits of renewable energy, like reduced pollution, less global warming, domestic and local economic development, and reduced dependence on foreign energy sources. Such a law must be part of electric industry restructuring legislation.[26]

We would add that such a law should include impacts on all eight forms of wealth and also require attention to the full range of costs.

During implementation, the wealth matrix provides a touchstone to ensure that all forms of wealth are kept in the picture, even if they are not all being addressed at the same time. *Using the wealth matrix helps us become aware when some forms of wealth are being undermined to build others. We do not know how to create some forms of wealth without exploiting others; but we have to figure it out to have a truly sustainable economy. It will require creativity and inventiveness as well as changes in our systems of production and consumption.* Our current systems are designed to deplete some stocks of wealth to create others. The underlying assumption of the wealth creation

What is Wealth? 21

approach to economic development is that investment in all stocks of wealth without undermining some to enlarge others will result in more "income" to consume and reinvest. As the quality of the underlying stocks improves, so will the quality of the "income," and vice versa as the higher-quality "income" is reinvested in the stock. The evaluation of a wealth creation approach seeks to provide information on how practitioners' efforts have contributed to increases and improvements in the stocks of various forms of wealth. Measurement is based on intended impacts on the stocks of each form of wealth as well as on the system as a whole. (See Chapter 8 for more on measurement.)

For instance, in 2012, 39 Deep South Community Agriculture Network (DSCAN) producers dedicated a total of 82.5 acres to growing for the market. In 2014, 34 producers dedicated 185 acres to growing for the market. This is tangible progress, showing increased utilization of an underutilized resource, cultivatable land or natural capital. In 2012, production methods were not classified. By 2014, DSCAN had begun to track impacts on natural capital with an emphasis on quality as well as quantity. They discovered that, of the 185 total acres, 84 were cultivated conventionally, 20 were certified organic, 24 used hardly any or no chemicals, and 57 used energy-efficient production methods. Production methods have a direct impact on the quality of natural capital (e.g. soil health; water quality). With a goal of improving natural capital, DSCAN is able to intentionally target resources toward wealth creating production practices while tracking impacts over time.

Using the wealth matrix as a tool throughout the process of wealth creation encourages practitioners to reach beyond the partners they typically work with and expand to find those that are familiar with and skilled in complementary areas. By doing so, practitioners are able to expand their view of the system in which they are working; better understand the interconnections between the eight foundational forms of wealth, find unexpected and unconventional partners in their work, and bring new resources to bear on their work.

The wealth matrix is particularly valuable in helping practitioners become "multi-solvers" and not exploiters. We already know how to build one stock at the expense of others. Exploitation is a well-established road to economic power. The problem is that it is fundamentally unsustainable. We are currently paying the price for past exploitation of natural and human resources, and for our failure to invest in maintaining and growing intellectual, individual, social, political, and built capital. We are seeing the results of our failure to invest in maintaining healthy stocks of wealth in increasing obesity and chronic disease, crumbling roads, bridges, water and wastewater systems, lack of fit between workers' skills and job requirements, etc. Each of these is taking a costly toll on our economy and society. The wealth matrix promotes consideration of the impact of our development approaches on all eight foundational forms of wealth.

One aspect of our exploitative approach to economic development is our over-reliance on consumption and under-reliance on investment as drivers of economic activity. We have become a society fixated on consumption, not

22 What is Wealth?

investment, as the driver of our economy. Remember when George W. Bush famously encouraged Americans to "go shopping more" to keep our economy going after 9/11? The percentage of the Gross Domestic Product (GDP) of the United States derived from household final consumption is around 70%. Household final consumption expenditure (formerly private consumption) is the market value of all goods and services, including durable products (such as cars, washing machines, and home computers), purchased by households. According to the World Bank, we rely significantly more on household final consumption than most other developed countries, including, for example, Germany, United Kingdom, Australia, France, Canada, and all the Scandinavian countries.[27] The fact is we cannot consume our way to a sustainable economy. Relying on consumption alone to fuel our economy is simply not sustainable. In fact, according to the New Economics Foundation, five planets would be needed if the rest of the world were to consume at the rate of the US![28] Our current rates of consumption are unsustainable and do not have a solid foundation. Nearly 50% of American households have credit card debt (the third-largest source of debt after student loans and mortgages) and the recent reduction in debt is not due to repayment, but write-offs by credit card companies.[29] In 1980, there were 287,579 non-business filings for bankruptcy. That figure was 1,181,016 in 2012.[30] Research has established a link between household expenditures on durable goods such as housing and automobiles and personal bankruptcy filings. "Consumption patterns make households financially overstretched and more susceptible to adverse events."[31]

How can we reconfigure our economic systems from their over-reliance on consumption to a sustainable balance between consumption, savings, and investment? First, we need to think more creatively about what investment is. Investment can occur in many forms; it is not always purely financial. The wealth creation approach to economic development defines investment to include any significant change in behavior and/or resource allocation that promotes wealth creation. This could include a change in policy (e.g. when a hospital decides to purchase X% of their food from local sources); a change in the use of infrastructure (e.g. when a distributor upgrades an underutilized building provided by a municipality to provide warehouse space or agrees to use its trucks to aggregate crops from growers); a sharing of social capital (e.g. when a partner uses his or her connections to open the door to new markets for the entire value chain); or a sharing of expertise or individual and intellectual capital (e.g. when a marketing firm agrees to assign a staff person to work with an emerging wealth creation effort on a pro bono basis). By considering "in-kind" as well as strictly monetary investments, there are more investment options available to more people and organizations and the pool of resources that can be brought to bear to improve the eight foundational stocks of wealth increases. As our stocks of wealth increase, the "income streams" also increase and portions of these, too, become available for reinvestment. In other words, over time, wise investments made by one generation can help the next generation "pay it forward."

How can we begin to use these changes in perception to create a new basis for economic development that embraces the principles of wealth creation? The first step requires us to be willing to learn to think about the economy in new ways. In other words, we need to change our mindsets. Systems thinker Donella Meadows identified a change in mindset as one of the highest leverage points in changing a system. Meadows defined "mindset" as the "paradigm out of which the system—its goals, power structure, rules, its culture—arises." She goes on to say:

> There's nothing necessarily physical or expensive or even slow in the process of paradigm change. In a single individual it can happen in a millisecond. All it takes is a click in the mind, a falling of scales from eyes, a new way of seeing. Whole societies are another matter. They resist challenges to their paradigms harder than they resist anything else.[32]

The good news is that societies are comprised of individuals.

One step in changing our individual mindsets, and thus putting ourselves in a position to help others change theirs, is to change our focus with respect to the development of our economy from just flows (jobs and income) to flows in relation to the underlying stocks and to the condition of the stocks themselves. We can learn to think in systems so we can identify the information and feedback we need to be able to see the ways that stocks are affected by one another. A systems perspective can help us find solutions that provide us with multiple benefits. Thinking in systems does not seem to come naturally to many people and it is not the way we are currently taught to think. For instance, an experiment in systems thinking with highly educated graduate students at MIT found that only about one in five grasped basic systems thinking concepts.[33]

In the real world, people often fail to recognize the systems they are part of. For example, in a recent study of asset accumulation among low-income rural families in Mississippi, a researcher found that professionals working in asset accumulation and financial education sectors and community development cited the "culture of poverty" among residents and their lack of motivation to get off government assistance, save, and pursue formal education, while residents in the community cited institutional factors such as eligibility requirements for receiving government aid, red tape, lack of access to infrastructure such as transportation and internet services as significant barriers to economic integration. In other words, professionals in the field failed to identify the systemic and structural barriers inherent in the system which they are a part of, instead focusing on the responsibilities of individuals, while individuals outside the system were better able to identify some of the conditions it creates.[34] This is why it is so valuable to bring people together in a value chain context. Multiple perspectives help reveal the true dimension of the system that shapes outcomes for everyone.

24   *What is Wealth?*

Systems thinking can be taught, learned, and applied by ordinary people. It does not require a PhD! The basic concepts of stocks and flows, feedback loops, and behavior change over time are all things we experience in our everyday lives. Sterman writes, "Learning about stocks and flows may go a long way in overcoming people's poor intuitive understanding of dynamics."[35] The wealth creation approach to economic development fosters systems thinking by encouraging attention to stocks and flows and to the inter-relationship of the eight fundamental stocks of wealth. We can use systems thinking to consider where an investment in one form of wealth can substitute for an investment in another and thus create new opportunities for its use elsewhere. Where do positive synergies exist between stocks of wealth? How can an investment in one form of wealth complement another form of wealth? Where is there a real danger of doing harm to one stock by using any given approach to improve another? What would it take to improve all the stocks over time?

For example, if we are going to maintain a stock of healthy water in the bathtub, how can we introduce behavioral changes that maintain healthy water in ways that also build other stocks of wealth? Craft3 (formerly Shore Bank Enterprise Cascadia) is a regional nonprofit that makes loans in Oregon and Washington to strengthen the resilience of businesses, families, and nonprofits, including those without access to traditional financing. In 2007, Shore Bank Enterprise Cascadia developed a program that allowed low-income homeowners to invest in septic system upgrades. The loan product is tailored to the unique situation of each borrower with eligibility requirements designed to be inclusive, not exclusive. The program was designed to provide multiple benefits by improving multiple stocks of wealth, not only individual wealth of homeowners, but many forms of community wealth as well. First, an upgraded septic system protects water quality and improves human health. But it doesn't stop there because the program intentionally involves many small subcontractors that inspect, repair, replace, and monitor the systems and provide training and skills development for their workers and it increases the value of the house itself, which is often the most valuable asset a low-income family owns. It also reduces the cost of regulatory compliance and publicly funded inspections and avoids costly cleanup efforts. This kind of thinking or "multi-solving" is at the heart of the wealth creation approach to economic development.

In Chapter 8 we will explore the role of measurement in helping us become more aware of how we impact stocks of wealth through the ways in which we do the work of development. In the example above, for instance, how many homes are in need of septic system inspections and upgrades? Of these, what proportions are owned by low-, medium- and even high-income households? What is the ambient water quality in the region? How prevalent are water borne illnesses? How many wells and water systems are contaminated as a result? What is the value of the homes with substandard systems? Knowing this type of baseline information at the outset is critical to being able to aggregate resources at the scale needed to make a meaningful impact. Baseline information allows us to measure progress over time and learn as we go about what is making a positive difference, what is making a negative difference, and what still needs to change in the overall system of water protection and wastewater management so that more positive outcomes can be achieved as a matter of course.

If we could build and maintain healthy stocks of all eight forms of wealth, without undermining any one to build another, we could create the "income" streams we need to satisfy the reasonable demand of current generations for a comfortable and fulfilling life, while maintaining generative stocks for the benefit of future generations. The challenge we face together is to learn how to build all stocks of wealth over time without exploiting any one to build another, and to learn to think in terms of *community wealth*, the wealth that supports us all, like the air we breathe and the roads we drive on that we all share, as well as individual wealth. As a society, we still have a lot to learn and, even as we struggle, our systems of production are changing around us driven by increased scarcity of resources, discoveries in biotechnology and materials science, information technology, and global communications. "Multi-solving" is one term, coined by Climate Interactive, to denote the ability to solve multiple pressing problems at the same time and with the same set of interventions, by understanding the inter-relationships of various forms of wealth as they affect and are impacted by specific circumstances.

For example, in Vermont where I live, changing the way people heat their homes from fuel oil to woody biomass can solve multiple problems including reducing dependence on fossil fuel, improving forest stewardship, stabilizing fuel prices and improving human health (as more people can afford to heat their homes to health-supporting temperatures on a regular basis and as polluting technologies are replaced with cleaner technologies), creating entrepreneurial and workforce opportunities within the state not only for fuel but for appliances, installation and maintenance, and reducing greenhouse gasses and other air pollutants by using state of the art technology. Success will require investments in multiple forms of wealth, including intellectual (understanding wood heat and research to develop high-functioning affordable appliances), individual (skills to produce, install, and use wood heat), social (relationships with wood product suppliers, forest land owners, neighbors, municipal governments, and more), political capital (supportive policies such as incentives for trading in old appliances) and natural capital (using best practices to maintain forest health). To achieve widely shared benefits, care will need to be exercised to ensure that investments in any one form of wealth do not undermine investments in any other.

WealthWorks is an aspirational framework and approach. It is not a silver bullet. It will not by itself correct or redesign systems overnight. However, based on the experiences its practitioners have had to date, it has the power to transform the way we think and approach our work and to produce positive changes at a meaningful scale.

26 *What is Wealth?*

The power of the wealth creation approach to economic development comes from connecting specific community assets to market demand to create sustainable livelihoods and using real world experience to identify "hidden" opportunities that can be unlocked by seeing the entire system and influencing the key leverage points that change it. The way that this focused and powerful learning happens is through exploring and building wealth creation value chains.

Notes

1   Managi, S. and Kumar, P. (eds.) (2018). *Inclusive Wealth Report 2018: Measuring Progress Toward Sustainability*, London: Routledge.
2   Boyd, D. R. (2004). *Sustainability within a Generation: A New Vision for Canada*. Suzuki Foundation. Retrieved from: https://davidsuzuki.org/science-lea rning-centre-article/sustainability-within-a-generation-a-new-vision-for-canada/
3   Hamilton, K. et al. (2006). *Where is the Wealth of Nations?: Measuring Capital for the 21st Century*. Washington, DC: World Bank Publications.
4   Flora, C. B. and Flora, J. (2004). *Rural Communities: Legacy and Change*. Boulder, CO: Westview Press.
5   Hudson, W. J. (1993). *Intellectual Capital: How to Build it, Enhance it, Use it*. New York: Wiley.
6   Porter, E. (2013). Stubborn Skills Gap in America's Workforce. *New York Times*, October 8. Retrieved from: https://www.nytimes.com/2013/10/09/busi ness/economy/stubborn-skills-gap-in-americas-work-force.html
7   Integrated Benefits Institute. (2012). Poor Health Costs U.S. Economy $576 Billion According to the Integrated Benefits Institute. *Cision PR Newswire*, September 12. Retrieved from: http://www.prnewswire.com/news-releases/poor-hea lth-costs-us-economy-576-billion-according-to-the-integrated-benefits-in stitute-169460116.html
8   Mendelsohn, R. and Muller, N. (2007). What Do Damages Caused by U.S. Air Pollution Cost? *Resources*, December 16. Retrieved from: https://www.resourcesma g.org/common-resources/what-do-the-damages-caused-by-us-air-pollution-cost/
9   Kiker, B. F. (1966). The historical roots of the concept of human capital. *Journal of Political Economy*, 74(5), 481–499.
10   For more information see http://www.better-angels.org. Many other organizations do similar work.
11   Economists refer to this as a reduction in transaction costs.
12   Hawkins, S. Social Capital: Bibliography. Retrieved from: http://science.jrank. org/pages/8084/Social-Capital.html
13   Banfield, E. C. (1961). *Political Influence: A New Theory of Urban Politics*. Glencoe, IL: Free Press.
14   Bourdieu, P. (1991). *Language and Symbolic Power*. Cambridge, UK: Polity Press.
15   Boehnert, J. (2013). The History of the Concept of "Natural Capital"—First Coined by E.F. Schumacher in 1973 #NatCap13. Ecolabs, November 21. Retrieved from: https://ecolabsblog.com/2013/11/21/the-history-of-the-concep t-of-natural-capital-first-coined-by-e-f-schumacher-in-1973-natcap13/
16   Flora and Flora (2004) defined cultural capital as people's understanding of society and their role in it, values, symbols, and rituals. An example is the "Protestant work ethic," which Weber (1905) argued was an important factor contributing to the rise of capitalism in the West. Choby defined cultural capital as "the rules for engaging other types of capital (human, economic, social)" see: http://pattichoby.wordpress.com/2010/06/05/what-is-cultural-capital

What is Wealth? 27

17 Bourdieu, P. (1973). Cultural reproduction and social reproduction. In: Brown, R. (ed.) *Knowledge, Education and Cultural Change*, London: Tavistock, pp. 71–84.
18 Economy. (2017). *The Kiplinger Letter*, 94(1) (January 6).
19 For Most U.S. Workers, Real Wages Have Stagnated Since 1960s. (2018). *Philanthropy News Digest*, August 18. Retrieved from: https://philanthropynewsdigest.org/news/for-most-u.s.-workers-real-wages-have-stagnated-since-1960s
20 Too Much of a Good Thing. (2016). *The Economist*, March 26. Retrieved from: http://www.economist.com/news/briefing/21695385-profits-are-too-high-america-needs-giant-dose-competition-too-much-good-thing
21 See the Vermont Small Business Offering Exemption: http://www.dfr.vermont.gov/press-release/vermont-small-business-offering-exemption-helps-small-businesses-raise-capital-promote
22 "Since roughly 1980, the growth of the U.S. economy has been proceeding with a diminishing supply of public assets on which to foster growth." Heintz, J., Pollin, R., and Garrett-Peltier, H. (2009). *How Infrastructure Investments Support the U.S. Economy: Employment, Productivity, and Growth*. Amherst, MA: Political Economy Research Institute.
23 Estimates from US DoT, Association of American Railroads, Airports Council International, EPA, and the American Society of Civil Engineers (Heintz et al., 2009).
24 The Royal Bank of Canada completed a study called *The Coming Skills Revolution, Humans Wanted: How Canadian Youth Can Thrive in the Age of Disruption*, which offers fascinating insights into transferable skills between traditional jobs that are disappearing and 21st-century jobs that are emerging:. See: http://www.rbc.com/newsroom/_assets-custom/pdf/03-2018-rbc-future-skills-report.pdf
25 Low-Income Communities More Likely to Face Childhood Obesity. (2016). University of Michigan School of Medicine, January 7. Retrieved from: http://www.uofmhealth.org/news/archive/201601/low-income-communities-more-likely-face-childhood-obesity
26 Public Utility Regulatory Policy Act (PURPA). The Union of Concerned Scientists. Retrieved from: http://www.ucsusa.org/clean_energy/smart-energy-solutions/strengthen-policy/public-utility-regulatory.html#.WIolDdIrKCj
27 Data from: https://data.worldbank.org/
28 See: http://bsd.net/nefoundation/default/page/file/41a473dfbe880a0742_ucm6i4n29.pdf, p. 40.
29 Tsosie, C. and El Issa, E. (2018). 2018 American Household Credit Card Debt Survey. Nerdwallet, December 10. Retrieved from: http://www.nerdwallet.com/blog/credit-card-data/average-credit-card-debt-household/
30 See:http://www.abiworld.org/AM/AMTemplate.cfm?Section=Home&TEMPLATE=/CM/ContentDisplay.cfm&CONTENTID=66471
31 Zhu, N. (2011). Household consumption and personal bankruptcy. *The Journal of Legal Studies*, 40(1), 1–37.
32 Meadows, D. H. (1999). *Leverage Points: Places to Intervene in a System*. Hartland, VT: The Sustainability Institute.
33 Sterman, J. D. and Sweeney, L. B. (2002). Cloudy skies: assessing public understanding of global warming. *System Dynamics Review: The Journal of the System Dynamics Society*, 18(2), 207–240.
34 Meikle, Paulette and Green-Pimentel, Leslie, and Liew, Hui. (2018). Asset accumulation among low-income rural families: Assessing financial capital as a component of community capitals. *Community Development*, 1–21. DOI: 10.1080/15575330.2017.1422529.
35 Sterman, J. D. and Sweeney, L. B. (2002). Cloudy skies: assessing public understanding of global warming. *System Dynamics Review: The Journal of the System Dynamics Society*, 18(2), 207–240.

3 What is a Wealth Creation Value Chain?

What is a Supply Chain?

Every product or service we buy comes into being as a result of a series of relationships between producers and an ultimate connection with consumers. For example, the can of tomato soup on the grocer's shelf depends on the producers that grow the tomatoes. They, in turn, depend on access to land and the businesses that supply them with seeds, fertilizer, equipment, training, insurance, financing, and more. Once the tomatoes are grown, they must be harvested, graded, processed, tested, and turned into soup. The soup maker must also create or purchase recipes, train workers, buy the cans and other packaging, develop label designs and purchase equipment for labeling, interact with food safety inspectors, and more. Once the soup is produced, it must be stored, transported, and stored again before it is delivered to the grocery store and stacked on the shelves for you to buy. When you take it home, you have to decide how you will heat it up (e.g. microwave vs. stove-top), how you will serve it, who you will serve it to, and how you will dispose of the packaging. You become a co-producer and your preferences have implications for how the soup is produced, packaged, and labeled.

In a typical supply chain, the businesses that sell seeds to the farmer, for example, probably do not know that the tomatoes the farmer grows are destined for a particular brand of tomato soup, nor do they know the characteristics of that brand that most appeal to you, the end consumer. Likewise, the tomato soup manufacturer may not know the producers that grow the tomatoes they buy in bulk through a broker. The company that transports that soup to the grocery store probably does not know anyone except the shipping clerks at the businesses they pick up from and deliver to. They may not even know that they are carrying tomato soup on the truck or train.

In the conventional supply chain, every business in the chain works independently and only knows the people they buy from and the people they sell to; for example, the farmer knows the company that supplies them with seed and fertilizer and the aggregator to whom they sell their tomatoes. They may have no idea what happens to the tomatoes after that, and only the grocer has direct contact with you, the end consumer. The information potentially available to the grocer about how your tastes are changing and what you are looking for in tomato soup (for example, less salt, more natural seasoning, smaller portion sizes, microwaveable containers, recyclable packaging, sustainable production practices that are water-saving, support for beginning farmers, etc.) may not be collected and, if it is, is unlikely to be shared with all the other businesses in the supply chain. This means that the businesses in the supply chain do not receive the information they would need to be able to adjust to changes in market demand on a timely basis. They also miss out on the other potential advantages of working together such as shared training, equipment, insurances, logistical support, etc. The grocer is at risk of not being able to find the products consumers really want, and you, the consumer, lose the chance to reward the businesses that are responding to your values while providing a tasty product. Producers lose out on opportunities to contain costs and keep up with market developments. They can easily fall prey to the "buggy whip" syndrome. This refers to the displacement of buggy whip makers that occurred when the automobile came along. There are many examples of the "buggy whip" syndrome in today's rapidly changing economy (think about telephone landlines, fuel oil deliverers, and realtors that specialize in coastal properties for starters).

We use the term "supply chain" to refer to this very common situation. Most of the efforts to develop jobs in rural areas that we have seen are based on a "supply chain" mentality. They begin with some good or service that an area has available (e.g. we grow tomatoes) and they assume that if they can only make or grow more of it, consumers will buy it. It's the "build it and they will come" approach, also known as the "push" approach because it involves pushing your product to market without any orientation to demand or what the market wants. Yet, in our market economy, demand is in the driver's seat.

Some companies participate in chains that are demand-oriented. However, the primary measure of their success is profits and the degree to which every business in the chain is able to buy low and sell high based on the value added at each stage of production. This is in accord with the concept of a value chain first introduced by Michael Porter as a model to analyze specific activities through which firms can create competitive advantage that leads to profitability.[1]

Value Chains vs. Wealth Creation Value Chains

The difference between this definition of a value chain and the concept of a wealth creation value chain is in the broader set of goals a wealth creation value chain intentionally seeks to achieve. Understanding demand not just in terms of price points and willingness to pay but more holistically in terms of the full range of values consumers want to support, is key to building the capacity to deliver and adjust to ongoing changes in demand. That capacity to adjust is a key component of the basis for sustainable livelihoods.

30   What is a Wealth Creation Value Chain?

Profit matters and a wealth creation value chain must be profitable to endure; however, the measure of success in wealth creation value chains is not profits alone but rather profits plus contributions to building the stocks of eight forms of wealth while doing no harm (see Chapter 2 for more information on the eight forms of wealth). The activities of the value chain such as research and development, procurement, logistics, operations, customer service, sales, and marketing are all designed to support and not undermine multiple stocks of wealth while intentionally engaging and benefiting economically marginalized people and places. The forms of wealth are built through the operation of the wealth creation value chain in the ways in which businesses and their support partners, including their demand partners, work together as multi-solvers. While financial profit matters, the goal is not to maximize financial profit alone, but to maximize the full range of positive investment and "income" generation throughout the value chain.

There are four types of businesses or organizations in a wealth creation value chain. The first are transactional players. These are the businesses or organizations that actually touch the product or service on its way to the buyers or demand partners. In our example, input suppliers, farmers, processors, warehouse operators, and transporters would all be transactional partners in a value chain in the agriculture sector.

The second type of business or organization is a supporting partner. Those that provide insurance, training, financing, inspections, legal services, and create the policy environment in which the value chain operates are all supporting partners. They do not touch the product or service directly, but without their contributions, the value chain cannot operate successfully at scale; multiple partners cannot work effectively together to meet demand that exceeds the capacity of any single partner to satisfy.

The third type of business or organization is a demand partner. Demand partners are not generally the end consumers, but rather the businesses and organizations that serve the end consumer. In the tomato soup example, the grocery store is one type of demand partner; others might include restaurant suppliers, institutional buyers like schools, colleges, and hospitals, and even tour guides if the value chain was created to include agro-tourism.

The fourth type of business or organization is an investment partner. Investment partners are entities that recognize a benefit to themselves from a fully functioning value chain that operates at scale. Investment partners may be in the same sector as the value chain itself; for example a distributor may see benefit in developing a pipeline of locally produced agricultural products at scale. Investment partners may also be in other sectors; for example, hospitals and other health care providers may see benefit in a value chain that improves nutritional options for their clientele. By thinking broadly about who might benefit from the value chain if it were operating at scale, the universe of potential investors grows. (See Chapter 6 for more on investors as partners.)

What is a Wealth Creation Value Chain? 31

A video game created by the Emergent Media Center at Champlain College provides players with the chance to experiment in creating relationships among transactional, support, and demand partners while maintaining financial profits and positively impacting multiple forms of wealth. You can find the game and a few instructional tools at http://www.wealthworks.org/resources/wealthbuilders-game

These categories—transactional, support, demand, and investment partners—are not immutable or exclusive. In fact, a single partner may fall into more than one category. The value of the categories is in helping you think deeply about the full range of actual and potential participants in the value chain. For example, in the transactional category, what about the waste collector who collects the waste at the tomato-processing plant? They touch the actual product, but not the part that goes to consumers in the form of soup. Is there another product that could be generated from that waste? What about animal feed or compost or biodegradable packaging, any one of which might use tomato waste as an input? We call these entrepreneurial opportunities that appear from close examination of a wealth creation value chain "chainlets," to distinguish them from the original value chain from which they spring. Chainlets can take on a life of their own that becomes part of the scalable impact of wealth creation.

In conventional economic development, the waste generated through the production process, whether it is physical waste like tomato skin and seeds or the harm that comes to humans and the environment through exploitive production practices like miners with black lung disease or mountain top removal, is an externality borne by society and often hidden from society. In the wealth creation approach to development, the goal is to identify all costs including externalities and then meet the challenge of internalizing the externalities (i.e. recognize the costs) and turning them into wealth. (In the case of tomato waste, this may be relatively easy; more creativity may be needed in the case of externalities like black lung disease. Here the challenge is both in how to inform demand and redesign production practices that meet our need for energy in ways that do not cause harm, but also to find a productive role for as long as possible for those with black lung disease, perhaps in research or education.)

In summary, a wealth creation value chain is a set of relationships among the people and businesses whose skills and contributions are essential to produce a good or service valued by buyers in the market. One way to think about a wealth creation value chain is as a horizontally integrated business. Economists use the term "horizontal integration" to refer to one business that performs the same function (e.g. trucking) at the same level of the value chain in multiple industries. In the context of a wealth creation value chain, we are using horizontal integration to describe something very different; a value chain comprised of multiple independent partners who see their self-interest in cooperating with one another.

32 *What is a Wealth Creation Value Chain?*

Each business or partner must benefit from the value chain or they will not continue to participate. Ownership is diffused throughout the chain, unlike vertically integrated businesses in which one large corporate entity owns and controls everything from input supply to final product (and often the demand channel as well). Horizontal integration offers many more entities an opportunity to own and benefit from participating in the production process and makes room for place-based entrepreneurship rather than control and exploitation by outside interests that have no vested interest in the places where development matters.

Wealth creation value chains can be built in multiple sectors, including, but not limited to agriculture, tourism, manufacturing, housing, energy efficiency, renewable energy, forest products, fisheries, craft beverages, transportation, and health care. Most wealth creation value chains produce a mix of products and services. Some, like manufacturing, are more oriented toward products and others, like transportation or tourism, have services at their core. Yet services, including customer service and product customization, are increasingly important to product producers, and service producers like tourism operators or training providers may distinguish themselves through association with specific products like local foods and produce manufacturers.

A wealth creation value chain is not a "system" by itself; rather it is embedded in a system of laws, regulations, behavioral norms, relationships, mental models, infrastructure, incentives, and technologies that together dictate the way in which the things we want and need are currently being produced, distributed, and consumed. The intent of wealth creation value chains is to make the larger system visible, identify its weaknesses (e.g. elements that lead to exploitation versus shared benefit; over-consumption versus investment, isolation and poverty versus productive engagement, etc.) and identify shared values that can engage people across the value chain as well as others that are not part of the value chain per se but would benefit if it succeeded.

For example, in a value chain organized to deliver energy efficient affordable housing to veterans, at first glance the primary beneficiaries might appear to be veterans and builders. However, if veterans who have safe and secure housing are less likely to occupy park benches, then one group that would benefit from a successful value chain may be the municipal Parks Department. What is the self-interest of the Parks Department in supporting the value chain? Their self-interest may be a measurable reduction in the time and money required to address disruption caused by homeless veterans and an increased ability to attract more people to events and activities in the parks. The Parks Department may even be induced to become investors in the value chain if the benefits are shown to be real and tangible.

It is possible to identify and engage other, often less obvious, beneficiaries by looking at the entire system and not simply at the transactional and support partners. The resources these partners have to bring to the table may surprise you! For example, when Michigan State University Extension teamed up with Fremont Area Community Foundation in Michigan to explore a tourism-based wealth creation value chain, they discovered a 47-mile recreation trail under development. This became the focus of their value chain. Thinking "out of the box" they built relationships on the demand side with a regional group and an international group that saw value in a new trail that could be developed to meet the needs of their constituents and become a world-class adventure destination trail for mountain bikers, hikers, and runners. The value chain coordinators also began to recognize the need for a comprehensive approach to branding for the region as a whole that went beyond the separate efforts of individual towns and the county. Thinking broadly about the wealth creation impacts of a recreation trail led them to a conversation with the local hospital, which in turn led the hospital to volunteer the services of its marketing department to support the value chain initiative. A more conventional approach to economic development typically defines partners much more narrowly and leaves unconventional resources such as this underutilized.

Four Phases of Implementation

The work of systems change takes place in the context of facilitating wealth creation value chains that provide specific goods and services in specific communities and regions. The information unearthed in the process of exploring, proving, implementing, and institutionalizing specific wealth creation value chains can lead to changes in overarching systems. We have defined four phases in the process of applying the wealth creation framework. Success in each of these four phases is critical to achieving systems change.

Exploration

The first phase is the exploration phase. During this phase, one or more potential wealth creation value chains are identified and mapped out, outreach to partners occurs, and there is a preliminary assessment of gaps, barriers, and underutilized resources. Gaps refer to functions in the value chain that are not currently being fulfilled. Barriers refer to obstacles such as regulation, lack of infrastructure, lack of skills, lack of knowledge, etc. that prevent the value chain from progressing. Underutilized resources refer to potential building blocks of a value chain that are sitting on the sidelines waiting to be engaged. Inclusivity must be intentional during the exploration phase and then it must carry through to every subsequent phase. The truth is exploration never ends; the more partners learn about the larger system in which they operate, the more opportunities to invest differently, change the system, bring in new partners, and positively impact multiple forms of wealth they discover.

The first challenge in the exploration phase of WealthWorks is identifying a market segment with potential or documented unmet demand in your region. There are many ways to explore demand, including secondary research and, most importantly, conversations with a range of potential buyers. The purpose of these conversations is not to sell products or services to buyers or even to "sell" them on

34 What is a Wealth Creation Value Chain?

the idea of a wealth creation value chain; it is to begin to understand the world from the buyers' perspectives. What problems are buyers trying to solve? What do they see as unmet demand and what would have to happen from their perspective to enable them to tap into that demand? What are their biggest headaches? What would they like to be able to source within the region that they cannot source currently? What initiatives do they already have underway to try and address any of these issues? (See Chapter 5 for more on what it means to be demand-driven.) You may explore several market segments before determining which has the greatest traction.

Once you have started to understand buyers' perspectives and a bit about market potential, it is time to conceptualize the transactional piece of the value chain by identifying all of the functions from design to inputs to primary production to processing to packaging, to waste management (and reuse), transportation and distribution to sales and returns and more that need to be in place to produce a good or service that meets buyers' needs and expectations. The best people to help conceptualize the transactional piece of the value chain are the potential transactional partners themselves. One way in which WealthWorks differs from conventional development is in engaging transactional partners early and often in defining the value chain functions, building relationships among themselves and with supporting partners and with demand partners, and collective problem-solving.

The conventional approach to economic development tends to start with supporting partners; often nonprofit organizations that produce studies showing what the opportunities are for a given community or region based on analysis of secondary data, sometimes accompanied by interviews with other supporting partners. Likewise, much community development work begins with community visioning that tends to attract a relatively predictable set of participants, few of which are private-sector businesses. Since nonprofits are often at least one step removed from mainstream markets and businesses that make things, the ideas that emerge from these exercises are generally not well-grounded in real-world thinking or experience.

This is not the process WealthWorks practitioners have used. Instead, they have first focused the discussion by identifying one or two promising economic sectors and market segments and then brought to relevant transactional partners some preliminary ideas about a wealth works value chain along with some information from the buyers' perspective. Next they worked with the transactional partners to conceptualize the rest of the chain, including the types of supporting partners that would be required to address challenges and fill in gaps.

In a wealth creation value chain, we are looking for a mix of transactional participants, some of whom are economically marginalized, while others are not. If we limit the focus only to those participants that are economically marginalized, the amount of investment required to bring the quality and quantity of production up to standards acceptable to buyers may be overwhelming. However, engaging only participants that are not economically marginalized does not meet the goals of the wealth creation

What is a Wealth Creation Value Chain? 35

approach. There is a "sweet spot" based on what buyers demand that brings economically marginalized participants to the table along with less marginalized participants. The relationship building between them is part of the wealth creation process. The work of identifying potential transactional players is an adventure in which new discoveries shape what is possible.

Proof of Concept

The second phase in applying the wealth creation framework is proof of concept. During proof of concept, the partners in a value chain actually work together to produce and deliver products and services to their demand partners and receive payment in return. Proof of concept is also when relationships with investors begin. Investors engaged early in proof of concept are able to share their perspectives on what the proof points are that would convince them to invest at scale. Understanding the perspectives of potential investors and using those to help shape the proof of concept sets the value chain up for the third stage of implementation. Investors can also be helpful in developing tools and approaches to mitigate risk. Proof of concept may apply to the value chain as a whole as well as to aspects of systems change. For example, as part of the exploration phase for a WealthWorks value chain to bring Appalachian sustainably grown, harvested, and processed wood products to market, Rural Action and Appalachian Sustainable Development discovered that one of the barriers to connecting regional producers to markets was the lack of a one-stop shop where buyers could order a full range of products. If for example, the buyer was building houses, they might need a wide variety of wood products, from wooden studs for framing to stairs to flooring and cabinets. It was too expensive in time, effort, and dollars for buyers to seek out individual regional producers for each item they wanted. In the proof-of-concept phase, Rural Action and Appalachian Sustainable Development came together to start Woodright, a brokering and distribution business for regional producers that met the value chain criteria. This change in the system was part of the value chain's proof of concept.

Apart from the logistics-related challenges of producing, aggregating, distributing, and selling goods and services within the WealthWorks value chain framework while building multiple forms of wealth, two critical challenges at the proof-of-concept phase are attention to scale and investability. The purpose of the proof-of-concept phase is to lay the groundwork for going to scale. (For a fuller discussion of scale, see Chapters 3 and 6.) This means that all the elements of the value chain, from input supply to production technologies to communications, aggregation, and distribution systems must be designed to be scalable. If they are not, there is a real danger that the value chain will be unable to respond in a timely manner to opportunities to scale up and may never progress beyond the "pilot" level. Many WealthWorks Coordinator organizations, especially small place-based nonprofits, are not used to thinking in terms of scaling up. This is a skill they must acquire. Many have done so by bringing someone with private-sector experience in the sector in which they are working on board.

The second challenge is in understanding what needs to be proven and to whom in order to aggregate the investment required for scaling up. (See Chapter 5 for more on relating to investors.) If these questions are not addressed in the design of proof of concept, there is the possibility of a loss of momentum moving into implementation.

Implementation

The third phase is implementation at scale. During this phase, the ability to attract investment increases based on a successful proof of concept, the number of partners may increase, and the quantity of goods and services that moves through the value chain goes up. The scope of the value chain may also change, with new products and services being introduced and new demand partners emerging. The impacts on multiple forms of wealth should also occur at a greater scale during implementation. For more on connecting with investors, incorporating technology, and rethinking measures of economic impact, all of which play a role during both proof of concept and implementation, please see Chapters 6, 7, and 8.

Institutionalization

The final phase is institutionalization. During this phase, the changed system for producing and consuming the goods and services of the wealth creation value chain become the "new normal." The system is no longer dependent on a few charismatic leaders or champions. It is codified in policies, rules, procedures, budgets, norms of behavior, and expectations that produce outcomes that are superior to those of the system it replaced. One credit union member of the National Cooperative Business Association described institutionalization of financial literacy work at their credit union as the difference between having one staff member that was its champion and did all the work from start to finish, including raising the money to support it, to having a line item in the credit union's annual budget for financial literacy along with trained staff to deliver programs.

The key to the ongoing resilience of WealthWorks value chains is to build enough feedback loops into the new system in which the value chain is embedded, so that information on what is changing is readily available, opportunities to use political capital to shape changes are identified, and enough flexibility exists so that the value chain can adapt to new information over time. Flexibility enables resiliency. Given the tendency of most human-built systems to become rigid over time, this is a task that again requires intentionality and commitment to measurement and information sharing by all partners in the chain, including supporting partners, investment partners, and demand partners, as well as transactional partners.

What is a Wealth Creation Value Chain? 37

Here is a story of a wealth creation value chain that has evolved through multiple phases. Fahe, formerly Federation of Appalachian Housing Enterprises, is a nonprofit organization serving the Appalachian portion of Kentucky, Tennessee, West Virginia, Virginia, Alabama, and Maryland through a Membership Network that consists of 50+ nonprofit housing organizations. When Fahe first began experimenting with a wealth creation approach to development, all the nonprofits in the network depended heavily on subsidies to support construction of affordable units of housing that met a nationally recognized green standard. Fahe's key measure of success was the number of units built and the number of families served. "The initiative has required that we look at our work through a different lens, focusing on value chains and inter-connectivity beyond the realm of our typical focus on outputs of units built or families served."[2]

The value chain Fahe initially thought they would develop was for green affordable housing. However, within the first year they learned:

[W]hat matters is how this endeavor and the ongoing work in affordable housing undertaken by our members impact the bottom line of the families who ultimately reside in these units. Long-term affordability in an environment rife with rising energy costs is a growing theme in Central Appalachia. We have found that one way to alleviate this widespread concern is to incorporate specific energy efficient features within all projects on the front end. Adhering to a green construction standard does not necessarily facilitate this in a direct and cost-effective way.[3]

Fahe redefined their value chain from green affordable housing to energy efficient affordable housing once they understood that prospective low-income home owners did not care how "green" their home was but cared very much about how much it cost to heat and cool.

During the first year, Fahe also discovered that:

The system for delivering an energy efficient housing unit to residents of Appalachia is broken. This includes the ability to build to a standard, inspect and certify to that standard, obtain an appraisal that recognizes the value of such certification, and finally, finance the unit through a mechanism that values this process.[4]

This process of envisioning what a fully functional system would look like makes existing gaps, barriers, and underutilized resources apparent. This, in turn, translates into defining the investments required to bring the value chain to fruition. Over the course of two years, as more and more information came to light, Fahe identified the need for investment in multiple aspects of the value chain, including, but not necessarily limited to:

38 *What is a Wealth Creation Value Chain?*

- better information on how to build energy efficient affordable housing;
- developing a standard for energy efficiency that could be built to and replicated;
- training contractors to build to the standard;
- training inspectors who could determine whether a house met a specific standard or not;
- sharing best practices information among housing developers;
- developing effective mechanisms to educate home buyers in how to live in an energy efficient home;
- educating government agencies regarding the standard and how it related to existing funding streams.

Fahe took on the task of finding partners in each of these critical areas and filling in the gaps, addressing the barriers, and engaging underutilized resources.

For example, early on Fahe identified inequities in the number of trained energy efficiency inspectors available in rural versus urban areas of their region. They decided to address this by paying for appropriate training for their members' staffs. First, they had to find a training provider. The community college system was unable to offer the type of focused, short-term opportunity for detailed, hands-on instruction of a more technical nature that was required. Eventually, Fahe identified New River Center for Energy Research and Training (NRCERT), a subsidiary of Community Housing Partners, a longtime member. In cooperation with NRCERT they put together a training package that includes three weeks of classroom training, a field monitoring component and a complete energy auditor toolkit and offers trainees and their organizations three separate BPI (Building Performance institute) certifications. Organizations with staff who complete the training receive equipment as well as certification so they can provide additional services (energy audits, energy efficient retrofits and repairs, etc.) in rural areas in the region. Fahe selected participants strategically so that at the end of the first year, home energy audits and related services could be provided by at least one member in each state. Between 2010 and the middle of 2015, Fahe trained 37 analysts and NRCERT trained 113 analysts and 14 auditors serving rural areas. The demand for training spread from nonprofit to for-profit developers as the demand for energy efficient housing began to emerge.

After about a year, Fahe's leadership began to realize that changing from a subsidy dependent, essentially supply-driven model of production to a demand-oriented, market driven model of production was going to change the entire way that Fahe as a whole approached its work. This was not a task for a single staff member but demanded engagement from the top of the organization on down. Once this shift occurred, more attention was given to the barriers that were leaving the demand for energy efficient affordable housing unmet. Chief among these was the lack of appropriate appraisals. Conventional appraisals made no distinction between energy efficient houses and energy inefficient houses; thus failing to capture the value of efficiency in terms of cost savings.

In the energy efficient affordable housing value chain, appraisal is a key to the difference between effective and ineffective demand. If financers do not recognize the added value of an energy efficient home, they will not lend enough money to cover the additional cost of construction to achieve energy efficiency. And financiers will not recognize that value unless it is embedded in the appraisals they receive and on which they base their financing decisions. Fahe worked with the Kentucky Association of Real Estate Appraisers to develop a training program in how to properly appraise energy efficient housing. USDA Rural Development is interested in adopting Fahe's methodology which adds an average of $9,000 to the value of an affordable, energy efficient home, of which $7,500 is needed to finance energy efficient construction.

Today, Fahe is defining success in terms of systems change. The materials used in the housing has changed, the way the housing is built has changed, the way builders and appraisers work together has changed, the way appraisers are trained has changed, the way mortgages are structured and held has changed, and the way buyers are educated about how to get the most out of their energy efficient homes has changed. In the process, Fahe has developed intellectual capital that supports its own work. Overall, the system for providing affordable, energy efficient housing has changed from one that was virtually 100% dependent on subsidy to one that is supported primarily by market forces.

The measure of success is not the number of energy efficient affordable housing units nonprofit developers build, but the number of energy efficient affordable housing units built by all developers, including private developers in response to market demand. Why would private developers build affordable energy efficient housing? Because it makes economic sense and the system supports demand through accurate appraisals and appropriate mortgage products instead of rendering it ineffective.

Fahe's role is that of a WealthWorks Value Chain Coordinator. A WealthWorks Value Chain Coordinator can be any type of organization that commits to understanding and applying WealthWorks on the ground. The many functions of the WealthWorks Value Chain Coordinator are discussed in greater detail in Chapter 9.

What Does it Mean to Be Inclusive?

There are as many dimensions to inclusion as there are to exclusion. Our society has raised barriers to economic inclusion for many groups. Poverty afflicts many people of color but also many white people, immigrants, older people, and LGBTQ+ people, among others. Exclusion can arise through cultural differences, prejudices, lack of education, ageism, poor health, structural issues (like lack of access to transportation or the internet, or policies like redlining), and more. Thinking about inclusion looks different in every community, region, and value chain. The comparative advantage to the wealth creation approach is in defining opportunities for inclusion concretely in terms of the requirements and opportunities related to specific wealth creation value chains. This takes the conversation out of the realm of wholesale societal change and into the realm of specifics that we can address in context. It is a place to start and a way to avoid the feeling of being overwhelmed that leads to inaction and even denial. Piloting successful wealth creation value chains creates ripples that contribute to societal change.

Community organizers often focus on giving voice to people whose voices have not been heard, while economic developers tend to focus on those who already have connections to the mainstream economy. WealthWorks focuses on building bridges between the two for the purpose of establishing and maintaining sustainable livelihoods and building community wealths. Being intentionally inclusive is part of every aspect of implementing WealthWorks. Without that intention, it is entirely possible to "create jobs" and engender investments that do little or nothing to address issues of poverty and even make it worse.

It is also possible to fail to learn from those who have succeeded under conditions that have crushed their peers. It is easy to assume that everyone who is marginalized responds to similar circumstances in the same way, but this is not true. Sociologists have come up with an approach to behavioral and social change that they call positive deviance, which is based on the observation that in any community there are people whose uncommon but successful behaviors or strengths enabled them to find better solutions to a problem than their peers, despite facing similar challenges and having no extra resources.[5]

We have seen positive deviance play an important role in developing wealth creation value chains. The Development Corporation of Brownsville, Texas (CDCB), the place-based partner of Community Resource Group of Arkansas (now merged into Communities Unlimited) recognized the low mortgage approval rate among low-income families as a significant barrier to a market-driven affordable housing value chain. They concluded that improved financial literacy among low-income families could be used to reduce the barrier and increase rates of mortgage approval. In designing and testing a bilingual financial literacy training program targeted to prospective low-income home owners CDCB discovered some low-income families who are able to budget successfully in the midst of many that do not. Investigation revealed that those families who budget successfully attribute their success to their own experiences as children in which their parents demonstrated how to set priorities and spend within limits. CDCB used this insight into positive deviance to help craft a bilingual curriculum that incorporated realistic and achievable behavioral changes, using illustrations recognizable to the target population.[6]

The practice of positive deviance helps us test our assumptions and learn to look more closely at any given group to discover deviant behaviors that are practical and produce positive outcomes. Since the people who engage in positive deviance are in other respects the same as the target population, their experiences are relatable and their strategies can be replicated, often without a significant influx of external resources. Positive deviance is not limited to people in low-income communities; people within large corporations can also develop deviant strategies that produce positive, inclusive, and wealth creating outcomes where they would not otherwise exist (see Chapter 7 for examples).

The power of a wealth creation value chain approach to impact poverty comes from adherence to the principle of inclusivity. As you will recall, one of the main assumptions behind this work is that poverty is a function of isolation; isolation from multiple forms of community wealth that make it difficult and sometimes impossible for individuals and households to become productive contributors to the larger economy. The principle of inclusivity is about overcoming isolation by recognizing that connecting unproductive assets to the larger economy and removing obstacles that prevent them from contributing to that economy benefits not only people and places that are economically marginalized, but the larger economy as well. Inclusivity is about much more than full participation in group decision-making;[7] it is about full and fair participation in the economy, whether as a business owner, worker, consumer, or service provider.

We can be inclusive in thinking about transactional partners, support partners, and demand partners. It is often effective to engage a mix of transactional partners, some of whom are economically marginalized and others of whom are not. Building social capital among them is an important step in wealth creation. Similarly, support partners can be a mix of providers of mainstream, non-mainstream, and highly innovative services to a range of different populations. We address the inclusive dimensions of demand in the wealth creation framework in Chapter 5.

We can also be inclusive in considering all the functions required for a value chain to succeed. For example, we know that businesses require financing, but how that financing is structured can make the difference between engaging limited resource producers or not. We can be inclusive in thinking about the full range of people and organizations that would benefit if our work was successful. For example, if we are working on energy efficient affordable housing, how could our work impact local governments? What might be in it for them to revise building codes, improve neighborhood security, remediate brownfields, or extend infrastructure in exchange for increased stability and tax revenues? How can our work help strengthen low-income representation in local governments as well as renew neighborhoods?

What Does it Mean to Be Place-Based?

There are several key aspects to the concept of "place-based" that have influenced the development of the WealthWorks framework. The first is the conviction that geographic place is one determinant of appropriate development. Every place is unique in its history, resource endowment, cultural context, power struggles, and accomplishments. In our experience, every wealth creation value chain requires a mix of some interventions that are place-specific and others that may apply more broadly, because, for example, they relate to sector as well as place or to skills needed regardless of

42 *What is a Wealth Creation Value Chain?*

place, or to public or private policies of institutions that exist in multiple places. Therefore, WealthWorks is a framework and not a cookie-cutter approach and is expected to look different in different places. The uniqueness of place is one reason why the sixth principle speaks to flexibility in application. Attention to place helps us look with fresh eyes at what we have to work with to create an increasingly sustainable economy. Being open to the uniqueness of place helps practitioners identify promising sectors and wealth creation value chains based on comparative advantage that already exists or can be brought into existence with targeted investment.

The second aspect of "place-based" that was on our minds as we developed the framework has to do with the often unrecognized flows of people, money, goods, and services between rural, suburban, and urban places within a regional context. Some of these flows are formal, i.e. based on the market economy, and others are informal, based on like exchange, barter, and non-monetized trade. While it was once common for people to spend their entire lives in either an urban or a rural setting, it is increasingly common for people to experience both over the course of their lives. Rural areas have higher rates of self-employed business proprietors (entrepreneurs) than their urban counterparts, largely out of necessity. [8] Rather than thinking of rural and urban as two distinct categories, researchers are increasingly conceptualizing a continuum between rural and urban.[9]

Thinking of economic development in a regional context that includes rural areas provides an opportunity to transform the urban-centric planning and economic development models that dominate today to models that heighten awareness of the synergies between rural, suburban, and urban areas. The air, water, soil, forests, wetlands, and other natural resource endowments of rural areas, if polluted, depleted, destroyed, or otherwise mismanaged threaten the survival of urban as well as rural areas.

The concept of an ecological footprint has been used to raise consciousness concerning the impact of a person or a community on the environment, and to raise a degree of awareness about the amount of resources it takes to support concentrated settlements. Ecological footprints are expressed as the amount of land required to produce the natural resources consumed and to absorb the waste created by a given settlement.[10] However, ecological footprints alone do not create social capital or provide guidance on how to bring about a change in perception and relationship between urban areas where consumption and waste generation is concentrated and rural areas where natural resources are exploited. Nor do they create an infrastructure for investment that supports rural areas in providing ecosystem services required by regions.

Rural communities have an important role to play in providing resource stewardship services and other goods and services such as food, fiber, energy, education, technological innovation, wildfire protection, flood protection, ecosystem diversity, tourism, and recreational opportunities for everyone. What types of investments in sector specific wealth creation value chains that connect rural and urban areas can redound to the benefit of both? How can urban waste be reduced and/or converted into inputs for reuse?

The Economic Development Administration and some other federal agencies have begun to promote regional development that is inclusive of rural areas,[11] yet most urban governments are focused on their day-to-day challenges and rarely foster strong relations with rural communities that they impact and are impacted by. In fact, the way some government agencies define regions exacerbates the very isolation that engenders ongoing poverty. For example, the Appalachian Region is defined by the Appalachian Regional Commission to include 420 counties in 13 states, but the line around the region excludes the major metropolitan areas on its borders.[12] Resources targeted to alleviate poverty in the region are not typically used to assist these communities to intentionally connecting with demand in urban areas. The very way regions are geographically defined and targeted has resulted in few institutions, social structures and policies that foster urban–rural economic development dialogue.

Economic Connections between Rural and Urban

Our urban-centric thinking is a natural outgrowth of the historic pattern of exploiting rural resources to meet the needs of urban areas. For example, Central Appalachia has long supplied mineral energy in the form of coal to urban areas throughout the country and beyond, but the cost for the region itself in black lung disease, mining disasters, polluted waterways and airways, and economic dependency on local monopolists has been very high. Going back to the primary aspiration of WealthWorks, which is to create market-driven economies that do not undermine some forms of wealth to create others and allow multiple forms of wealth to stick in the places where they are created, we can see the need to rethink and re-envision the urban–rural continuum from one of exploitation to one of *mutual benefit*. We need to begin with a better understanding of rural/urban interconnections.

As part of the WealthWorks exploration of rural–urban linkages, Brian Dabson and others at the Rural Policy Research Institute used social accounting matrix tools to measure the flows of production, consumption, savings, and investment, and the stocks of capital and wealth across Central Appalachia's economic, social, and environmental dimensions and estimate the degrees of connectedness between rural and urban areas in and adjacent to the region. The key findings from this work include the following.

- Rural peripheries have negative trade balances because the value of the goods and services they produce is insufficient to pay for their consumption of goods and services from both the core and the outside economy.
- Rural peripheries tend to have positive Federal accounts. Federal accounts are the flows of transfer payments (primarily Social Security and unemployment) and non-transfer payments (direct payments, grants, procurement,

44 *What is a Wealth Creation Value Chain?*

salaries and wages) from the federal government. A positive federal account means that rural peripheries generally receive more in Federal payments on a per capita basis (generally transfer payments more so than non-transfer payments) than they pay in federal taxes. This is due to relatively lower incomes and higher rates of poverty.

- Rural peripheries tend to have lower assets income flows. Assets income flows include dividends, interest and rent payments that go disproportionately (on a per capita basis) to core (i.e. more urban) economies.[13]

One take-away from this analysis is that persistent lack of competitive connection to the mainstream economy is not costless for society as a whole and that opportunities exist to restructure the nature of investment in rural and urban areas to improve overall economic performance. There are opportunities to develop inclusive wealth creation value chains that connect and benefit both rural and urban economies. WealthWorks was developed with rural areas as initiators; this role could be played just as well by urban or suburban partners if those partners reconceive their connections to the rural areas on which they depend.

The Sacramento Model

The Sacramento Area Council of Governments provides one notable example of an exploration of rural–urban connections in the context of regional planning and economic development.[14] In 2008, the Sacramento Area COG shifted its paradigm to more explicitly include rural areas and began to create a Valley Vision encompassing 6 counties, 22 cities and 2.2 million people. Among the data gathered were land uses and themes (commodity agriculture, open space/recreation, large lot residential with agriculture, small-scale local market agriculture), overall acreage and value of agricultural commodities produced, and return on investment by acre in agriculture. The development scenarios took into account water demand, labor demand, transportation requirements, demand for infrastructure such as sewer, flood control, streets, and wastewater, carbon emissions, and more and modeled potential responses to changes conditions such as continued drought.

The Sacramento Area COG engaged more than 8,000 participants in multiple forums and conducted research establishing baseline and desired conditions through 2050. Baseline conditions were established through an assessment of current conditions and trends. One significant outcome of this work was a desired reduction in additional urbanized land of some 357 square miles or more than half the anticipated urbanized area likely to exist in 2050 based on historic trends. In other words, participants including a preponderance of urban dwellers want to see fewer densely developed acres and more working landscape.

Among the innovations in investment patterns identified that would support the desired future of limited urbanization were city–county agreements that direct urbanization to cities in exchange for sharing tax increment revenue with counties. Investments by urban areas in open space conservation were another example, particularly when tied directly to mitigation of development impacts. In addition, they identified market driven investments in the food system that would support maintaining land in agricultural uses, including increased local distribution, local processing capacity, and local institutional purchasing and the mismatch between what they grow and what they eat. Among the barriers identified was the lack of adequate transportation for farm workers. Forests were analyzed as well and the multiple contributions of sustainably managed forests in providing a variety of materials, food, and bioenergy. The Sacramento COG also identified a reality facing nearly every rural area in the country; namely the small size of rural populations relative to the large number of road miles they are expected to maintain, many of which support provision of goods and services to urban areas. Many of these investment opportunities and mechanisms could be shaped to support wealth creation value chains connecting rural and urban areas for mutual benefit.

Individual wealth creation value chains provide a context in which to get specific about the sourcing of inputs, generation and reuse of waste, and connections to demand that connect rural and urban production capacity and rural and urban markets. Specific wealth creation value chains offer tangible opportunities to promote dialogue between urban and rural decision-makers that can result in increased awareness of interdependencies and innovative approaches to complementary investments in rural and urban areas. For example, the Deep South Community Agricultural Network has begun to explore connections between agricultural producer groups in the Deep South and urban agricultural producers and consumers in Detroit, many of whom have families that trace their roots to the Deep South and value southern foods. Given the differences in growing seasons between the Deep South and Detroit, what would it take for limited income producers in the South to become the source of southern crops like sweet potato greens and collard greens for Detroit residents during the parts of the year when local production is not feasible? What kinds of structures can be developed that would allow urban dwellers to invest in the capacity of southern producers to meet demand on a sustainable basis? What goods or services might be provided by Detroit producers to residents in the Deep South?

Specific wealth creation value chains offer tangible opportunities to promote dialogue between urban and rural decision-makers that can result in increased awareness of interdependencies and innovative approaches to complementary investments in rural, urban, and suburban areas.

What We Mean by "Scale"

Scale matters. If we are serious about re-inventing capitalism we need to think big, even as we use grounded, place-based experiences to inform systems change

46 *What is a Wealth Creation Value Chain?*

through changes in partners, policies, incentives, and more. One of the criteria for deciding which of the many potential wealth creation value chains that could move to proof of concept in a given place at a given time is its potential for going to scale.

"Scale," of course, means different things in every situation. In the practice of wealth creation, scale is not defined by absolute numbers (e.g. 1,000 jobs created or 1 million consumers reached) and it is not confined to the impact of a single project. There is no single definition of what constitutes scale in this work; however, scale is more than a matter of size. Scale is a fluid concept that looks different depending on context; it has certain characteristics that include moving beyond dependence on one or a handful of individuals who are champions of change to sustainable, market-driven solutions that are integrated into private, public, and nonprofit institutions as a new normal. Achieving scale means not only impacting a relatively wide range of producers and consumers, but changing the systems in which production and consumption occur from systems that are fundamentally exploitative to systems that are synergistic and inclusive. The potential for scale is directly related to the likelihood of creating a "new normal" through systems change that opens up benefits to many that were not part of the original work and may never know how it influenced their lives.

This approach to scale does not focus on attribution (i.e. we can prove that our work caused this), but rather on contribution (i.e. we can prove that the work we did contributed to this positive change). That's because we (and others) recognize the futility and small-mindedness that results from an attachment to attribution as the litmus test for success in work that is about systems change.

Scale also has an important geographic component that differentiates WealthWorks from conventional community development and economic development. Wealth creation value chains do not need to be, nor do they tend to be, comprised of partners from a single community. Instead, the geography of note is the geography required to connect the right producers with one another and with market demand at a scale that leads to sustainability and institutionalization. Demand must be greater than any single partner can meet alone; otherwise there is no shared benefit from participation in a value chain.

WealthWorks was conceived of as a strategy for rural economic development in a regional context. The framework recognizes the economic connections and gaps between rural, suburban, and urban places and the existence of both marginalized and mainstreamed populations in rural, urban, and suburban places. Although the WealthWorks approach was built from a rural foundation, potential for scale exists in connecting value chains to regional (not only local) demand while creating wealths that stick among currently economically marginalized people and places with varying population densities. Helping value chain partners understand the concept of scale at a regional level can secure "buy-in" where it would not otherwise exist. As value chain partners begin to envision the potential for an increasingly sustainable regional economy through investment in a specific value chain and its chainlets, what may have started out as an unfamiliar and even abstract concept, quickly becomes tangible.

The goal of wealth creation work is not just a successful pilot, but rather exploration, proof of concept, implementation, and institutionalization of wealth creation value chains that sustain the livelihoods of those engaged from the start, build multiple forms of wealth while not undermining any to build others, and result in systems changes that unlock new opportunities for many to become engaged over time. The same visioning muscles used in community development to help communities imagine a better future have a place in wealth creation work in visioning what a wealth creation value chain would look like at scale, who would benefit, and what needs to change to get there. One of the elements of change often required relates to structures of ownership and control.

Notes

1 Porter, M. E. (2008). *Competitive Advantage: Creating and Sustaining Superior Performance*. New York: Free Press. (Republished with a new introduction, 1998.)
2 Fahe, *Wealth Creation in Rural Communities, Year One Reporting Template*, submitted to Yellow Wood Associates, internal report, 2010.
3 Ibid.
4 Ibid.
5 https://positivedeviance.org/
6 *Wealth Creation through Financial Education: Empowering Families through Information and Knowledge Sharing*, 10 modules, Community Resource Group in collaboration with Community Development Corporation of Brownsville, 2013.
7 This is the definition of inclusion offered by the D5 Coalition in the context of philanthropy's commitment to advance diversity, equity and inclusion: http://www.d5coalition.org/tools/dei/. It should not be confused with the definition and principle of inclusion offered here.
8 Thiede, B., Greiman, L., Weiler, S., Beda, S., and Conroy, T. (2017, March 16). Six charts that illustrate the divide between rural and urban America. *The Conversation*. Retrieved from: https://theconversation.com/six-charts-that-illustrate-the-divide-between-rural-and-urban-america-72934
9 Dabson, B. et al. (2009). *Briefing Paper on Wealth Creation and Rural–Urban Linkages in Central Appalachia*. Columbia, MO: Rural Policy Research Institute.
10 Global Footprint Network. *Ecological Footprint*. Retrieved from: http://www.footprintnetwork.org/our-work/ecological-footprint/
11 U.S. Economic Development Association. (n.d.). *Investment Priorities*. Retrieved from: https://www.eda.gov/about/investment-priorities.htm; see section on Collaborative Regional Innovation.
12 Appalachian Regional Commission. (2011, August). *Population Change in Appalachia, 2000–2010*. Retrieved from: https://www.arc.gov/research/MapsofAppalachia.asp?MAP_ID=63
13 Dabson, B., Johnson, T. G., Miller, K. K., and Robinson, D. P. (2009). *Rural–Urban Interdependence in Central Appalachia*. Yellow Wood Associates. Retrieved from: http://yellowwood.org/assets/resource_library/resource_docs/rural%20urban%20interdependence.pdf
14 Shabazian, D. (n.d.) *Rural–Urban Connections Strategy*. Retrieved from: http://www.sacog.org/rural-urban-connections-strategy

4 How Do Ownership and Control Change the Game?

Making Wealth Stick

When it comes to place-based wealth creation, ownership matters. Ownership and control over various forms of wealth is central to making wealth "stick" in economically marginalized places. The location and composition of ownership and control of the enterprises within the chain and the resources on which businesses and consumers depend determines who benefits from investments, how the benefits are distributed, and how reinvestment happens. In order to realize the promise of wealth creation value chains, ownership and control of resources needs to belong to the places and the people where we want wealth to stick.

One way to think about a wealth creation value chain is as a horizontally integrated business. Economists use the term "horizontal integration" to refer to one business that performs the same function (e.g. trucking) at the same level of the value chain in multiple industries. In the context of a wealth creation value chain, we are using "horizontal integration" to describe something very different; a value chain comprised of multiple independent partners who see their self-interest in cooperating with one another. Each business or partner in a wealth creation value chain must benefit or they will not continue to participate. Unlike vertically integrated businesses, in which one large corporate entity owns and controls everything from input supply to final product (and often the demand channel as well), in a wealth creation value chain ownership is diffused throughout and across the chain.

Horizontal integration offers many more entities an opportunity to own and benefit from participating in the production process and makes room for place-based entrepreneurship rather than control and exploitation by outside interests that have no vested interest in the places where they operate. Various structures exist to support shared ownership of enterprises that may be part of the transactional, support, and/or demand section of the value chain. Shared ownership has the potential to spread wealth further into communities and include people who would not otherwise have the experience of ownership in a productive economic enterprise.

Since value chains begin with raw materials and extend through to wholesale buyers and ultimately final consumers, ownership and control matters throughout the chain. A wealth creation value chain that is dependent on resources beyond the control of the business entities that are part of the chain is more vulnerable to exploitation and disruption than one that is not. Often, strengthening a wealth creation value chain requires engaging supporting partners in developing and implementing the policies, tools, and regulations that support individual, shared, and/or community ownership and control of multiple forms of wealth. This may include forging agreements between entities with different ownership structures and even changing existing ownership structures to better serve the financial and wealth creation goals of the value chain.

The Power of Ownership

Ownership is the legal and governance framework that determines who has decision-making power over any given asset or resource. It is the owner of a resource who decides how that resource will be used, who will directly benefit from its use, if and how it will be maintained and how any "income" it generates will be distributed and/or reinvested. The question of "how" is central to the WealthWorks approach. There are many ways to provide any given good or service; some are generative and create wealths, while others are exploitative and destroy wealths. (Some, of course, do a mix of both, generally creating wealths for those who already have more and destroying wealths of those who have less.) Changing from exploitative to equitable generative solutions requires behavioral changes in how we use our resources, and the decisions over how resources are used are generally controlled to a significant extent by those that own them.

Most value chains require resources that may be owned or controlled by people and organizations other than the value chain partners. The dialogue between those who own and control resources and those who don't is often challenging. One way to address this challenge is for value chain partners to establish, formalize, and/or reveal their ownership stake in one or more of the resources critical to the success of the value chain. Even a relatively small ownership stake in, for example, real estate, intellectual capital, or a business critical to the success of the value chain can bring otherwise marginalized voices "to the table" where policy decisions that would impact the value chain are being made. Getting to the table is half the battle; once there, the partners can begin to form relationships that can influence decisions for mutual benefit. In this way, ownership can contribute substantially to social capital and political capital that can in turn be used to further expand opportunities for ownership or control.

Since owners of assets, whether physical, financial, intellectual, or other, are the ones that get to decide whether and how to invest in those assets and whether and how to reinvest or distribute the returns on initial investments,

50 *Ownership and Control Changing the Game*

the way ownership is structured matters. The structure of ownership sets the stage for those decisions. For example, a rural electric cooperative is owned by its members who elect a board of directors, which together with management, set policies regarding investments and distribution of benefits to members. They are not set up as profit-making entities. By contrast, privately held utilities are profit-making entities and some portion of the profits they make each year is distributed to shareholders rather than reinvested in the utility and its infrastructure. Therefore, over time, a greater amount of money must be squeezed out of consumers to cover required investments plus profit-sharing. The structure of ownership can be the determining factor in whether investments flow back to the places and assets that generated value to begin with and thus grow local stocks of wealth or whether the value generated is simply extracted and re-located away from the point of origin, leaving local stocks of wealth depleted.

The structure of ownership may also be related to the time horizon for investments. A recent study documented the shift to "short-termism" among publicly traded firms in the United States from 1980 to 2013. Short-termism, meaning prioritizing immediate profits to shareholders over investments in long-term productivity, is correlated with a decrease in investments in research and development, capital equipment, employee training, and environmental and community stewardship. It is also correlated with high turnover in corporate leadership and an increase in large share repurchases, which provide returns to investors but do nothing to build productive stocks of wealth.[1] Changing the emphasis in our economy and society from how much we can consume to how much we can invest in multiple stocks of wealth will require a combination of incentives for long-termism applied to all ownership structures, as well as some reimagining of ownership structures.

Ownership and Place

WealthWorks strives to tie regional wealth to place through place-based ownership and control. Understanding the difference between place-based wealth and people-based wealth can help practitioners identify relevant ownership patterns and create strategies to tie more wealth to place.[2] Place-based wealth refers to the combination of private, public, and communal assets of a region regardless of their ownership. Some forms of natural capital, for example, soils and minerals, are particularly tied to place. People-based wealth refers to the cumulative value of individuals' multiple capitals, less liabilities. While some people-based wealth, such as individual capital (skills and health) may be tied to place insofar as they belong to people who live in a place; even individual capital may not be invested in the place in which people actually live (think of bedroom communities). This is even truer when distant markets can be readily tapped from anywhere offering strong internet capabilities. When people leave a place; they take their individual capital with them.

Financial wealth, in particular, is a form of people-based wealth often invested over long distances and away from the places where people live. This distinction explains, in part, why there are financially wealthy individuals even in very poor places in rural America.[3] Financially wealthy individuals living in poor places typically invest substantially outside the areas where they reside. People-based wealth, which is all about ownership and control, does not necessarily enrich a place, though it has the potential to do so.

From the perspective of the wealth creation approach to economic development, resources do not represent community wealth unless communities own and/or control them. If, for example, the place-based wealth that is solar or wind resources is controlled by a few companies based outside the community it is not as likely to be used, maintained, and reinvested in for the good of the communities in which it is located as if it were owned or controlled locally. We have seen this in Vermont, where locally owned municipal utilities in Stowe and Hyde Park (among others) have developed renewable solar energy infrastructure that directly benefits their communities by providing energy and stabilizing rates without reducing the value of adjacent properties, while developer-owned industrial wind installations sell renewable energy credits outside the state, undermine the value of adjacent properties without compensation (depleting social and individual capital as well as the financial assets of affected property owners) and provide no local rate stabilization benefits. Similar examples abound in every sector of our economy.

Successful implementation of the WealthWorks approach does not depend on a wholesale change in ownership patterns. There is room for all types of ownership within the WealthWorks framework. The difference between a conventional approach to economic development and WealthWorks is in: 1) raising awareness about the significance of ownership and control; 2) being intentional about understanding existing patterns; and 3) identifying opportunities for changes that can induce increases in productive investments in places that and people who are currently isolated from the mainstream economy.

Ownership and control are different. Ownership means just that: having legally defensible rights over and responsibility for any given asset. Control is a matter of degree. If, for example, a community offers a developer a tax break in exchange for creating jobs, this may seem like a form of control but in actuality, unless the community is prepared to invest in defending their rights, the control is generally illusory. There are far too many examples of communities that have given away tax breaks with the hope of more jobs, only to have companies fail to provide those jobs. Once the tax breaks are no longer available, many companies pull up stakes and leave.

Ownership and control apply not only to physical property and business entities but to intellectual property as well. The most successful wealth creation value chains are breaking new ground in the ways business is done that create intellectual property that can be patented, trademarked, and/or copyrighted. These forms of protection for intellectual property are valuable ways to both ensure the integrity of process and outcomes and create wealth

52 *Ownership and Control Changing the Game*

that can be used to continue to support the growth and development of the value chain.

For example, Fahe had to fill a gap in the energy efficient affordable housing value chain through research to determine exactly which building practices produced the greatest impact on energy efficiency by dollar invested. Was it the insulation, the windows, the foundations? Well, it turned out to be the caulk used to seal openings in the building frame. High-quality caulk makes a huge and measurable difference in building performance. By carefully documenting the precise construction methods required to achieve an energy efficiency affordable dwelling that meets specific measurable standards of performance, Fahe created intellectual capital that has become the basis for a unique mortgage product and has unlocked a significant stream of financing for energy efficient affordable housing in Appalachia.

At the same time, having intellectual capital has allowed Fahe, as value chain coordinator, to develop a potential income stream related to sharing, teaching and training others in the use of the well-documented process they have developed. Having this type of intellectual capital available contributes to systems change in markets by expanding the range of choices available to developers and consumers. Because wealth creation value chains almost by definition require innovation in products, processes, and market relationships, there is a high likelihood that they will produce novel intellectual capital. The difference in intellectual capital produced through wealth creation value chains, and intellectual capital produced in a vacuum (as is the case for so many patents developed in garages and workshops around the country each year that never become commercialized) is that the intellectual capital produced through value chain development is already embedded in a set of market relationships and is therefore more likely to be used and further developed to scale.

Ownership can also apply to a brand. For example, a group of fishermen in Georgia worked together with a facilitator to develop and promote a brand for local fish. Once all their hard work had begun to pay off with customers, the facilitator stepped forward and revealed that they, not the fishermen, actually owned the brand. Furthermore, now that the brand had traction, they were going to use it with other fishermen, thus undercutting the initial participants. Since no one had asked who owned the brand at the start, there was nothing that the initial group could do about it. They had to invest in creating another brand for themselves and begin the process of market penetration all over again.[4]

There are a variety of ways to structure ownership and/or control of assets that can help channel the benefits from those assets and decision-making over how they are maintained over time to those that need them the most. These structures can connect place-based assets with people-based assets in ways that keep wealth local and mitigate the tendencies toward extraction of wealth and exploitation of communities. *A single wealth creation value chain may encompass a variety of ownership structures, including conventional individual and/or corporate ownership plus shared ownership and/or structures that provide influence over wealth flows.* Shared ownership structures can offer more people the opportunity to participate as owners than would otherwise have that opportunity.

Shared ownership can take many forms. *It can mean that ownership is shared among individuals, as in cooperatives or employee-owned firms. It can mean that ownership is shared between an individual and a collective entity like a land trust. Or it can mean a sharing of certain ownership duties—like marketing dairy goods or managing wind rights—while other aspects of property ownership remain in individual hands.* The form of business ownership that makes the most sense will depend on a number of factors including, but not necessarily limited to: the nature of the business and its value proposition; the management capabilities available; and the willingness, interest, and capacity of participants to assume an element of ownership. All these factors can change over time.

In addition to structures for shared ownership, there are frameworks that offer communities a degree of control over the allocation of resources that does not require outright ownership. Structures that provide influence or control over stocks and flows of wealth can result in reinvestment of wealth in place rather than wealth extraction.

Structures of Shared Ownership and Control

We have identified seven structures of shared ownership and six shared control structures with track records that are worthy of consideration. These structures are rarely considered in the same breath, yet they are all forms of shared ownership and control that can benefit both the community and the individual. Many are more widespread in our economy than you might think. Wealths owned and managed through these structures may be a place to start in aggregating resources to support wealth creation value chains. These structures may also be appropriate for consideration by existing businesses in the value chain and/or for use in structuring emerging entrepreneurial opportunities. What follows is a very brief description of each structure; more information, including a list of sources of expertise related to each structure is available in *Keeping Wealth Local: Shared Ownership and Wealth Control for Rural Communities* (http://www.wealthworks.org and http://www.yellowwood.org).

1 Cooperative Ownership

A cooperative is a democratically controlled enterprise owned and governed by the people it serves. Cooperatives allow members to pool resources for shared benefits. In general, cooperative members control profits, business reinvestment, and business services. Cooperatives put service to members before profits.

54 *Ownership and Control Changing the Game*

Cooperatives exist and thrive in a variety of sectors. Nationally, the most widely used form of cooperative is the credit union. Marketing co-ops, also known as producer co-ops, include such well-known names as Ocean Spray, Land O'Lakes, and Organic Valley, as well as many smaller entities. Value-added processing co-ops own manufacturing facilities that add value to member products. Consumer co-ops provide retail services to consumers such as coffee shop services, grocery services, hardware services, etc. Purchasing or service co-ops allow businesses to collectively purchase materials or manage services. Rural electric co-ops provide electrical power in rural areas. Worker co-ops are businesses that are cooperatively owned by their employees. The Island Employee Cooperative in Deer Isle, Maine is the largest worker cooperative in Maine and the second-largest in New England.[5] Multi-stakeholder cooperatives draw their membership from more than one group of stakeholders such as consumers and producers, or raw materials providers and processors, or producers and community members. As of 2007, there were more than 300 multi-stakeholder cooperatives in Quebec, Canada operating in around 22 sectors from leisure to computing to farming and manufacturing.[6]

2 Employee Ownership

Another form of employee ownership in the United States in addition to cooperative ownership is through an employee retirement plan called an Employee Stock Ownership Plan (ESOP). According to the National Center for Employee Ownership, there were about 7,000 ESOPs covering about 13.5 million employees in 2015. Through ESOPS and other related mechanisms, the Center estimates that employees now control about 8% of corporate equity in the United States. Reputable studies have found that firms with ESOPs that actively practice participatory management experience above-average growth in productivity, while those that have plans in place but do not engage employees show no significance changes in performance. Successful participatory management requires ongoing investments in the intellectual and individual capital of employees so that they have the understanding and skills required to participate effectively. Employee ownership is not restricted by size or sector (as long as the costs of establishing the plan do not outweigh the advantages). The largest employee-owned firm listed by the Center is Publix Super Markets with more than 182,000 employees; others have tens of thousands of employees and fewer.[7]

3 Community Land Trusts

A community land trust is a nonprofit organization formed to hold title to land in perpetuity, allowing the community to provide permanently affordable housing and plan land use to meet other community needs such as agricultural production or recreation, while houses remain under private ownership. According to the Center for American Progress, today there are about 220 active community land trusts in the United States.[8] Many, though

Ownership and Control Changing the Game   55

not all, community land trusts include an affordable housing component that creates built wealth for the community in ways that benefit individual households as well as the community itself. Benefits of safe and stable housing have been documented in improved physical and mental health, educational and social outcomes for adults and children.

4 Municipally Owned Enterprises

Municipally owned enterprises are businesses owned by local public authorities that provide services to citizens and bring in revenue to cities. Municipal enterprises typically do not seek to maximize profits but rather to provide services that would not otherwise be available, or, if available, would be restricted to higher-income residents. There are many different types of municipally owned enterprises, including, but not limited to, electric utilities, telephone companies, hospitals, liquor stores, airports, transit systems, broadband companies, and recycling and composting enterprises. The scale of municipally owned enterprises varies. The most recent type of municipal enterprise in the US is the municipally owned cannabis store. North Bonneville, Washington, a city of 1,000, established The Cannabis Corner in 2015 as a municipally owned enterprise after cannabis was legalized in Washington State. Governance is modeled after Seattle's famous Pike Place Market. Austin Energy in Austin, Texas is the eighth-largest community-owned electric utility in the nation, serving around 420,000 customers, while Swanton Electric in Swanton, Vermont serves a population of about 6,500 in the village and surrounding areas.

The difference between a municipally owned enterprise and public ownership (described below) is in the expectation that municipally owned enterprises will operate as businesses with streams of non-tax revenue that contribute substantially to offsetting costs of operation. Municipally owned enterprises can contribute to many forms of community wealth, including, but not necessarily limited to: social capital (e.g. improved connectivity within and among communities); natural capital (e.g. improved soil quality through use of compost, or reduced reliance on fossil fuels through renewables); individual capital (e.g. improved human health); and built capital (e.g. accessible transportation using non-polluting vehicles). Because these enterprises are municipally owned and operated, decisions regarding investment and reinvestment as well as other ways in which the enterprises can further community goals, as for example, by serving as a site for worker training, can be made through a democratic process. Municipally owned enterprises offer an alternative to the more conventional model of business attraction, offering municipalities the option of investing directly in providing goods and services rather than subsidizing others to do so.

5 Public Ownership

Public ownership refers to infrastructure and programs supported primarily by tax dollars. Schools, libraries, fire stations, and town halls are forms of

56 Ownership and Control Changing the Game

public ownership common in many rural communities. Public ownership is often overlooked as a form of shared ownership but that is exactly what it is. As communities seek to support wealth creating value chains, they may find that public ownership provides opportunities to strengthen demand, by, for example, increasing the amount of locally grown food in local schools or locally produced fuels in local transit systems. Publicly owned infrastructure and equipment can also be repurposed or shared to support production of goods and services. For example, the city of Espanola, New Mexico had a list of properties sitting unused. The value chain coordinator for a value chain in the agricultural sector identified an appropriate building for sorting, washing, and storing regional produce and was able to secure a 30-year lease from the City Council. The same value chain was able to work with support partners and transactional partners to restore and utilize a ten-year-old commercial kitchen owned by a local college that had previously failed and was mothballed.[9] Value chain analysis can be used to identify underutilized assets such as these whose owners have self-interest in bringing them back online.

Land banks are another variation on public ownership. Michigan has the most developed land bank system in the country, with public authorities that capture property transfer taxes and may reinvest in community property or convert tax delinquent property into community forests.

6 Local Ownership

Local ownership (also known as resident ownership) refers to the ownership of enterprises or resources by people who live in a given locality or region. In most counties in the US, the percent of workers employed by locally or resident-owned businesses outweigh the percent of workers employed by nonresident-owned businesses. But this number varies widely among counties. The share of employment in nonresident businesses varies from 0% in 24 counties across the nation to 85% in Tunica County, Mississippi.[10]

Local ownership is the wedding of place-based and people-based wealth. Local ownership is not necessarily "shared" in the same sense as the other forms of ownership, since a single local person or family may be sole owners; however, local ownership may create a climate of greater sensitivity to local needs and support for local opportunities when compared with non-local ownership.

A paper published by the Federal Reserve Bank of Atlanta in 2013 specifically tested the hypotheses that: 1) local entrepreneurship in general has a positive effect on county per capita income growth and employment growth and a negative effect on change in poverty in counties; and 2) smaller local businesses have a more positive effect on local economic performance (measured as per capita income growth, employment growth, and change in poverty) than larger local businesses. The author concludes,

> I find that the percent of employment provided by resident, or locally-owned, business establishments has a significant positive effect on

county income and employment growth and a significant and negative effect on change in poverty in the all counties and nonmetro counties samples ... the results show that smaller resident establishments are more favorable for county economic performance (while) results for medium and large businesses are mixed.[11]

Local ownership may also lead to other forms of shared ownership. For example, when a locally owned community store closes due to the retirement of its owner, the community may choose to form its own entity to purchase and maintain it. Another story of local ownership that transitioned into shared ownership is the Green Bay Packers, an NFL football team that has made its home in Green Bay, Wisconsin since 1919 when it was founded by local enthusiasts. In 1923, the Green Bay Packers became a publicly owned nonprofit corporation. Today the team is entirely owned by some 112,000 local fans and generates $241 million in revenue. Its shares do not increase in value nor pay dividends and can only be sold back to the team. If the company were ever sold, all profits would be earmarked to go to the American Legion. This arrangement keeps the team local in a small market with a nation-wide fan base. [12]

7 Mission-Controlled Ownership

Mission-controlled enterprises design the protection of their social mission into their legal frameworks to ensure that the social mission remains intact through time. The legal stipulations that govern ownership of shares and any future sale of the Green Bay Packers, described above, is one example of mission-controlled ownership.

There are a wide variety of legal frameworks that can be used to imprint the mission into an enterprise while still allowing changes in investors over time. Dual-class share structures that place control of super-voting shares in the hands of a family, a trust, a foundation, or a nonprofit underlie the structure of the *New York Times*, with its mission of serving an informed electorate, and Novo Nordisk A/S, a Danish pharmaceutical company with a mission of defeating diabetes, among others. B Corporations, where the "B" stands for "beneficial," are another option. B Corporations are distinguished by requiring a bylaw provision that states that directors will consider the welfare of stakeholders such as the environment, customers and the community as well as the financial interests of shareholders. In addition, B Corporations must receive a passing grade on a scorecard of social and environmental practices developed by B Lab, a nonprofit organization that certifies B Corporations. Another recently developed legal framework is the low-profit, limited liability corporation or L3C Corporation first enacted through legislation in 2008 in Vermont and now authorized by ten states, three tribes, and Puerto Rico.[13] L3C Corporations are designed to attract both private capital and philanthropic capital for enterprises that deliver a social benefit. Unlike charities, L3Cs can distribute profits, after taxes, to owners or investors.

58   *Ownership and Control Changing the Game*

Mission-controlled ownership can be used to tie a business to a place if the mission itself is place-based, as in the case of the Green Bay Packers, but may not necessarily achieve that objective if the mission is not place-based.

The Organically Grown Company (OGC) in Eugene, Oregon, a mission-driven company since its inception in 1978, recently revised its ownership structure to address the disconnection between its mission and existing options for investors. OGC was looking for an ownership structure that would put purpose ahead of profits, create accountability to many different stakeholders including workers, growers, and allies (instead of only to financial investors), and exist in perpetuity to remove any pressure on owners to exit the company. The structure they came up with is a Perpetual Purpose Driven Trust. The Trust raised the money to buy out existing investors so that it became the single shareholder of the company. The Trust is accountable to five stakeholder groups—investors, workers, growers, customers, and community allies—and all five jointly elect a committee to oversee the Trust. Rates of return for investors are established at the outset but investors are limited to no more than 40% of any profit above the pre-established rate of return, thus ensuring that all stakeholders benefit from any upside.[14]

We have also identified six structures that can be used to provide a measure of influence and control over stocks and flows of wealth without taking complete ownership.

1 Community Fees and Taxes

Community fees and taxes are charges levied by local or state governments that are earmarked to be used outside the general fund to create community wealths. Examples of community fees and taxes include taxes on the depletion of natural resources (also known as severance taxes) that can be earmarked for specific investments in reclamation, education and worker training, etc.; real estate transfer taxes that can be earmarked for affordable housing, land conservation, etc.; impact fees; systems benefit charges such as efficiency fees added to utility bills and reinvested in efficiency measures and value recapture taxes used to recapture a portion of the value created through public investment in infrastructure such as a sewer or water line extension. Value chains that contribute to the goals for which community fees and taxes are levied may be able to tap into these resources directly or indirectly.

2 Community Covenants and Easements

Community covenants and easements are binding contracts stipulating that development rights will be held in perpetuity by a community institution, while property ownership remains in individual hands. Covenants and easements create shared ownership by separating out different categories of ownership rights. While these are most often development rights, they can also apply to mineral rights, wind rights, water rights, rights to biomass growth, and more. Community covenants and easements can protect an underlying resource from uses that are not specified in the easement. They cannot, however, guarantee beneficial uses. For example, an easement that protects a working waterfront cannot, by itself, ensure that there will be enterprises available to make use of the facility in the long run. For example, in a 2006 study, the American Farmland Trust found that easements on farmland had protected 1.1 million acres from development, most of which continued to be farmed despite purchase of properties by non-farmers. However, the easements often failed to offset the decline in the overall economics of the farming communities in which properties were located. In addition, the study found that most easement programs were unprepared for the long-term job of governing holdings and responding to problems with non-compliance.[15] Typically, easements or covenants affect the value of the property and provide individual owners with tax benefits. The legal framework governing covenants and easements varies from state to state. Easements and covenants must be held and managed by some entity with capability to enforce their provisions over the long term. Such entities can be units of government or nonprofit organizations. The decision-makers of the organization holding the easements may be more or less inclusive and may or may not be oriented toward productive as well as protective objectives.

3 Community Endowments

Community endowments are a mechanism for transferring stocks of wealth from individuals to communities for long-term community benefit. They are one mechanism to convert people-based wealth into place-based wealth. The difference between community endowments and public ownership is in the control of stocks of wealth by entities that are not governments and are, more typically, nonprofit institutions such as community foundations and/or national conservation groups. In the case of community foundations, donors may designate how they wish their endowments to be used or they may contribute to a general fund to benefit a particular community or region.

4 Community Benefits Agreements

Community benefits agreements are legally enforceable agreements between developers and community groups or local governments detailing the benefits that the developer agrees to provide the community. Depending on the type of value chain and the type of development under consideration, there may be opportunities to tie the two together for mutual benefit. For example, in a region working on a value chain in the recreation sector, the redevelopment of a regional airport may provide opportunities to shape the infrastructure to benefit local aviation entrepreneurs including balloonists, gliders, and more. In addition, a program for advertising, marketing, and shuttle services that support the value chain could be negotiated. Workforce

60 *Ownership and Control Changing the Game*

training and/or vacation packages with participating airlines are other possibilities. Although the airport re-developer is not likely to be able to negotiate on behalf of airlines, he/she can use their social and political capital to create relationships of benefit to the value chain and help value chain participants understand how best to communicate with and listen to airline executives.

5 *Community Currencies*

Community currencies are currencies not linked to government that are backed by a local or regional organization. Community currencies are generally designed to promote local trade and bartering and prevent consumer dollars from leaking out of local economies. Some community currencies, such as Ithaca HOURs in Ithaca, New York, are not convertible to dollars, while others, like BerkShares in western Massachusetts, are. Time banks (also called Time Dollars and LETS) offer participants service credits based on time donated. In areas where community currencies have been established, they may provide another means of tapping into demand or converting ineffective demand into effective demand.

6 *Sharing Finite Common Resources*

In some communities in the US and abroad, including tribal communities, there are resources such as forestland, rangeland, irrigation water, fishing waters, etc. that are considered communal resources over which no individual or single entity has ownership or exclusive control. In 1968, Garrett Hardin introduced the concept of "the tragedy of the commons" showing that resources that are not protected by private property rights tend to become debased and depreciated through overuse.[16] Global warming can be interpreted as a "tragedy of the commons," in which the shared resource of a healthy planetary atmosphere has become debased through millions of individual decisions that have resulted in overburdening the atmosphere with carbon. The right to pollute has been protected; the shared right to a healthy atmosphere has not.

In the work for which she won a Nobel Prize in 2009, Elinor Ostrom used real-world examples to show that the "tragedy of the commons" is not inevitable. There are, in fact, many examples around the world where communal resource-sharing has been successfully sustained over multiple generations. In the US communal resources might include wildlife, town forests, waterways, beaches, rangeland, night skies, solar, wind, geothermal resources, and more. In the United States, when we hear the word "ownership," we tend to think of private ownership. Even shared ownership, though not as uncommon as you might think, seems like a conceptual stretch. However, there is unrealized potential in increasing the health and productivity of our underutilized communally owned resources as well. Realizing this potential will require investments in governance structures, as well as the resources themselves.

One wealth creation value chain exploration supported by WealthWorks was based on the communal resource of waste in the form of large appliances abandoned to decay in fields and along streams. No one claimed ownership of the appliances; they were leaching poisons into the surrounding water and soils, and, if they could be rehabilitated, they could be reused. A value chain in rehabilitated appliances could employ local youth, teach valuable mechanical and business skills, and improve the quality of life of local households that could benefit from working appliances. While this is not exactly the same as governing the use of a fishery, it demonstrates the type of creative thinking that can develop into new opportunities based on changing the existing patterns of resource use.

Elinor Ostrom identified eight principles for how communal resources can be governed sustainably and equitably.

1 Define clear group boundaries.
2 Match rules governing use of common goods to local needs and conditions.
3 Ensure that those affected by the rules can participate in modifying the rules.
4 Make sure the rule-making rights of community members are respected by outside authorities.
5 Develop a system, carried out by community members, for monitoring members' behavior.
6 Use graduated sanctions for rule violators.
7 Provide accessible, low-cost means for dispute resolution.
8 Build responsibility for governing the common resource in nested tiers from the lowest level up to the entire interconnected system.[17]

These principles can also be applied to the governance of wealth creation value chains, a collaborative effort that requires buy-in and responsiveness from all partners and often includes shared use of resources.

It is critical to understand the ownership landscape for those resources most essential to the success of any wealth creation value chain. The ability to implement a wealth creation approach to economic development is significantly enhanced when accurate and timely information regarding ownership is readily available, but that is not always the case. Lack of transparency regarding ownership is one of the roadblocks in our current system that contributes to inequality and allows extreme consolidations of wealth that fly under the radar of regulation. Ownership is not always easy to determine but it is essential to understanding the relationships that must be built to ensure the success of any given wealth creation value chain. Owners of underutilized resources may have surprising self-interests in supporting wealth creation value chains if value chains have the potential to improve the quality of those resources and bring them back into productive use.

62 Ownership and Control Changing the Game

Ownership Transitions

WealthWorks opens up the opportunity to consider ownership transitions. For example, in designing a wealth creation value chain there may be opportunities to transition from sole ownership to one or more forms of shared ownership, or from ownership by an absentee or remotely headquartered nonprofit or for-profit owner to ownership by local people. There are many elements to ownership transitions. Some that are important from a wealth creation perspective include the following.

1 Ownership and structure—the legal and organizational form of the enterprise and who actually owns its assets.
2 Investment and financing—the source(s) of investment and the financing arrangements that support the enterprise.
3 Governance and distribution of benefits—who controls the enterprise and how economic benefits are distributed and how the mission is maintained over time.
4 Supply management—how raw materials and support services are procured.
5 Management and staffing—who manages and staff the organization and how they are trained and prepared to be successful.
6 Profitability, products, and markets—the overall profitability of the enterprise and the degree of diversification among products, services, and markets.

The implications of transitioning ownership need to be considered in all of the areas listed above. Each area offers opportunities for wealth building through careful and intentional transition.

Wealth Works developed resources to assist practitioners in navigating the intricacies of ownership and control in collaboration with Wake Forest University School of Community Law and Business Clinic. They include: *Formalizing Your Business: A Wealth Works Guide for Coordinators and Coaches*, and *Wealth Works Value Chain Business Law Guide.* [18]

Ownership and control are essential factors in how the wealths created are managed and maintained, who benefits from those wealths, and how they are anchored to economically marginalized people and places. However, creating the wealths in the first place depends, first and foremost, on creating effective relationships with the demand side of the market.

Notes

1 Sampson, R. C. and Shi, Y. (2018). Are investor time horizons shortening? *Seattle University Law Review*, 41(2), 543–550.
2 I am indebted to Thomas G. Johnson for his work on people and place-based wealth. See: http://www.mcrsa.org/Assets/Documents/Proceedings/2015_Proceedings_Presentations/Johnson.pdf

Ownership and Control Changing the Game 63

3 Hamilton, L. C., Hamilton, L. R., Duncan, C. M., and Colocousis, C. R. (2008). *Place Matters Challenges and Opportunities in Four Rural Americas*. University of New Hampshire. Retrieved from: https://scholars.unh.edu/cgi/viewcontent.cgi?referer=&httpsredir=1&article=1040&context=carsey

4 I am indebted to John Littles of McIntosh SEED for sharing this story with me.

5 Island Employee Cooperative. *Project Equity*. Retrieved from: https://www.project-equity.org/owner-retires/island-employee-cooperative/

6 Lund, M. (2011). *Solidarity as a Business Model: A Multi-Stakeholder Cooperatives Manual*. Kent, OH: Cooperative Development Center, Kent State University.

7 ESOP (Employee Stock Ownership Plan) Facts. National Center for Employee Ownership. Retrieved from http://www.esop.org/

8 Zonta, M. (2016, June). *Community Land Trusts*. Center for American Progress. Retrieved from: https://cdn.americanprogress.org/wp-content/uploads/2016/06/14141430/CommunityLandTrusts-report.pdf

9 Roger Gonzalez, personal communication, April 9, 2014.

10 Rupasingha, A. (2013). *Locally Owned: Do Local Business Ownership and Size Matter for Local Economic Well-Being?* (No. 2013–01). Federal Reserve Bank of Atlanta, Atlanta, GA.

11 Ibid.

12 Team History: Green Bay Packers. *Pro Football Hall of Fame*. Retrieved from: http://www.profootballhof.com/teams/green-bay-packers/team-history/

13 https://nonprofithub.org/starting-a-nonprofit/jargon-free-guide-l3c/

14 Ben-Ami, A. (2018). Heads up, investors: It's not all about you. *ImpactAlpha*, December 10. Retrieved from: https://impactalpha.com/heads-up-investors-its-not-all-about-you/?utm_source=Pico&utm_campaign=d3a49de881-EMAIL_CAMPAIGN_6_1_2018_12_25_COPY_01&utm_medium=email&utm_term=0_57980c6bda-d3a49de881-105595273&mc_cid=d3a49de881&mc_eid=b856eaa0d2

15 Sokolow, A. D. (2006). *A National View of Agricultural Easement Programs: Measuring Success in Protecting Farmland – Report 4*. December. American Farmland Trust and Agricultural Issues Center. Retrieved from: http://aftresearch.org/research/publications/detail.php?id=b939970b7b60e9da138bcc9164f6ca41

16 Hardin, G. (1968). The tragedy of the commons. *Science*, 162(3859), 1243–1248.

17 Walljasper, J. (2011). Elinor Ostrom's 8 Principles for Managing a Commons. *On The Commons*, October 2. Retrieved from: http://www.onthecommons.org/magazine/elinor-ostroms-8-principles-managing-commmons

18 The business law guide can be found here: http://www.wealthworks.org/economic-development-resources/how-tos/wealthworks-value-chain-business-law-guide-wealthworks-guide, and the coordinators and coaches guide can be found here: http://www.wealthworks.org/economic-dev : delopment-resources/how-tos/formalizing-your-business-wealthworks-guide-coordinators-and

5 What Does It Mean to Be Demand-Driven?

Being demand-driven means several things. First, understanding what buyers want and need while helping buyers understand what producers need to be able to meet buyers' demands. Second, it means organizing the value chain to meet the needs of buyers and producers while simultaneously building multiple stocks of wealth. Perhaps the most significant distinguishing feature of the wealth creation approach is its emphasis on market demand as the driving force for inclusive development. *It is only by connecting people at the economic margins and underemployed individuals and other underutilized resources to genuine market demand in a non-exploitative manner that we will move the needle on poverty.* Only when the demand side of the market is well understood and relationships with buyers are formed, can businesses begin to understand how and why they need to work together to satisfy demand and where there are opportunities to invest in multiple forms of wealth while doing so.

In the wealth-based development framework social services, subsidy programs, and other familiar efforts to ameliorate poverty are not the focus; rather they are legitimate supporting partners only to the extent that their contributions strengthen the functioning of specific wealth creation value chains. All too often, they do not. For example, when alt.Consulting (now Communities Unlimited, Inc.) began to explore their wealth creation value chain for alternative energy in Arkansas, they discovered there was already a two-year community college program training students for work in the renewable energy sector. However, since the market for renewable energy was not yet established in Arkansas, there were hardly any businesses offering renewable energy services and program graduates could not find jobs. That is the all-too-familiar kind of mismatch between well-intentioned resources with economic realities that a wealth creation approach can address by *first* identifying the market opportunity and then figuring out what it will take to connect multiple businesses to realize that opportunity at scale.

As a society, we have condoned a myriad of programs that offer one or another form of "assistance" to under-privileged people that frequently results in further isolation from rather than integration into the mainstream economy. These programs are generally needs-driven or rights-based and do not begin with an understanding of specific and actionable market conditions. They are

What Does It Mean to Be Demand-Driven? 65

dependent on subsidies of one kind or another and rarely become self-supporting. Workforce training is only one area in which well-intentioned programs often fail to move the needle on poverty at scale. Public housing is another. Rather than being a stepping-stone to economic integration, all too often, public housing has become a trap, keeping its residents socially and geographically separated from meaningful economic opportunities.

An alternative approach to workforce development using the WealthWorks framework began in 2011 in the Lower Rio Grande Valley. Detailed employment projections in the health care sector prepared by a local workforce development board focused on entry-level jobs such as personal and home health care aides, nursing aides, orderlies, and attendants, and medical assistants. It showed that the projected rate of growth in these areas was over 30%, with thousands of new jobs anticipated by 2018. This became the basis for a WealthWorks value chain exploration that began with interviews with eight area employers in the health care sector to better understand their needs, expectations, and realities with respect to entry-level staffing, and to begin to identify their self-interests in a potential value chain.

The value chain coordinator, South Texas Adult Resource and Training Center, discovered widespread employer dissatisfaction with the quality and availability of entry-level employees. Employers recognized the need for improved training for a variety of entry-level workers in the health care sector. Their job applicants by and large lacked the "soft skills" necessary for working in a medical practice. The technical training that applicants received from local institutions was often out of date by the time they arrived on the job. Local institutions were not keeping up with the fast pace of change in the industry, yet they had a lock on public training-related resources. Some employers had already developed their own training due to dissatisfaction with the training available from local institutions. Others provide informal on-the-job training by peers, only to see bad habits transfer from trainers to trainees. Hospitals, clinics, colleges, senior care programs, migrant health promotion programs, state agencies, insurers, workforce development boards and private-sector pharmacies all had interest in the concept of a value chain that would produce a pipeline of trained workers that met market demand.

The exploration phase pointed toward an employer consortium organized to pool and leverage resources to build a pipeline qualified entry-level workers in the health care sector. Members of the employer consortium would be both demand partners and, to some extent, transactional partners actually providing training. Other transactional partners would include recruiters like institutions providing High School Equivalency Certificates or GEDs to those with demonstrated competencies but no high school diploma, institutions certifying community health workers, temporary employment agencies and more; trainers to address specific requirements identified by employers, certifiers, job coaches, and more. Support partners would include the media and politicians among others. The relationships built among employers were anticipated to lead to common solutions to other shared

66 *What Does It Mean to Be Demand-Driven?*

problems beyond filling entry-level positions, such as creating career paths for health care workers within a regional context. The value chain would be considered successful if it resulted in employees that were better trained, more effective, and stayed on the job longer, thus reducing turnover and increasing the cost effectiveness as well as health outcomes of providers.

Unfortunately, the organization spearheading this effort lacked adequate resources to bring it to the proof-of-concept stage. In addition, as a social service agency, it was difficult for them to shift from a social service delivery approach to an economic development approach. This, in turn, made it difficult to distinguish transactional partners from support partners; a critical distinction in this work. Relying too much on input from support partners made it difficult to move beyond networking to the business negotiations required to put in place the functions needed to make the value chain work to create a profitable, self-sustaining set of economic activities while building multiple forms of wealth without exploitation. Wealth creation value chains have the potential to help supporting partners in workforce training, housing, and many other areas succeed by building direct relationships with employers engaged in building and growing value chains that are connected with market demand, but this requires recognizing the difference between a supporting partner and a transactional partner, and keeping the focus on the building the capabilities of transactional partners to deliver what the demand partners really need. The core of any value chain is the relationships formed among and between the transactional partners, without which the goods and services of the chain cannot reach the market, and the demand partners, without whom there is no economic driver.

It takes strong leadership, vision, energy, and perseverance to first change one's own way of thinking about what is possible and then to help others change theirs. It is all too easy to get stuck treading water in the existing system, sometimes without even being aware that is what is going on. (See Chapter 10 on coaching for value chain coordinators. The role of coaching is to help value chain coordinators see where they may be getting stuck and figure out how to keep moving.)

What Is Demand?

Effective Demand

Demand refers to the buyers' side of the market. Ultimately, it is the tastes, preferences, and behaviors of buyers that determine winners and losers in the marketplace. Market demand is a nuanced concept. Economists think of demand as either effective or ineffective. Effective demand exists when buyers have the means to pay for the goods and services they desire. Sometimes value chain coordinators and participants can identify effective demand that is unmet. For example, in many parts of the country there is more demand for locally sourced food than there is supply. Customers are able and willing to pay for locally sourced food when they can get it, but there just isn't enough to go around. This is a relatively straightforward scenario in which the challenge is in building a value chain that effectively utilizes local resources in ways that grow a usable and desired supply. Much work is being done in this arena and many lessons are being learned about the accommodations needed on the supply and demand sides of the market to make this work. It can be done; like all the work of changing economic systems, it isn't easy, but it is possible. The Farm to School program is evidence of this. According to the US Department of Agriculture, in 1997, there were five states with some schools using locally or regionally produced foods. All around the country, growers and school systems have come together to negotiate changes in crops, planting regimes, planning, post-harvest handling, packaging, pre-processing, labeling, certifications, insurances, on-site preparation, staffing, menu planning, storage, consumer education, and more that are often required to increase the volume of locally or regionally grown products available to students and faculty in public schools. As of 2014, 42% of all US schools in all 50 states and Washington, DC, serving more than 23.6 million students are engaged in farm to school programs that spend $789 million a year on local food.[1]

Ineffective Demand

Wealth creation value chains can also successfully target ineffective demand. Ineffective demand exists when people or companies want a good or a service and lack the means to pay for it. The conventional approach to addressing ineffective demand, when it is addressed at all, is through direct subsidies. Providing food stamps, for example, increases the effective demand for food. WealthWorks takes a very different approach to ineffective demand, using market forces, the structure of the markets, and innovative product and service designs to convert ineffective demand into effective demand for specific goods and services.

The work that MACED has done is a perfect example of addressing ineffective demand by finding a way to make it effective. Many people in Kentucky live in homes that are not energy efficient. In 2007, Kentucky had one of the lowest costs per unit for energy in the country, yet households used well above the US average kWh per month, making the cost of energy much higher than it needed to be due, in large part, to energy inefficiency.[2] Many home owners in Kentucky do not have the financial resources to invest in improving the energy efficiency of their homes even if it would substantially lower their energy bills and pay them back over time. It is reasonable to assume that they would want the benefits of energy efficiency if they could afford it, but they can't. Therefore, their demand for energy efficiency and related services is ineffective. MACED realized that it was not only home owners but also utility companies that were losing revenue due to inefficiencies. In fact, one of the first utility companies to enter into the value

68 *What Does It Mean to Be Demand-Driven?*

chain conversation with MACED, a rural electric cooperative, reported increasing problems with members who could not pay their bills. Utility company costs in dollars and public relations of trying to work with such members were increasing to the detriment of the company's own bottom line. This was their immediate self-interest in coming to the table as a value chain demand partner. Private, non-member utility companies in the Appalachian region were finding the costs of adding new energy sources going up, so increased energy efficiency was a way to contribute to significant cost avoidance while maintaining revenue flow.

MACED staff researched alternative approaches to implementing energy efficiency improvements and discovered a process called on-bill financing. On-bill financing eliminates the need for home owners to invest dollars up-front to install efficiency measures in their homes. Instead, the up-front costs are paid by utility companies that receive repayment from home owners through a portion of the savings on future bills. While MACED's motivation in establishing this program was to improve the finances, health, and security of lower-income home owners, by making the program inclusive home owners at every income level are able to benefit and a larger percentage of the housing stock is permanently improved. The obligation to pay the utility company back stays with the home and is taken on by any new owner (along with low energy bills) as a condition of ownership.

Another approach to making ineffective demand effective, sometimes known as "frugal innovation," involves starting with the needs of poor buyers and working backward to products that meet those needs yet are still affordable. More than two decades ago, an entrepreneur introduced shampoo sachets in India, creating a market for a product that was not affordable in larger volumes. By repackaging an existing product, shampoo, into small units that sold for a fraction of the cost of larger units, millions more people could afford it. Ineffective demand became effective demand. Since then, many more examples of "frugal innovation" have expanded the markets for everything from cars (e.g. the Tata Nano, which eliminates frills, reduces the use of steel and can be assembled from a kit), to water purifiers, to hand-held electrocardiogram devices to mobile banking.[3] This approach to tapping into the unmet demand for goods and services offers additional opportunities for the emergence of viable wealth creation value chains by combining technological, institutional, and social innovations.

Nascent Demand

Demand can also be nascent, meaning that consumers are unable to clearly articulate what they want or need. For example, how many consumers could have described their need for an smartphone before they saw one? The same can be said of many game-changing inventions for end consumers and producers. Here's a lower-tech example: Mamava is a company that produces privacy booths called lactation pods and suites for mothers who need to breastfeed and/or pump in public places like airports, military bases, train stations, and workplaces. Until Mamava designed their product, mothers were breastfeeding and pumping in all kinds of inconvenient and uncomfortable locations. The inconvenience of breastfeeding discouraged many women from doing it at all or continuing to do it past a short period of parental leave. There were no organized groups of lactating women demanding "lactation pods" since nothing like it had been seen before. However, once Mamava came up with the idea and developed their product, the market emerged.

Nascent demand is harder than effective or ineffective demand to measure, understand, or predict, but listening closely to the needs and circumstances of potential buyers can lead to the types of innovations that address nascent demand. For instance, Mamava was inspired by an article that appeared in the *New York Times* in 2006 describing the challenges certain mothers faced trying to continue breastfeeding after returning to work. Though individual mothers do not purchase Mamava's product, satisfying mothers' needs is in the self-interest of the institutional customers who do.

Location, Location, Location

Another important dimension of connecting with demand has to do with its proximity to production. WealthWorks recognizes that changing systems at scale and helping economically marginalized people and communities become productive contributors to the mainstream economy cannot be solely a matter of import substitution. Import substitution refers to the idea of concentrating investment to produce goods and services locally that would otherwise be imported into a given community or region. Efforts to rely on import substitution as an engine of economic development, particularly in rural areas with limited populations and underdeveloped access to markets have proven largely ineffective due to the restricted size of local markets.

On the other end of the spectrum, international value chains that link production in underdeveloped countries with consumers in developed countries are often exploitative. The Fair Trade movement is one effort to counter this, but it applies to a very limited proportion of overall international trade. In international development circles, emerging wisdom suggests that building connections with producers and consumers within the same country by focusing on connecting rural and regional urban markets offers opportunities to build personal relationships as well as shape the flow of benefits from value chains in ways that are more conducive to creating shared wealth. Regional urban markets are much larger than local rural markets, yet not as large as international markets. In developing countries in particular, customers in regional urban markets often come from the rural areas in which producers live and maintain ties to and goodwill toward those areas that can affect their behavior as consumers.

70   *What Does It Mean to Be Demand-Driven?*

Interest in connecting urban/suburban demand to rural production in a regional context is mirrored to a degree in the renaissance of interest in local/regional food and food systems in the United States where consumers are often willing to choose a locally or regionally produced product over an imported product, even though they may be many generations removed from rural living. In another example, the Leadership in Energy and Environmental Design (LEED) Certification Process granted by the Green Building Certification Institute awards extra points for regional sourcing of construction materials.

There are also many examples of "buy local" initiatives from Small Business Saturday (the day after Black Friday), created by American Express to boost local businesses and increase transactions using the Amex card, to local currencies like Ithaca bucks that are generally only accepted by businesses in a specific community. Reframing how we think about markets from a limited "buy local" perspective to a perspective that includes local markets and regional markets and connects rural and urban producers and consumers within a regional context creates greater opportunities for inclusive market diversification.

Thinking broadly about demand, including effective, ineffective and nascent demand, offers a wider range of possibilities for connecting to the mainstream economy than simply competing to fulfill demand that is already present.

What Does it Mean to Connect to Demand?

In the WealthWorks framework, connecting to demand means actually meeting face to face with decision-makers in businesses and organizations that sell directly to consumers. These are the buyers that must have their fingers on the pulse of what consumers want (and how consumer preferences are changing) if their own businesses are to flourish. Secondary research and market surveys may provide guidance in a preliminary determination of the sector and focus of a wealth creation value chain, but they are no substitute for building a personal relationship with buyers. This usually requires value chain coordinators to move outside their comfort zones and interact with people and organizations they may never have worked with before or even imagined they would be in the same room with.

In our work with Ford grantees, we identified several commonly held assumptions, which, if untested, make it more difficult for value chain coordinators to implement the demand-driven aspect of the WealthWorks framework successfully. These assumptions include: 1) perfect information; 2) immutability of current policies; 3) omniscience of investors; 4) narrow, exclusively profit-maximizing motivations of decision-makers in the private sector.

Test Assumptions: Perfect Information

Connecting to demand is the key to harnessing the power of markets for social change. Yet the assumptions so many of us hold about the inherently

What Does It Mean to Be Demand-Driven? 71

exploitative nature of capitalism and the pervasive cynicism among many about the selfish motivations of any and all big businesses (and, by extension, private-sector business of any size) makes it difficult for some to recognize and consider shared interests across the public, private, and nonprofit sectors to be credible. Many of the assumptions of neo-classical economics are so baked into our world view of capitalism that they are seldom challenged, yet I would argue that they have had a very distorting impact on the way our economy has developed.

One assumption of neo-classical economic theory that does not hold up in the real world is the assumption of perfect information, which means that everyone in the market has exactly the same correct information available to them at all times. Actually, this is very far from the case. Poor places, in particular, often lack access to information, sometimes exacerbated by a lack of access to modern information infrastructure. One of the most powerful functions of wealth creation value chains is to create new information and new patterns of information flow among the partners to improve not only efficiency but commitment and accountability to wealth outcomes. As Donella Meadows notes, "missing feedback is one of the most common causes of system malfunction ...We humans have a systematic tendency to avoid accountability for our own decisions. That's why so many feedback loops are missing."[4]

WealthWorks value chains add information and create feedback loops where they have been missing. First by building direct personal relationships between producers and buyers so that communication is ongoing and producers know what to produce to meet ever-evolving consumer demand, and buyers know what to adjust in their own behavior to make this possible. These relationshps build resilience into value chains. Second, by introducing all the transactional partners in the value chain to each other and allowing them to understand each other's self-interest in participating in the chain and making each other successful. As relationships form among and between transactional players, transactional partners often discover opportunities for shared infrastructure that increases efficiencies and shared wealths. They also learn how to problem-solve collectively, as illustrated by the Carolina Textile District.

The Carolina Textile District identifies itself as a value chain defined as a network of manufacturers that collaborate to meet modern demand. In the 1990s the North American Free Trade Agreement went into effect and many American clothing brands moved production to areas with lower costs. By around 2011 the limitations and hidden costs of offshore production had become apparent to some and a first wave of fashion designers became interested in producing American-made goods as an alternative to the tidal wave of offshoring. The hidden costs of offshoring include, but are not limited to: lag time in transit, poor quality control, and the cost of holding very large inventories to mitigate supply chain disruption. By around 2011, many of the larger players in North Carolina's textile sector had either folded or downsized and the old infrastructure for meeting designer demand was no longer operational.

72 What Does It Mean to Be Demand-Driven?

At the same time, some new smaller producers were beginning to emerge. One of the emerging smaller producers was Opportunity Threads, a worker-owned cooperative that employs Mayan immigrants (intentionally inclusive of otherwise marginalized people), recycles all fabric scraps back into the textile supply chain (positive impact on natural capital), and promotes local sourcing of raw materials to reduce shipping costs and support local industries (positive impact on natural and built capital and regional livelihood opportunities) and is committed to product innovation (building intellectual capital) and a high level of craftsmanship for mass-produced items (requires individual capital being fostered through connections with school systems).

Through information-sharing, the director of the Manufacturing Solutions Center in North Carolina and Opportunity Threads recognized there was more demand for domestic production than any single small firm could handle. Work opportunities were going unfilled and individual buyers were left trying to figure out who to call for which textile-related services and how to coordinate between them, which increased their cost of doing business. The idea of creating a single point of contact for potential clients seeking manufacturers was born. Many smaller businesses came together to cover the cost of this shared infrastructure. The success of this solution to a common problem led to creating a value chain that provides a range of services, including qualified sourcing of materials, connections to qualified contractors from designers to sew facilities, a docent program that connects established and scaling companies seeking long-term relationships with appropriate cut-and-sew factories, and a mill network that allows multiple cut–and-sew facilities to take on larger contracts. The Carolina Textile District serves clients and supports businesses and entrepreneurs that are new entrants to the sector.

Improved and focused communication between transactional and support partners allows support partners to improve the effectiveness of their interventions. For example, working with North Carolina schools to modernize and improve training for textile industry workers helps the schools and the industry succeed. An open relationship between businesses and schools provides feedback for continuous improvement.

Test Assumptions: Immutable Policy

Policies at all levels of society shape the system in which wealth creation value chains operate. Too often, practitioners approach their work with a sense that the policy framework is immutable. It may, in fact, be very difficult to change some policies from the top down. Yet many opportunities exist to experiment with alternative policies and resource allocation decisions when they are identified as important to the success of a tangible wealth creation value chain with potential to create multiple forms of wealth and improve livelihoods. Providing information to policy and decision-makers that was not previously available to them can influence resource allocation decisions.

What Does It Mean to Be Demand-Driven? 73

The process of exploring, proving, and scaling a wealth creation value chain typically unearths policy constraints that are often not evident before the exploration begins. Sometimes, these constraints exist at the level of individual businesses or institutions that have purchasing policies that make it difficult to do business with an emerging value chain. For example, schools may not have planning horizons for food purchases that are sufficient to allow farmers to plant appropriately to meet their needs. A change in school purchasing policy that includes collaborative annual planning with farmers timed so that farmers can prepare to grow the crops the schools would like to be able to purchase the following year serves everyone's interests. A state-wide, county-wide or district-wide "buy local" policy will not work unless the changes required in policy to allow implementation at the ground level also happen.

In other instances, existing policies are simply misunderstood and that misunderstanding has led to missed opportunities. For example, as Fahe began to understand the extent to which undervalued appraisals of energy efficient affordable housing represented a significant gap in the value chain, they also began to uncover the gaps in communication between appraisers and builders. Apparently, appraisers had been led to believe that they were not supposed to communicate with builders and vice versa as a matter of regulation. This meant that critical information about the nature of construction and building performance were not part of the information appraisers received as the basis for their work. Upon investigation, it turned out there was no regulatory prohibition against communication between builders and appraisers; it had just become an accepted norm and people *believed* there was such a policy. When Fahe worked with appraisers to design and develop training on how to appraise energy efficient homes, they were able to address this myth head-on. These kinds of myths that result in gaps, bottlenecks and underutilized resources are much more common than you might imagine.

A wealth creation value chain provides a focused context within which all the partners can identify policies that are helpful and harmful to the success of the value chain in terms of wealth creation, systems change and profitability and each can speak to the utility and impact of those policies on their own situation. These conversations are often enlightening to those who enact policies as well as to those affected by them and can lead to a willingness to change. Sometimes the change may be on a trial basis and sometimes it is more permanent. By bringing multiple partners with a shared interest in very specific policy changes into communication with decision-makers, changes can happen relatively quickly. As the impacts of changes in specific policies are felt, that can provide leverage and motivate a more comprehensive assessment of policy options. The potential for another critical feedback loop for a sustainable economy is created when decision-makers that create policies become more connected to the actual and specific real-world impacts of particular policies on real businesses, people, and places and discover alternatives that are better all around.

74 *What Does It Mean to Be Demand-Driven?*

Test Assumptions: Investor Omniscience

Perfect information is often notably lacking between investors and investable opportunities and among investors with similar interests but different priorities and constraints. Silos exist in the investor sector as in every other. Investors are not omniscient and they often do not know what other investors are actually doing, even in the same sectors or with interests in the same forms of wealth or geographies. Wealth creation value chains offer the opportunity to present a wide variety of potential investors with a range of outcomes related to stocks of eight forms of wealth as well as the potential for a fully functioning value chain at scale. Identifying specifics ways in which the value chain will impact several forms of wealth can broaden the base of potential investors for whom sustainable wealth-related outcomes may be as or even more important than maximizing profitability or the more common metric of economic development that is job creation. Creating relationships among and between different types of investors with diverse interests and capabilities can increase the efficiency of investments through shared understanding of the appropriate role and tools for risk mitigation, which is often a key to unlocking greater investment. It can also enable investors to better understand how their investments drive the outcomes they care about, including, but not limited to profitability. Relationships between value chain partners and investors can also help identify strategic and complementary investments. (See Chapter 6 for more on how to connect with investors.)

Test Assumptions: Profit-Maximizing Behavior

Another key assumption of neo-classical economics is that all businesses are profit-maximizing, meaning that every decision they make is for the purpose of squeezing the last possible penny out of the market and then distributing those pennies to owners. In fact, the vast majority of businesses in the United States are small businesses and very few (if any) small businesses are actually profit maximizers; i.e. willing to sacrifice all other values for an extra penny of profits. In fact, many small businesses contribute intentionally to the welfare of their communities, employees, and even customers in ways that do not result in increased short-term profit.

Even large businesses may recognize the need to factor sustainability into their operations, to keep their own costs of production under control, to meet the expectations of their buyers, and to protect profitability over the long term. It is easy to become cynical when confronted with instances of "greenwashing" or other unethical business practices, so it is important to remember that even business people can genuinely strive to do the right thing. If it just so happens that the right thing also contributes to business sustainability and profitability, so much the better. Often it takes courageous leadership to figure this out. For example, the leadership team for Tecate (a Mexican brand of beer), decided to disassociate their brand from violence against women in Mexican culture. They had the support of the CEO of Heineken Mexico. Tecate made a hard-hitting commercial that made it clear that they did not want men who abuse women as their customers. They did not know how such a stand would be received or how it would impact sales, particularly since their brand was associated with machismo, but they did it anyway. As it turns out, sales rose after the commercial came out and went viral on social media.[5] Remembering that such people exist even within large businesses can help foster curiosity about the self-interests of the "other" that is needed to bridge the culture gap between government, business, and the nonprofit sector.

Testing Assumptions: People with Power are Always Corrupt

Connecting with demand in person is one of the very first steps in exploring a wealth creation value chain. Yet it is also one of the biggest stumbling blocks in introducing the wealth creation approach to community and economic development practitioners, particularly those without a business background and/or those working in the public or nonprofit sector.

Those who have worked in the nonprofit sector tend to have deeply rooted suspicions (and even fear) of for profit businesses, particularly large corporations, that often lead them to demonize and exclude such businesses from lists of potential partners. Even when nonprofits are willing to reach out to people that work in large businesses and corporations, they often go into the conversation with self-defeating assumptions. For example, they may be telling themselves, "So-and-so will never take the time to talk with me" and "So-and-so will not care about anything that matters to me," or, even worse, "So-and-so only wants to take advantage of me and people like me." We often spend considerable time coaching coordinators before they sit down with potential demand partners. Coaching provides an opportunity to practice asking good questions and listening attentively as well as uncovering self-defeating assumptions. There is a balance to be struck between self-defeating assumptions and ongoing vigilance. Not every demand partner is the right partner and some will (and have) tried to take disproportionate advantage of wealth creation value chains without being mindful of impacts throughout the chain. However, just because some partners are not the right partners does not mean that there are no good partners.

Likewise, some businesspeople may question the value of some nonprofit endeavours, or, at the very least, their relevance. Distrust of government and politicians can also be an issue for smaller businesses and nonprofits. We have seen too many situations in which the assumptions made by each group about the other have resulted in failure to tap the power of markets to address inequalities and unsustainable practices. It is important to recognize and name distrust where it is present and then work to figure out the steps that can be taken to build trust over time, rather than simply rely on untested assumptions to assume there is no way forward.

76 *What Does It Mean to Be Demand-Driven?*

In our experience, the process of actually connecting with buyers is often profoundly revealing. For example, while teaching a workshop for ActionAid on access to markets in Myanmar based on WealthWorks principles, several workshop participants had the opportunity to accompany women who were local village crafters to a nearby trade center to meet with potential buyers face to face for the first time. They returned astonished to have learned that, not only did the buyers have many useful suggestions for how the women crafters could improve the marketing of their products, but the buyers themselves were willing and even eager to help since many of them came from the same villages and were genuinely concerned about conditions in those places.

While there is no denying that there are profit-maximizers in the world, greed is real, and markets can and do create externalities and exploitation, it is also true that there are corporate leaders that have a genuine interest in inclusion if it can be done in a way that is consistent with increased business stability and sustainability as they perceive it. There are groups like the Sustainable Food Lab and Ethical Corporation and others that work with multinational businesses to help them investigate, experiment with, and share information with their peers about how to do business in ways that reverse exploitation and actually strengthen many forms of wealth.

In 2005, Costco's corporate counsel became involved with the Sustainable Food Lab. This led her to wonder about the equitability of Costco's supply chains with respect to small farmers. Thus began an analysis and ongoing set of interventions in Costco's supply chain for French green beans that begins in Guatemala. The first step in the work was a thorough exploration of the supply chain to understand who the transactional partners were, what they did (i.e. the functions they served, such as credit provision, technical assistance to farmers, risk management, packaging, and marketing), how much it cost them, and what they earned as a percentage of the total revenue from sales to the end consumers. Mutually agreeable protocols for confidentiality were in place before the research began. The exploratory included quite a bit of work on the ground in Guatemala undertaken by CIAT, an international agricultural research center and Counterpart International, an American NGO that contributed a Quiche-speaking anthropologist to the endeavor. It also involved time spent building personal relationships among and between Costco personnel at different levels, farmers and their cooperatives, non-member farmers, an aggregation cooperative, and an intermediary buyer. Since completing the initial exploration phase and sharing results in 2007, a new foundation has been chartered to support health care access and educational scholarships for workers' families in Guatemala, building on a legacy of project already begun by local groups and funded, in part, by green bean revenues.

One of the many lessons learned through this work was the impact of personal experience on decision-makers. Before the work on the French green bean value chain began, Costco's corporate counsel had already experienced rural poverty in Viet Nam. The direct experience of rural

What Does It Mean to Be Demand-Driven? 77

poverty in Guatemala was transformative for the American Costco buyer and his assistant who helped establish the supply chain. It caused them to rethink the work they were doing and how they were doing it. The CIAT researcher also changed his perspective from one of viewing big box stores as exploitative monolithic organizations to groups of actual people that make decisions with very limited information. In that sense, they are not so different from the farmers that provide them with French beans. Only by coming together and sharing information are they able to see ways to improve the system that affects them all.[6]

One of the interesting facets of the Costco story is that it did not begin with Costco's CEO, but rather with the corporate counsel who saw an opportunity to create a win–win–win situation for producers, customers, and the company. She has since changed jobs within the company to work more closely with the French green bean value chain and spread lessons learned to other value chains that supply Costco.

Change agents within companies are sometimes called intrapreneurs. The Aspen Institute began a program called First Movers in 2009 that brings together "high potential midcareer social intrapreneurs (executives pursuing social or environmental goals from within a company)" to support and equip them to effect change in their companies. As intrapreneurs encounter obstacles and constraints in their work (sometimes including obtaining corporate support to simply participate), and begin to fashion workarounds, they are changing the structure of our economy one step at a time. Knowing that such intrapreneurs exist opens up the possibilities of different types of value chain partnerships, even with large corporations. Companies that have engaged with First Movers include Colgate-Palmolive, Microsoft, MetLife, Dow Chemical, and Walmart Stores.[7]

Maria Popova, author of *Brain Pickings*, said in an interview on NPR with Krista Tibbett, "Evil only prevails when we mistake it for the norm."[8] To successfully implement the wealth creation framework at scale, one must be willing to believe in the possibility of good, even in what one might consider to be the most unlikely places.

Not only are there many business leaders who already recognize connections between the financial bottom line and other forms of wealth creation, there are also societal forces afoot influencing consumers in ways that *require* them to care. When consumers decide to boycott firms that use child labor, those firms need to reconsider how they produce their products. Likewise, when consumers want to avoid fossil fuels, or corn syrup and other food additives, or want to be assured that the processes used in production of the goods they buy are environmentally friendly, firms that want to remain competitive must find ways to respond. When consumers begin to turn away from the throw-away culture, firms will need to rediscover how to build products that last.

In 2015, Nielson Global surveyed 30,000 people in 60 countries across the globe and asked consumers how much influence a variety of factors including environment, price, packaging, marketing, and health or wellness claims

78   *What Does It Mean to Be Demand-Driven?*

had on their purchasing decisions with respect to brand name products: 66% of global respondents said they are willing to pay more for "sustainable"[9] goods, up from 50% in 2013. Those with lower earnings (under $20,000) are actually 5% more willing than those with higher incomes (over $50,000) to pay more for products and services that come from companies perceived to be committed to positive social and environmental impacts. Millennials and the even younger Generation Zs are even more willing than their elders. Consumers in the Middle East, Africa, Asia, and Latin America are more willing than North Americans and Europeans.[10] I have put the word "sustainable" in quotation marks because I do not believe that the factors included in the survey represent true sustainability; nor do I believe that the work of incorporating sustainability into every aspect of production and consumption is done. In fact, it is just beginning. Nonetheless, it is worth noting that more consumers than ever before are influenced by corporate claims of sustainability.

In a world in which it is increasingly difficult to know who and what one can trust, establishing transparency and reliability with consumers gives producers a competitive advantage. If you as an economic development practitioner can create a value chain that helps the demand side of the market respond more effectively to changing consumer preferences, and you build trusted relationships while you do it, you have built in a degree of resilience that can serve you well.

Farmers who work with Red Tomato learned this lesson several years ago. Red Tomato is a nonprofit that uses existing wholesale distribution to deliver fresh regional produce to a wide range of buyers. One of the brands that Red Tomato has developed is Eco Fruit (originally Eco Apples). Eco Apples are sustainably grown using integrated pest management to minimize the use of chemicals. Farmers had been growing and selling Eco Apples through Red Tomato to stores that valued the farmer connection and Red Tomato's branding efforts for many years. One year the apple crop was severely depleted due to bad weather. Rather than choosing to buy replacement apples from another broker or another group of farmers, Red Tomato's buyers decided to let Red Tomato's growers purchase replacement apples grown under comparable conditions in other parts of the country to sell to the buyers so that a) the growers would receive the revenues they counted on to survive, and b) the buyers could continue to build loyalty to the Eco Apple brand over time.[11] While the profits were not as great as they would have been had the local crop not failed, the growers received enough revenues to sustain their operations, which would not have happened had the buyers gone around them entirely. This is one small example of the kind of resilience that a market-driven approach based on long-term trusted relationships can create.

Notice that the motivation for buyers to continue to do business with Red Tomato and its growers was not altruistic; rather it was in their own self-interest to maintain the growers' capacity to produce in the future to meet increasing market demand. The self-interest of the buyers and the self-interest of the growers resulted in shared interest in keeping the entire value

What Does It Mean to Be Demand-Driven? 79

chain in business. Red Tomato has imprinted the concept of resilience for growers into their business model by setting prices based on what farmers would like to see their products sell for and never lower than the price a farmer can accept without compromising his or her dignity. They call it "The Dignity Deal."

Unfortunately, competitive forces can and do win out, particularly when sectors like agriculture and retail food sales face increasing consolidation and there are fewer buyers in a market with very tight margins. This can mean that the partner that was the right partner isn't any longer. This happened to Red Tomato in 2018 when their largest customer for regional apples chose to source elsewhere for, in the case of one variety, a reported $.01 per pound difference. This happened, at least in part, because of increasing consolidation in the retail food industry. Red Tomato is in the process of rethinking how to connect regional growers with less affluent consumers. Their leader, Laura Edwards-Orr, recognizes that this means they will have to "collaborate beyond our comfort zones and navigate difficult conversations."[12]

The key to connecting with demand is in understanding the world from the perspective of the buyers and appreciating the constantly changing nature of markets. What are the problems buyers are trying to solve? What keeps them up at night? What are their "pain points"? Sometimes the investments in multiple forms of wealth that a WW value chain requires to succeed can benefit buyers' bottom lines in ways they may not be aware of. For example, until we worked with them to measure the impact of investments in individual capital through an onsite day care center at a rural electric cooperative worksite, the cooperative had not recognized the reduction in turnover experienced at that site relative to its other sites and the substantial cost savings that went with it. Once they did, they realized that onsite day care literally paid for itself in avoided costs associated with turnover.

Business Trends and Inclusive Business

There are many indications that some businesses and business leaders are searching for less exploitative and more inclusive ways of doing business because it is in their self-interest to do so, and the trend seems to be accelerating. See, for example, the number of businesses that have adopted one or another form of social responsibility metrics and reporting, such as The Sustainability Scorecard, ISEAL Alliance Sustainability Standards, Global Reporting Index and many more. While there is no standard set of metrics across the world, sustainability metrics generally include internal measures such as corporate governance as well as corporate impacts on society and the environment. Business schools such as the University of Oxford in England, the University of California, Berkeley, Cornell University in New York state, IE Business School in Spain, Rotterdam School of Management at Erasmus University in the Netherlands, the University of British Columbia

80 *What Does It Mean to Be Demand-Driven?*

in Canada, and others offer MBA students the opportunity to focus on issues related to corporate responsibility and sustainability.

New business structures such as B Corporations and multi-stakeholder cooperatives are also emerging along with the concept of social enterprise as a step toward market-based businesses that create, rather than undermine, various forms of wealth for social as well as personal good. Alliances and networks of like-minded entrepreneurs such as Business for Social Responsibility, Network for Business Sustainability and others are also active, as are sector-specific networks like the National Good Food Network and The Forum for Sustainable and Responsible Investment and The Forest Stewardship Council. All of this activity indicates that there is a growing collective awareness that we cannot keep doing business in the way we have in the past. Change is never easy, nor does it proceed along a steady path. Setbacks are normal and there is always a strong undercurrent pulling us back into the exploitative systems we know best. But the drive for improvement, however imperfectly executed, is there.

A movement in the business world that seems particularly relevant to WealthWorks is called "inclusive business." As Robert de Jongh writes:

> Inclusive businesses are profitable businesses that integrate the low-income segments of society into their mainstream business activity as consumers, producers/suppliers or employees ... Inclusive business focuses not only on profitability but also on the extent to which the low-income segment is able to participate in, contribute to, and benefit from the performance of the business, as measured by changes in overall standard of living while having neutral to positive impacts on the environment.[13]

Inclusive businesses are not motivated by altruism; they are typically large, well-established businesses seeking to: a) accelerate growth by pursuing new market segments and distribution channels; and/or b) mitigate supply chain, labor, and/or reputation risks. If an inclusive business is a social enterprise, they may be seeking to scale up a proven model. Inclusive businesses do not trade financial returns for social returns; rather, they seek solutions to optimize both simultaneously. Inclusive business use measurements to track their social and economic performance. Some even maintain "scorecards," like the Balanced Scorecard or the Social Business Scorecard.

There are a wide variety of inclusive business models, including, but not limited to: a) deep procurement from multiple small producers; b) investments in training in which inclusive businesses use third parties who identify, train, and place employees in job openings at the edges of the formal and informal sectors; and c) distribution and sales through informal shops and/or a dedicated sales force that reaches deep into communities, providing access to those that would not otherwise have it.[14] All of these models design from the needs of low-income producers, employers, employees, and consumers up rather than from the top down and all are looking for scale through localization rather than centralization.

Both WealthWorks and inclusive businesses rely on value chain development processes to identify key partners and dynamics among and between partners of different types and both focus on leveraging market-based solutions to create shared value. However, inclusive business begins with an assessment of what will best serve the company and the specific value chain it is a part of while WealthWorks begins with an assessment of what type of value chain in which economic sector or subsector will best serve specific economically marginalized people and places. WealthWorks intentionally designs the value chain process to collectively contribute to each form of wealth in a meaningful manner, and to ensure that the wealth that is created and maintained is reinvested in strengthening the value chain and the communities in which it is embedded. WealthWorks value chains are often being created from the ground up and go through a pilot stage in which standards are developed and refined as skills and capacities improve.

Since inclusive businesses are operating within an already established value chain with standards in place, a relatively high degree of skill and capacity may be needed to participate effectively. Some inclusive businesses are willing to invest in building the capacities of economically marginalized communities to integrate into a mainstream value chain because they see it in their business self-interest to do so. Since many inclusive businesses are large, well-established companies, they may be effective partners in attracting additional investment because their engagement may help other investors perceive less risk than they otherwise might.

Identifying inclusive businesses in sectors under consideration for Wealth-Works value chain development can result in engagement by relatively large, well-resourced companies that are open to broader partnerships. The conversation begins with the question asked by the value chain coordinator of value chain partners, "What are we ready to do to support the anchor company in its business development effort that will also help us and the community?" As the relationship develops, WealthWorks practitioners will want to pay attention to issues of ownership and control as well as impacts of all proposed actions on all forms of wealth. Inclusive businesses may also have experiences relevant to engaging economically marginalized people as producers, employees, suppliers, and consumers, including how to design products, services, and delivery systems that unlock ineffective demand, lower barriers to entry, and reduce the "poverty penalty" that results in poor people paying more than others for basic goods such as food, energy, transportation, and communication. The "poverty penalty" is multi-dimensional and includes lower quality goods, being priced out of the market, having to choose between basic goods, and having to buy goods on expensive credit.[15]

WealthWorks created a *Private Sector Engagement Toolkit* to provide practical guidance to WealthWorks practitioners in how to approach and work with private-sector entities based on shared values that provide benefits to your value chain and their business.[16]

82 *What Does It Mean to Be Demand-Driven?*

Understanding and connecting with demand begins with building actual personal relationships with intermediate buyers that are connected with end consumers. This approach is very different from relying solely on secondary market research to determine the likelihood that there will be buyers for the products and services you plan to produce. It requires reaching beyond one's comfort zone and learning the language, world view, constraints, and aspirations of individuals and organizations that have the power to drive economic transformation. The more time spent building a wealth creation value chain, the deeper the knowledge and detailed understanding you will and must acquire about your demand partners and the world in which they operate. The more you learn, and the more trust you build, the better the odds of finding shared interests. The same basic concept applies to investors as well.

Notes

1 Growth of Farm to School in the U.S. (2014). National Farm to School Network, June 1. Retrieved from: http://www.farmtoschool.org/resources-main/growth-of-farm-to-school-in-the-u-s-1997-2014-graphic
2 This was still the case in 2018: see https://www.chooseenergy.com/electricity-rates-by-state
3 India's Frugal Dynamism. (2012). *New Times*, July 14. Retrieved from: http://www.newtimes.co.rw/section/article/2012-07-14/89887/. And
    Soman, D., Stein, J. G., and Wong, J. (2014). *Innovating for the Global South: Towards an Inclusive Innovation Agenda.* University of Toronto Press, Toronto.
4 Meadows, D. H. (1999). *Leverage Points: Places to Intervene in a System.* Hartland, VT: The Sustainability Institute.
5 Thanks to Hal Hamilton of the Sustainable Food Lab for sharing this example on their blog: https://sustainablefoodlab.org/the-3-barriers-to-business-sustainability/?utm_source=SFL+Main+Contacts+List&utm_campaign=eceac0c156-EMAIL_CAMPAIGN_2018_11_07_07_15&utm_medium=email&utm_term=0_03d98741b6-eceac0c156-202116041
6 For a more detailed analysis of The Juan Francisco Project, see http://sustainablefoo.wpengine.com/wp-content/uploads/2016/02/Costco-and-CIAT%E2%80%99s-Exploration-of-Guatemalan-Green-Beans.pdf
7 Murray, S. (2017). Fellowship for Change. *Stanford Social Innovation Review.* Retrieved from: https://ssir.org/articles/entry/fellowship_for_change?utm_source=Enews&utm_medium=Email&utm_campaign=SSIR_Now&utm_content=Title
8 *Maria Popova—Cartographer of Meaning in a Digital Age.* Radio show broadcast February 7, 2019. Retrieved from: https://onbeing.org/programs/maria-popova-cartographer-of-meaning-in-a-digital-age-feb2019
9 Quotation marks added.
10 McCaskill, A. (2015). Consumer-Goods' Brands that Demonstrate Commitment to Sustainability Outperform Those that Don't. Nielsen, October 12. Retrieved from: https://www.nielsen.com/us/en/press-room/2015/consumer-goods-brands-that-demonstrate-commitment-to-sustainability-outperform.html
11 Personal communication from Michael Rozyne, founder of Red Tomato, http://www.redtomato.org/fairness/
12 https://redtomato.org/blog/good-food-movement-in-the-face-of-consolidation/
13 Red Mantra. (2014). Building Rural Wealth Through Inclusive Business, A Primer on Private Sector Engagement for Community Impact. Retrieved from.

http://www.wealthworks.org/economic-development-resources/how-tos/buildin g-rural-wealth-through-inclusive-business-primer.

14 More information on inclusive business models is available from Building Rural Wealth through Inclusive Business: http://www.wealthworks.org/economic-deve lopment-resources/how-tos/building-rural-wealth-through-inclusive-business-primer

15 Paxton, J. (2017). The poverty penalty in action—less for your money. Phys.org, January 19. Retrieved from: https://phys.org/news/2017-01-poverty-penalty-a ctionless-money.html

16 Red Mantra. (2015). Private Sector Engagement Toolkit. WealthWorks, June 12. Retrieved from: http://www.wealthworks.org/economic-development-resources/ how-tos/private-sector-engagement-toolkit

6   How Do We Connect with Investors?

Investment as the Basis for Sustainability

The drivers of economic success and sustainability are ongoing investment in multiple forms of wealth and connection to demand. The wealth creation economic development framework relies on the power of investment and reinvestment in multiple stocks of wealth as the foundation for a truly sustainable economy. *All stocks of wealth become depleted over time and all require periodic or ongoing reinvestment to remain capable of benefiting the larger economy.* When our stocks of wealth are healthy (and thus truly "wealth" and not "liabilities") they can provide sufficient income or income equivalents to support our consumption needs with enough left over to reinvest as required to maintain, grow, and improve the stocks.

This is difficult to see in the current situation in the US, in which we privilege consumption over investment, not only as individuals but as a market system. According to ImpactAlpha, of the $976 billion in net income generated by the S&P 500 in 2014, $571 billion—nearly 60%—was used to buy back shares (further concentrating financial wealth) and, when dividend payments to shareholders are included, total payout ratios topped 93%, leaving just 7% for reinvestment.[1] Personal savings rates are also down from an average of roughly 11% in the 1960s and early 1970s to an average of roughly 6.5% from 2010 to 2019. Generally speaking, US savings rates are lower than those of many other countries. China, for instance, had a personal savings rate of just over 37% in December of 2015.[2]

This habit of privileging consumption over investment has allowed so many of our stocks of community wealth, whether social, natural, individual, intellectual, built, political, cultural, or financial, to become badly depleted. For example, according to the American Society of Civil Engineers 2017 Infrastructure Report Card, the US gets a D+ grade on the quality of our infrastructure (built capital) due to deferred investment of over $2 trillion over ten years.[3] According to the Center for Disease Control, as of 2015–2016, 39.8% of adults and 18.5 % of children in the US were obese and obesity rates among adults were still rising. The medical cost of obesity in the US was estimated at $147 billion.[4] Other trends affecting the quality of individual capital include increased diabetes and physical inactivity (both related to obesity) and the opioid epidemic. Increased polarization in the US is a symptom of disinvestment in social capital. In 2016, participants in the World Economic Forum at Davos recognized the potential environmental and economic benefits of increased investment in soil health (natural capital). Why? Because most agricultural soils around the world have lost 50–70% of their original organic carbon levels and, as a result, are significantly less productive than they would otherwise be. One example of decreased investment in intellectual capital is federal spending on non-defense research and development as a percentage of the federal budget, which has fallen from a high of 5.8% in 1966 to 1.6% in 2017.[5] Since 1990, the proportion of university-based research and development funded by public dollars has also decreased by over 10%.[6] Building wealth creation value chains from the ground up highlights areas where specific investment can result in bringing underutilized and/or depreciated resources of all kinds into productive engagement with the mainstream economy.

What Investment Can Look Like

When we use the word "invest" we tend to think of the allocation of financial wealth, but investing in wealth creation value chains can take many different forms. For example, in Michigan a WealthWorks value chain developed around a 47-mile recreational trail that was already under development but had no clear relationship with demand. The WealthWorks value chain coordinators from the Michigan State University Cooperative Extension Service and the Fremont Area Community Foundation approached the West Michigan Mountain Bikers Association and the International Mountain Biking Association as potential demand partners. Both Associations offered their expertise in trail design and construction as well as volunteer hours to get the job done. They became investors in the value chain from the demand side because they could readily envision a return on their investment in the form of a unique resource well-suited to their membership.

Another gap in the recreational trail value chain in Michigan was a lack of comprehensive and consistent marketing for all the players in the value chain. Many were small businesses with limited resources and expertise. The value chain coordinators identified the local hospital as a potential beneficiary of the value chain and conversations with the hospital confirmed their interest from the perspective of making the community more attractive to employees and promoting active lifestyles. The hospital loaned their marketing expertise to the value chain partners to fill the gap. This is an example of local investment in a wealth creation value chain.

In addition to investing by contributing expertise and/or labor, some organizations and/or individuals that see their self-interest in a successful value chain can contribute access to decision-makers whose choices will impact the value chain by introducing representatives of the value chain to key decision-makers. Sharing political capital in this way can lead to changes in resource allocation decisions and policies that make a real difference in the success of the chain. For example, an introduction to the then chair of the Kentucky Appraisers Association was a critical link in Fahe's ability to generate support from USDA for developing a systemic approach to training appraisers to account for the full value of affordable energy efficient housing. Appropriate training increased the average appraisal by more than enough to pay for energy efficient construction, unlocking the missing link between market demand and construction financing.

Demand partners can also invest in wealth creation value chains by changing the way they do business by, for example, choosing to substitute local purchases for imports, changing payment or returns policies, providing access to a warehouse, changing a delivery route or adjusting a curriculum to strengthen the value chain. Demand partners can provide contracts to purchase goods and services from the value chain that the value chain can use to obtain financing. Offering credit to producers based on contracts to purchase is called factoring and can be a solution to the hurdle of lack of collateral for economically marginalized producers.

There is another category of potential investor in wealth creation value chains that may not be a transactional, support, or demand partner; the potential beneficiaries of a successful wealth creation value chain. For example, if you are developing a wealth creation value chain that involves recreational services, who else in your community and/or region would benefit if your value chain was successful? This depends, of course, on what the success of your value chain would look like. If, for example, you are developing an inclusive recreational trail system that serves as a focal point for casual recreation, competitions, equipment trials, equipment donations and refurbishing, training programs, educational opportunities, and lessons and engages multiple businesses as well as providing an attraction for tourists, there may be many potential beneficiaries you haven't thought about. For example, the medical community could benefit from increased access to customized recreational services for patients, and employers could benefit by being able to use the value chain to attract employees. What about non-recreational businesses that would benefit from increased tourism? Would local restaurants or lodging establishments see their self-interest in investing in the value chain?

Thinking broadly about who has self-interest in investing, what that self-interest might be and what investment can look like opens up new ways of thinking about how to aggregate resources that can make the difference between success and failure. By asking the question, "Who in this community or region would benefit if this value chain was successful?" you may identify several potential investors you would otherwise ignore. The more you understand about the relationship between your value chain and the full range of activities and resources in your community, the better able you will be to align interests and attract place-based and people-based investment.

Investing in Coordination

The most critical function in a value chain is its coordination (see Chapter 10 for more on value chain coordination). A value chain coordinator is the entity (or entities) with the staff that holds the big picture of the entire system and creates the relationships with demand, value chain partners, beneficiaries, and investors needed to move from business as usual to a new more inclusive normal. *The reason there are not more wealth creation value chains is not because there is a dearth of opportunity; it is because in our current highly interconnected yet fragmented and inefficient economy it is no one's job to connect the dots and build the relationships that will lead to a more inclusive economy.* Coordination is a multi-faceted, creative and challenging job that requires persistence and the capacity to learn and adjust. The coordination function cannot and will not be sustained without resources. Early investors have a critical role to play in supporting the coordination function, including coordinator training and training for coaches who work with and support coordinators (see Chapter 9 for more on value chain coordinators and coaches).

What about Financial Wealth?

There's no getting around it; building and maintaining wealth creation value chains requires direct financial investment as well as other forms of investment. During the Exploration Phase, financial investment may come from private-sector partners in the value chain but often "soft" money in the form of grants or donations is used to support a value chain coordinator or coordinators to conduct the research and build the relationships needed to determine the preliminary feasibility of the value chain. "Soft" money may continue to have a role through the proof-of-concept phase, but the goal of wealth creation value chains is to become market-driven and not dependent on public or private subsidies to the greatest extent possible. For value chain coordinators, this means learning to work with an investment landscape that extends well beyond foundations and private philanthropy. Many transactional and support partners become financial investors; to achieve scale, there will likely be partners that are primarily financial investors.

Philanthropic Investment as a Step toward Market-Driven Value Chains

In the mid-1990s, the Rensselearville Institute introduced the concept of outcome funding to philanthropic donors and grant-makers.[7] The basic premise of this approach is that grant-makers will be more impactful if they think of themselves as investors in social change, not simply donators of funds. Shifting from a donator mindset to an investor mindset fundamentally changes the relationship between philanthropic entities and their partners in implementation. Instead of providing funds for a specified set of activities, the providers of funds invest in a specified set of outcomes. As

88 How Do We Connect with Investors?

investors, the providers of funds expect to see a measured and documented return on their investments. They accept the high likelihood that the recipient of the funds will learn better ways to achieve the outcomes to which they have committed as they work towards them. Therefore, rather than insist that implementers follow a preordained a set of activities, the providers of funds build in the flexibility for fund recipients to respond to emerging conditions and lessons learned by changing activities so that they are more impactful in realizing desired outcomes. Furthermore, the investor expects to be informed as lessons are learned and is prepared to locate and help access additional support whether in the form of dollars, contacts, expertise, technology, or other. This was the approach taken by the Ford Foundation to the Wealth Creation in Rural America initiative and to the grants made under it. It allowed for the flexibility and learning that is required for successful implementation of WealthWorks.

The outcomes relevant to WealthWorks pertain to systems change and economic inclusion through wealth creation value chains that improve stocks of up to eight different forms of wealth at scale through the way they operate. Specific outcomes differ by value chain and location and are always broader than just financial profitability. Fortunately, there are trends afoot among private, public, and philanthropic investors that suggest the possibility for transforming the types of investment considered worthy and the nature of returns on investment considered legitimate.

Many people and organizations around the world are trying to figure out how to invest to support the types of multiple outcomes that WealthWorks intentionally delivers. There is a varied and extensive world of social impact investing (also known as socially responsive investing and impact investing) including organizations such as Impulse, based in Belgium with investments in Poland, Albania, Kosovo, Romania, Bosnia, Serbia, Lithuania, Bulgaria, Moldova, Macedonia, and Morocco; and Acumen, with offices on four continents and investments in North America, East Africa, India, Latin America, Pakistan, and West Africa.[8] Social impact investing is a subset of the development investment landscape, whose very existence suggests the importance some investors are placing on investing for impacts compatible with but separate from profits. Even though there has been considerable growth in social impact investing, there remains a gulf between the outcomes that even social impact investors think they need and what wealth creation value chain coordinators know about how to pitch their value chains to investors.

The wealth matrix and the entire WealthWorks framework is consistent with and can be responsive to social impact investors as well as to less progressive investors and those that are part of the conventional finance landscape with self-interests that align with specific investment opportunities. The ability to measure and report on those outcomes as well as measure and report on systems change and profitability is one piece of the investment puzzle, but not the only piece (see Chapter 8 for more on measurement). An opportunity exists to engage experienced investors in training value chain coordinators in how to communicate effectively to attract sufficient investment to scale past proof of concept.

A detailed analysis of the landscape of potential investors in wealth creation value chains is beyond the scope of this chapter; instead the purpose is to gain passing familiarity with the wide range of actors in the investment arena and highlight a few examples of investment approaches that are compatible with wealth creation value chains. We will also share some of the lessons learned with respect to attracting financial investment and the opportunities to restructure relationships among and between investors to contribute to wealth creation goals as well as profitability.

A Place-Based Investment Value Chain

The WealthWorks framework promotes a flexible, place-based approach to aggregating investment, as exemplified by the wealth creation value chain work of Emerging Changemakers Network (ECN) in Alabama led by Jessica Norwood and initially supported by the Ford Foundation. The value chain, originally known as the "Alabama Impact Investing Initiative" and now known as SOUL'utions, was intended to connect demand for small business financing and capital in agricultural value chains emerging in the South with local and regional institutional and individual impact investors. As ECN's leader, Jessica began with little to no experience or understanding of how private financial capital works to support communities, value chains, and businesses, but with a real passion to learn. The models that influenced the development of ECN's work included Slow Money, Calvert Foundation's Community Notes program, Community Development Financial Institutions (CDFIs) with loan funds, the Grameen Bank, and savings and burial and other targeted loan clubs. The Exploration Phase included working with a content coach with expertise in private investing and the Wake Forest University Community Law and Business Clinic, as well as building relationships with institutions outside the region. This provided ECN with the intellectual capital lacking in their region. ECN has continued to use to the strategy of relationship building with experts inside and outside their region to identify creative solutions to place-based challenges.

The first year of ECN's exploration uncovered a number of gaps and bottlenecks in the proposed value chain on both the demand and supply sides. On the demand side, emerging value chains were too new to have the structures in place required to receive investment as a group; therefore the focus shifted to funding individual businesses operating within a value chain. For example, while emerging agricultural value chains could benefit from shared investment in infrastructure such as a refrigerated truck, the value chains in question were too new to have development the trust and structures to be clear about who would have responsibility for repayment and maintenance. It was easier to start with small loans to individual farmers. However, it soon became apparent that many would-be

90 *How Do We Connect with Investors?*

entrepreneurial farmers lacked skills, networks, and support systems critical to their success as business people and as borrowers. This led ECN to create an accelerator program to support entrepreneurs in becoming investment ready. The accelerator curriculum covers business planning, market assessment, staffing, understanding financials, business value propositions, presenting to investors, and more.

As ECN got closer to farmers active in emerging value chains (some of which were also supported by Ford), they discovered additional bottlenecks. Farmers in the South, and particularly minority farmers and women, have long faced documented discrimination from banks and US government lenders. This, along with the precarious financial position farmers are often in and the uncertainties inherent in agricultural production, has led to extreme reluctance to borrow money, particularly if it requires using one's property as collateral. Too many farmers have lost their land this way. Conventional loan applications were not structured to meet the needs of farmers. ECN had to come up with an unconventional approach to lending that farmers would be willing to use. This involved a search for models that offered greater flexibility as well as ongoing communications with potential borrowers until the right approach was found.

The solution is a system that provides small loans ($500–$2,500) not based on credit scores to businesses involved in an agriculture or food system value chain. All members of the value chain that receive small loans participate together in the accelerator program and repayment is linked to the group. Everyone in the group must repay the loan or no one in the group is eligible for future borrowing. Repayments are used to help strengthen credit ratings. Participating borrowers receive coaching, technical assistance, and hands-on business development strategies. Graduates of the accelerator have all repaid their small loans and received recommendations to borrow from ECN's lending partners in the future if needed.

On the supply side, ECN's initial focus had been on working with individual investors to create pathways for people who wanted to invest directly in their own community. EMC knew such potential investors and believed there were more out there; however, others with stereotyped views of the region found this hard to believe. This is a great example of how a mistaken assumption (that there are not enough individuals in Alabama who want to invest in their own communities) that goes untested can result in missed opportunities. Too often we fail to test our assumptions.

As ECN began to understand the functions in the value chain, it became apparent that an institutional connection would be needed to provide due diligence for individual investors. The challenge of including Security and Exchange Commission (SEC) accredited investors (individuals that can show income of $200,000 for three straight years or a net worth of $1 million) and non-accredited investors also surfaced, as did the lack of a single CDFI headquartered in Alabama that had a community loan fund. (The CDFIs in Alabama at the time were all depository institutions, not lenders.) Rather

How Do We Connect with Investors? 91

than choose to become a CDFI, ECN concentrated on building relationships with the North Alabama Revolving Loan Fund, which was itself seeking to become a CDFI, to change the lending system to accommodate the needs of businesses in the agriculture and food sector.

By working with place-based financial institutions and other partners, ECN was able to catalyze place-based investment clubs, one in Selma and one in Birmingham that allow local people with varied resources to invest alongside local financial institutions in building their own communities. SOUL'utions Investment Clubs build on strategies found in investment clubs, crowdfunding, cooperatives, and legacy funds like savings clubs to reintroduce a culture of reinvestment.

In addition to filling gaps and addressing bottlenecks in the value chain to bring the underutilized resources of farmers, entrepreneurs, and investors into the mix, ECN intentionally worked at building political capital by becoming part of the Alabama Healthy Food Coalition and developing and maintaining relationships with individual organizations and state legislators with potential to impact policy related to financing for healthy food initiatives. Relationship-building led to ECN's successful partnership with the American Heart Association and others to bring the Health Food Financing Initiative to Alabama seeded with $300,000 in state funding for healthy food retail projects across the state.

> There were so many gaps in that entire system (of local investment in agricultural and food value chains), we were able to identify them and see what our resources were and what we could do to fill the gaps. Now people are looking at how it the system works at different levels for different groups in the system. We can share their perspectives even if they aren't in the room. They haven't seen the cutting edge stuff we've seen. But we're there to share it.
>
> Jessica Norwood[9]

ECN built a wealth creation value chain around investment to support other sector-specific value chains in their region. There was a steep learning curve and many challenges in learning what was possible and how to find and then work with the right partners to make it happen. Every value chain coordinator, no matter what sector(s) their value chain is in, or what the scale of investment is that they seek, faces the challenge of building relationships with investors and aligning investors with investable opportunities.

Aligning Investors with Investable Opportunities

Building relationships with investors hinges on understanding what each investor views an investable opportunity. Even in poor areas there is often capital available, however, bringing it to bear means understanding the needs and preferences of those who control it. For example, in an informal investigation of potential venture capital investors in West Virginia it became apparent that many of them had made their money in sectors such as retail that were not the focus for emerging entrepreneurs. Understandably, potential investors wanted to invest in sectors and in businesses that they could understand. Work was needed to help those with resources to invest become comfortable with present day investable opportunities in their region in sectors like information technology or biotechnology that were outside their "wheelhouse."

Value chain coordinators and their partners need to learn how to approach and make connections with investors at many different levels. This is another way in which the WealthWorks framework pushes practitioners beyond their comfort zones and can provide them with powerful new insights into how market-based economic systems work. Some value chain coordinators, like ECN, were working with institutional and individual investors at a modest scale to start; others were trying to attract larger amounts. Everyone discovered that they needed to learn a new vocabulary to understand investor self-interest, constraints, and the larger systems in which investments are determined.

Jim King, President of Fahe, learned how little nonprofit leaders know about talking with investment professionals including investment bankers. Investors like Goldman Sachs, TIAA CREF and others are used to getting information in a succinct and specific format that is not familiar to most nonprofit executives. Investors often try to be respectful of nonprofits because they are seen as "doing God's work," but, from an investor perspective, nonprofit staffs are also (often correctly) perceived as having no idea how money really works. Nonprofits live with the illusion that they are dealing with the banking industry when really they are often just interacting with banks that are required by law to implement the Community Reinvestment Act.

Trusted investment advisors can help investors make connections to place-based demand, but only if they are aware of the opportunities. Without those connections the people-based wealth of a region will remain locked up. To attract resources to inclusive development, we need to create many more relationships among and between potential investors and engage them in helping us create investable options and opportunities. To do this, we need to understand much more clearly what investors are looking for. This applies not only to the type, extent, and time frame for financial returns, but also to the range of other values investors would like to see manifested through their investments. As with the mental models about demand partners that too often prevent us from engaging them directly as value chain partners, practitioners often lack experience with investors and may also have self-limiting mental models about investors that are inaccurate and, at the very least, not universal.

The proof-of-concept phase is a key stage at which investor engagement can make a big difference in whether or not a wealth creation value chain can achieve scale over time. During the proof-of-concept phase, goods and

How Do We Connect with Investors? 93

services move all the way through the chain to buyers and their customers and revenues move back along the chain to producers. The proof-of-concept phase demonstrates the capacity of the value chain to execute, solve problems, and move forward. There is typically a steep learning curve between the exploration phase and the proof-of-concept phase, as partners learn how to work together, how to achieve efficiencies, and how markets react to what they produce. Although the proof-of-concept phase itself may not require extensive investment, getting to scale generally does. Therefore, if the proof-of-concept phase is designed to answer the questions posed by potential investors in getting to scale, the likelihood that it will become a full-fledged value chain instead of a boutique experiment is greatly increased.

One of the key leverage points in unlocking investment for wealth creation value chains is risk mitigation. Aligning investors with investable opportunities has a lot to do with understanding how investors think about risk and what it takes to build their confidence in the face of risk. Some investors have a relatively high risk tolerance and others do not. The answer is different in each instance, but the principle of understanding the investor's perception of risk and figuring out what it will take to manage that risk in a way that increases investor confidence is the same. Just as it is the value chain coordinator's job to understand what keeps demand partners up at night and use that information to shape the value chain, it is also their job to understand what keeps investors up at night (risk) and how to de-risk the value chain without undermining the wealth creation approach. De-risking investment often means bringing in different types of investors. For example, one investor may be willing to offer debt-financing if another investor is willing to provide a loan guarantee. If one or more investors are willing to offer loan loss reserves, loan guarantees or other forms of risk mitigation, this can be a real boon in attracting more risk-averse investors into the conversation. Likewise, innovative strategies that allow investment profiles to change over time and offer exit strategies to early investors may also encourage engagement of a wider variety of investors.

The best time to do this work with investors is prior to proof of concept, not after. If you begin building relationships with investors before you need their investment, it gives you the chance to learn more about what it could look like to adequately de-risk future investment. You have the opportunity to build some of that into a demonstration of proof of concept which can result in being much better prepared for scaling-up.

Different investors are likely to need answers to different questions before they are ready to invest. Knowing what those questions are can help value chain partners and their coordinators not only in designing their pilot appropriately, but in knowing which information they need to capture and how they need to capture it to be able to demonstrate outcomes to investors as well as to partners and other stakeholders. This, in turn can help value chain coordinators work with value chain partners to customize a "pitch" to investors that will resonate. Making a pitch for an entire value chain is not the same as making a pitch for an individual business since value chains are often looking for investment in infrastructure that will be shared across the chain. If you wait until after the proof-of-concept phase to begin conversations with investors, you run the risk of not having answers to the very questions on which their investment decisions will be based. This will make it that much harder to get to scale.

There are many factors that may influence the types of investors with whom you will want to connect, including the sector you are working in, the stage of value chain development you are in, and the types of investors and institutions in your place. The agriculture sector, for example, has catalyzed a wide range of investment vehicles to address specific gaps in financing to support re-regionalization of food production and consumption. For instance, the Fair Food Network has established the Fair Food Fund to provide financing and business assistance to food enterprises that are growing vibrant local food systems.[10] The focus of the Fair Food Fund is on building the infrastructure needed to connect regional producers and consumers at scale. This includes aggregation, distribution, processing, and marketing infrastructure that has disappeared in many places in the United States. Interestingly, the focus on agricultural re-regionalization and the rebuilding of infrastructure to support food-related value chains that is gaining traction in the United States is also emerging in the field of international development where there has begun to be a backlash against conventional value chains that export to international markets and renewed recognition of the potential for greater in-country benefit from serving regional markets in-country. The way you have defined scale for your work will also influence the types of investors you will want to approach (see Chapter 3 for more on scale).

Building a sustainable and inclusive market-driven economy will require social change agents and investors to work together in new ways with give and take on both sides. This is not just about moving money from one place to another; it is as much about building relationships that result in trust, loyalty, ongoing support and transfers of other types of wealth including social, political, and intellectual capitals. A more impactful system of investment will go beyond binary relationships between investors and implementers to relationships among and between investors as implementation partners and co-learners.

Systems Change with Investors

Opportunities for investing are changing as new tools and approaches are developed. Fortunately, some of these tools and the new systems of resource aggregation they allow seem well-suited to some wealth creation value chains. One such tool is crowdfunding, with which Ford grantees experimented. Social impact bonds, although not yet flexible enough to support wealth creation value chains per se, are another example of an emerging investment aggregation vehicle with a social outcome orientation.

Crowdfunding

Crowdfunding, unimaginable in its present form without the internet, allows practitioners to offer individuals opportunities to support wealth creation value chains that interest them. Black Belt Treasures, a cultural arts center in Alabama's Black Belt, coordinates a WealthWorks value chain to meet the market demand of tourists for authentic crafts and related experiences by engaging area artists, youth, and tourist businesses in co-producing goods and services for local and tourist customers. One gap in the value chain was the lack of adequate studio space for producers.

Black Belt Treasures launched a crowdfunding campaign in 2014 to raise $10,000 to build the studio they needed. The campaign resulted in contributions from local schoolchildren as well as others inside and outside the region and raised awareness of Black Belt Treasures as a regional resource. The Tellus Institute developed a Guide to Crowdfunding for WealthWorks value chains.[11]

Crowdfunding can be effective at multiple points in the evolution of a value chain any time a specific tangible need is identified which, if met, will unlock additional resources and opportunities. Sometimes, investments will be needed in individual businesses within the value chain and sometimes investments will be needed in shared infrastructure.[12] For example, if a value chain is producing wood products, the entire chain might benefit from a sort-yard, where multiple species of wood are aggregated and inventoried. The availability of this type of infrastructure could reduce the need for importing raw materials, as well as the cost to individual businesses of each maintaining their own inventories. It could also provide an additional source of revenue to the value chain. Sometimes infrastructure as basic as a shared vehicle can make the difference between success and failure at the pilot stage. Other forms of shared investment might include training programs that serve multiple value chain participants, shared insurances, certifications, and more. Considering investment in a wealth creation value chain context opens up opportunities for economies of scale that otherwise would not exist.

Social Impact Bonds

A social impact bond (SIB) is a tool pioneered in the UK in 2010 that allows government agencies to use private capital to pay for programs that deliver results. The government sets specific, measurable outcomes and promises to pay an organization to achieve them. A third party evaluator determines whether outcomes are met. If the outcomes are met, the government releases funds to the organization, which then repays investors with a return for the risk they have taken. If the outcomes are not achieved, the government does not pay the organization and investors lose their money. In the US, social impact bonds are also known as "Pay for Success" financing and have been used in 16 states and Washington, DC for programs related to health care, child care, homelessness,

96 *How Do We Connect with Investors?*

workforce development, and juvenile justice, among other things.[13] Over 100 social impact bonds had been launched worldwide as of January 2018.[14]

The SIB model as currently configured is not well-suited to wealth creation value chains (because value chains are not programs nor are they controlled by a single organization); however it does demonstrate the potential for aggregating funds from private investors to achieve outcomes that have an intentional social inclusion component. The SIB model is also increasing contacts and communications between private investors and nonprofit implementers. Using a SIB or SIB-like mechanism to finance wealth creation value chain development may provide an alternative approach that engages marginalized populations in actually producing the goods and services from which they benefit.

Another emerging concept is that of Social Justice Bonds (SJBs). SJBs are designed to change the system by which public infrastructure is funded, constructed, and used. Today, municipal public works are typically financed by wealthy investors and built by large, well-established firms that often employ people from outside the affected municipality and do business with large financial institutions. Some public works projects result in measurable improvements and benefit lower income and economically marginalized communities, but others cause disruptions such as: business closings and layoffs, traffic jams, destruction of neighborhood amenities, and pollution of water and air. Infrastructure improvements in previously undesirable areas often culminate in increased property values leading to displacement.

Social Justice Bonds seek to change the existing system that reinforces economic inequiteis to one that redirects a portion of the benefits away from established institutions to investors, businesses and workers that have been excluded to date with the intention of generating greater place-based wealth for local communities. Activest, an organization taking the lead in this area, describes itself as, "having the potential to leverage the same market forces that contribute to American inequality to now create more equitable and responsive governance."[15]

Collaborative Investing

Financial resources exist even in very poor communities. Even more resources exist if we look at wealth creation as a regional opportunity. The issue is not lack of resources; it is a societal failure to allocate resources inclusively. Many existing and eligible financial resources are significantly underutilized or misallocated due to the lack of coordination among different types of organizations that do or could provide investments to create an inclusive economy. For example, many investors require financial matches to obtain investments, and money goes unallocated due to the inability of potential borrowers to raise matching funds. At the same time, foundations that have the ability to provide matching funds are often unaware of the difference their dollars could make if the money were made available in a timely and targeted manner. Many communities have revolving loan funds that are

How Do We Connect with Investors? 97

underutilized for reasons that may include lack of awareness as well as lack of technical expertise in fund administration.

Wealth creation practitioners can help address this failure by encouraging conversations not only between value chains and investors, but among investors themselves. Instead of treating the conversations with investors as one-on-one conversations in which it is up to the recipient to figure out how to mix-and-match investments, it is high time to begin to engage investors in learning how they can work with each other more effectively to support implementers that can help them realize their own often inter-related objectives. Rural Development Initiatives in Oregon reached out to many different types of investors as they began to embrace the WealthWorks framework. They discovered investors eager to be engaged as co-learners, not only about the value chains in question, but about each other and what they each had to bring to the table. They were interested in the question of how they could improve their own effectiveness by working with other types of investors to achieve specified outcomes.

We call this "collaborative investing." Through collaborative investing, value chains can encourage new and unprecedented conversations between and among investors based on opportunities, gaps, bottlenecks and underutilized resources discovered in the course of exploring and implementing actual wealth creation value chains. Investors themselves can become a brain trust as well as a source of financing. By understanding each other's institutional capacities and constraints they can begin to design more effective systems for complementary contributions that produce more robust results over time.

Collaborative investing offers value chain coordinators the opportunity to engage investors in considering a host of questions, including:

"Who is eligible to invest in this value chain and what are the structures that support that investment?"
"Who receives the financial and non-financial benefits from the investment and how are those benefits distributed?"
"Who assumes the risks related to the investments and how are those risks distributed?"
"How do we measure the financial and non-financial returns on investment in a wealth creation value chain?"
"What kinds of investment beyond dollars can meet the interests of investors and the value chain?"
"What are the gaps, bottlenecks and underutilized resources related to required investments and how can we create relationships between different types of investors to address them?"

WealthWorks value chain coordinators have an important role to play in introducing investors to a range of ownership and control structures and models that can maintain shared place-based wealth over time. (See Chapter 4 for more on ownership models.) Helping investors recognize the connection between their own self-interests in multi-solving and shared ownership and control contributes to a market-driven economy in which financial investors no longer receive an outsize proportion of all profits; rather those profits and stocks of wealth created are shared by many different types of stakeholder/investors including workers, entrepreneurs, and other transactional and support partners in the value chain. Importantly, it also means that, over time, it will drive decisions about reinvestment to maintain forms of wealth into the spotlight and reduce the current pattern of wealth extraction to satisfy external investors.

Of course, collaborative investing requires investors to be willing to share the limelight as well as the heavy lifting and to be comfortable knowing that they have contributed toward improved outcomes. Investors that believe they must take sole credit for outcomes are not good fits for this work. Investors who insist on operating with a "project" framework may not be good fits for value chains. *Inclusive value chains are not projects; they are ongoing business operations engaged in systems change that produce positive outcomes for multiple forms of wealth.*

The MacArthur Foundation is one group actively rethinking its role in capital markets on the world stage. It recognizes that, "while there are proven and pioneering enterprises capable of dramatically improving health, reducing poverty, expanding education, or tackling the challenge of climate change, many have unconventional investment profiles that leave billions of dollars in potential investment on the sidelines." It has concluded that it has a role to play not only as a direct provider of capital but as "market makers for mission." "Our goal is to drive impact well beyond what we can achieve with our capital alone, and to create high-impact investment opportunities for other investors who are unwilling or unable to engage on their own."

MacArthur recognizes the need to intervene on both sides of the market, to create investable opportunities *and* networks of complementary investors and investments. The MacArthur Foundation's work as market makers for mission is in its early days. It is a promising model that could be replicated at the regional level by finding a partner with the skills and commitment to bring a wide variety of investors to the table around specific wealth creation value chain opportunities.

Community Foundations as Catalysts and Conveners

Like wealth creation value chains, collaborative investing does not just happen out of thin air; it requires a catalyst to coordinate, facilitate, and support the process of discovery and implementation among and between investors and investable opportunities. Community foundations are one type of institution that can be an effective catalyst in these conversations. For example, the Community Foundation of South Central New York (CFSCNY) began working with Council of Churches to see what could be done to address a food desert (i.e. a neighborhood in which it is difficult to find a place to buy affordable or good-quality fresh food) in Binghamton,

New York. The answer will be a new bargain grocery store that provides food, jobs, and training to local residents while helping to finance other food-security programs in the community. As a result of effective exploration and relationship building, financial resources are coming from three different foundations, three banks, and the city; CFSCNY's role as convener and catalyst was much more influential that direct funding would have been.

Similarly, the Fremont Area Community Foundation played a key role as a convener as well as provider of financial resources in the early stages of value chain exploration and development of proof of concept for the recreational trail value chain in Michigan. Community foundations (and other foundations with a community focus) often have the credibility, resources, facilitation skills, and physical infrastructure to invite potential partners into unprecedented conversations. These conversations allow partners to "kick the tires" of a wealth creation approach to development and begin to imagine a new way of doing business with each other. Community foundations can also provide resources to train staff and potential value chain partners in the wealth creation approach. Training develops a shared language that helps partners imagine new opportunities together.

Some community foundations have gone even further. The largest community foundation in Central Appalachia, The Greater Kanawha Community Foundation (TGKCF) in West Virginia, acts as a value chain coordinator for the Charleston Area Medical Center Local Foods Value chain that includes local growers, a distributor, an aggregator, and the Charleston Area Medical Center as the demand partner. The value chain taps into a sizable market for locally grown herbs and produce, and has introduced patients, their families, and staff to healthier foods that substitute herbs for salt and fat.[16] As TGKCF learned more about the power of the wealth creation approach, it chose to integrate wealth creation into its grant-making framework. To be eligible for discretionary grants an applicant must demonstrate the ability to build one or more forms of community wealth. TGKCF provides guidance and training to past, present, and potential grantees that spreads understanding of the wealth creation approach among many different actors in the region. The forms of wealth feature prominently on TGKCF's website.[17]

To catalyze collaborative investment, the convener needs to understand that each type of investor has his or her own goals, their own self-interests, and their own sets of restrictions that may be regulatory as well as institutional. Public funding sources, for example, may have regulatory restrictions attached to them tied to criteria like income eligibility, location, or economic sector. Some private funding sources may require a financial return on investment while others may not. Some investors may be restricted in terms of the types of investments that can make. Can they invest in equipment? Real estate? Training? Operations? Can they only invest over a set time period? Are they only able to invest in certain categories like health care or environmental justice? How much flexibility do they have to mix funds with other investors? What is

100   *How Do We Connect with Investors?*

the lead time required to obtain investment? How flexibly can they respond to lessons learned and new needs that emerge as the value chain develops? Can they underwrite risk by, for example, providing loan guarantees or setting up risk mitigation funds in escrow? What kinds of reporting requirements do your potential investors have?

Reporting requirements can place a large burden on value chains, particularly in early stages of development. Ideally, a collaborative approach to investors might result in, among other things, streamlining the reporting requirements for implementers. Today it is not unusual for nonprofit organizations in particular to maintain staff positions that are solely dedicated to preparing reports for funders. Each funder has its own system, time schedule, and reporting requirements. The opportunity cost of this kind of administrative waste is high and it undermines the capacity to achieve meaningful outcomes. Perhaps by agreeing to work together to achieve shared goals, funder investors can also agree on a shared reporting standard.

It is critical that coordinators and conveners understand what investors can and cannot do with the funds they control and what pre-requisites must be met to allow them to engage. It's also important to help investors understand each other's goals, constraints, and opportunities. Too often, investors are kept at arm's length from one another and have no real understanding of the priorities and objectives of other investors. They may not even know who the other investors are. Building social capital among investors can lead to developing enough political capital to impact each other's resource allocation decisions, even when this may require variances or waivers to try something different. When different types of investors come together and each sees their own self-interest in the success of the value chain as a whole, they can work together to forge innovative investment solutions.

Timeliness Matters

Market conditions can change rapidly and value chain partners often need to make decisions and act within a constrained period of time; they do not have time to wait for lengthy review processes and permissions. Wealth-Works is more likely to succeed when some investors understand how important timeliness is and have the institutional mechanisms in place that provide them the flexibility to respond rapidly when needed. One of the features that contributed to the success of the Ford experiment was a discretionary re-granting fund managed by two Ford grantees that was intentionally set up to help value chain coordinators address emerging needs that were not in evidence when they began their value chain explorations. The fund was relatively small, as were the grants made from it, but the turnaround was fast and the process was very straightforward. These small grants allowed coordinators to bring in experts, conduct research, and access resources in a timely manner that were critical to their ability to maintain momentum.

Investors may also provide introductions to technologies and technology providers that can help wealth creation value chains incorporate state-of-the-art production practices that improve stocks of multiple forms of wealth.

Notes

1 Ben-Ami, A. (2018). Heads up, investors: It's not all about you. *ImpactAlpha*, December 10. Retrieved from: https://impactalpha.com/heads-up-investors-its-not-all-about-you/?utm_source=Pico&utm_campaign=d3a49de881-EMAIL_CAMPAIGN_6_1_2018_12_25_COPY_01&utm_medium=email&utm_term=0_57980c6bda-d3a49de881-105595273&mc_cid=d3a49de881&mc_eid=b856eaa0d2

2 For latest savings rates, see: https://tradingeconomics.com/country-list/personal-savings

3 Infrastructure Report Card. American Society of Civil Engineers. Retrieved from: https://www.infrastructurereportcard.org/.

4 Adult Obesity Facts. Centers for Disease Control and Prevention. Retrieved from: https://www.cdc.gov/obesity/data/adult.html

5 Historical Trends in Federal R&D. American Association for the Advancement of Science. Retrieved from: https://www.aaas.org/programs/r-d-budget-and-policy/historical-trends-federal-rd

6 Ibid.

7 For more information, see Williams, H. S., Webb, A. Y., and Phillips, W. J. (1993). *Outcome Funding: A New Approach to Targeted Grantmaking*. Rensselaerville Institute, Delmar, NY. Retrieved from: http://www.rinstitute.org/product-page/outcome-funding

8 Social impact investing is not the same as using screens to avoid investing in specific activities or products such as guns, prostitution, resource degradation, or big box stores.

9 Personal communication with the author, September 22, 2014.

10 Fair Food Fund. Fair Food Network. Retrieved from: https://fairfoodnetwork.org/projects/fair-food-fund/

11 See: http://www.wealthworks.org/economic-development-resources/how-tos/guide-crowdfunding-wealthworks-value-chains

12 How-tos. WealthWorks. Retrieved from: http://www.wealthworks.org/economic-development-resources/how-tos/enterprise-financing-wealthworks-value-chainswork/

13 Costa, K. (2014). Fact Sheet: Social Impact Bonds in the United States. Center for American Progress, February 12. Retrieved from: https://www.americanprogress.org/issues/economy/reports/2014/02/12/84003/fact-sheet-social-impact-bonds-in-the-united-states/

14 Zaroulis, A. (2018). Social Impact Bonds reach global mass: 108 projects launched in 24 countries. *Social Finance*, January 30. Retrieved from: https://globenewswire.com/news-release/2018/01/30/1314226/0/en/Social-Impact-Bonds-reach-global-mass-108-projects-launched-in-24-countries.html

15 Activest. Retrieved from: https://www.activest.org/

16 A short video describing this work is available at: https://tgkvf.org/special-initiatives/value-chain/

17 Seven Forms of Wealth. The Greater Kanawha Valley Foundation. Retrieved from: https://tgkvf.org/grants/

7 Where Does Technology Fit into Wealth Creation Value Chains?

Paying Attention to *How* We Produce and Consume

Economics is the study of how we use available resources to meet human wants and needs. Economics is changing and so are opportunities for economic development. Whether we like it or not, we must find new ways of producing goods and services; it's a matter of survival. Production practices based on the exploitation and degradation of our natural resources and the use of materials hazardous to human and ecosystem health continue to pose significant threats to human health and settlement and lead to increasingly unstable climate conditions. We are running out of some of the raw materials we have come to rely upon, such as available potable water, sand, healthy soil, and copper, not to mention intact environmental systems.

We are also living through a period of rapid technological change in information technologies, robotics, artificial intelligence, DNA analysis, sensors, big data, materials identification and sorting, customized production, energy and building technologies, transportation technologies, and more. New opportunities are opening up in both *what* we produce to meet our wants and needs, and in *how* we produce it. New technologies are also changing our ability to understand and monitor the impacts of our production and consumption decisions.

The challenge for those of us who wish to pursue a wealth creation approach to sustainable development is in connecting the dots to: 1) ensure that the benefits of new technologies are shared and used to integrate and include rather than further exclude economically marginalized people and places; and 2) produce and consume in ways that create and sustain rather than exploit and deplete multiple forms of wealth. We must find new ways to satisfy human wants and needs around the world without destroying our world as we do it. We can no longer afford planned obsolescence and a throw-away society; we need to find new ways to create goods that last and can be remade into new goods when they are no longer useful. We need to help the inventors, manufacturers, and distributors of new technologies connect with people and businesses they would not otherwise know who can use their technologies to create a more inclusive economy.

Technology in Wealth Creation Value Chains 103

With change comes opportunity. We have the opportunity to reshape our economy, not only in terms of how we produce and consume, but also in terms of who is engaged in and rewarded for producing and who has the choice to consume. Wealth creation is as much if not more about *how* we produce as *what* we produce. For example, when the green affordable housing value chain in the Lower Rio Grande Valley in Texas was seeking an architectural firm that would work with residents in colonias (subdivisions of substandard housing in the Southwestern US, often lacking basic infrastructure and services) in designing green homes that met their needs, they were unable to find a firm within their immediate region that was qualified and interested in this type of participatory design. The closest firm they found with the right kind of experience and values was in Dallas. Rather than simply hire that firm to come into the Lower Rio Grande and complete the task at hand, they negotiated to have the firm open an office in the Valley and provide mentoring to local architectural firms so that the capacity to work in a participatory design mode was created among local firms. This type of capacity-building approach builds wealth that sticks in place. Either approach would have gotten the job done in the short run; only a wealth creation approach intentionally builds wealth that sticks.[1]

The Deep South Community Agriculture Network (DSCAN) also transferred technology to change the way in which farmers grew produce for wholesale markets. The Deep South Community Agriculture Network is a network of five organizations in Mississippi and Alabama that work with low income women and minority farmers in two of the poorest states in the US. Each partner serves as the coordinator of its own value chain and the network as a whole is supported and managed by McIntosh SEED. Many of the farmers are land-rich and cash-poor and most had limited, if any, connections with wholesale markets at the start. The value chains work together to meet wholesale market demand for local and regional produce that is greater than any one of the value chains can meet on its own.

During the exploration phase, one of the many gaps identified in the value chain was the lack of uniform growing protocols among growers. Uniform growing protocols are needed to ensure products of comparable quality within and across value chains. Hoop houses are one feature of the uniform growing protocols that were new to many of the small and marginalized farmers who were part of DSCAN. By engaging experts from Tuskeegee University to introduce farmers to uniform growing protocols, farmers were able to increase yields by at least 40% while meeting buyers' quality standards. Farmers who used the protocols to grow collard greens were able to produce around 2,200 pounds per acre compared to 300 pounds per acre for farmers who decided not to use the protocols. This is an example of the difference that can be made by connecting marginalized producers with technology that already exists but to which they have not had access.

Adopting uniform protocols also contributed to farmers' being able to meet USDA certification standards required by wholesale buyers. Between

104 *Technology in Wealth Creation Value Chains*

2012 and 2014, the value of products sold to wholesale buyers by DSCAN members grew from a baseline of zero to $168,065. Increased production, decreased food waste, and more effective utilization of existing resources including land and labor all helped to create more place-based wealth, but none of this would have been possible without first building trust (social capital) within and among the five value chains as well as between the value chains and the network coordinators. Without the hard, ongoing, and often frustrating work of building and maintaining trust, misunderstandings, habits of mind, inexperience, and behaviors that contribute to marginalization such as resistance to measuring profitability and failure to recognize opportunity, not knowing how to run effective meetings, unwillingness to share information, untested assumptions about potential partners, and the tendency to "talk a good game" to philanthropic funders without building and maintaining a functional business will continue to prevent economic integration even where there are clear market-drive opportunities, willing buyers, and profit potential. Changing the system requires working from the inside out as well as from the outside in.

A Circular Economy Approach

The concept of a circular economy aligns well with the wealth creation approach, since it strives to eliminate waste and reduce consumption of finite resources. Companies like Dell, Aquafil, and Horsehead are among those practicing a circular economy approach. For example, Horsehead uses hazardous waste as an input, extracts precious metals, and converts them into industrial inputs while seeking to employ the most environmentally and economically efficient conversion processes. Dell Corporation looks across their products' life cycles for opportunities to drive out waste by designing for repair, reuse, and recycling and taking recovered materials and putting them back into new products. This can be something as seemingly simple as minimizing the number of screws holding a computer together, thus making it easier to repair and disassemble or minimizing the different varieties of plastics used in production to and limiting them to the varieties with the greatest recycling potential. Dell recently launched a third-party-certified closed-loop plastic recycling program. Aquafil works at the molecular level to regenerate human-made fibers that they sell to make carpets and swimwear. Currently more than 33% of their production comes from regeneration of materials and they think they have a great opportunity to arrive at 100% regeneration.

These companies have found that it is critical to engage all the stakeholders in the value chain, including suppliers, packagers, shippers, customers, and financial analysts, as well as manufacturers, to truly understand the costs and savings involved in changing the way business is done. Profits come from cost savings and customer loyalty. Customers want superior products that are better for the environment. As Scott O'Connell, Director of Environmental Affairs at Dell is quoted as saying,

> I think at the onset when you're going to incorporate atypical materials
> you need to get all your stakeholders involved and the key is to get an
> accurate cost analysis. You have to dive in and figure it out as you go.
> It's a method of survival. If you don't become sustainable, you will be
> kicked out of the market.[2]

Although the examples above are of very large corporations, the same thinking can apply to value chains comprised of smaller transactional partners.

Rural Action, a nonprofit development organization in Appalachian Ohio, has used circular economy thinking to identify the opportunity for a WealthWorks value chain connecting stream restoration with paint manufacturing. Rural Action has been working for years to clean up waterways polluted by coal mining. Using a wealth creation framework they were able to help others connect the dots between investing in natural capital by cleaning up streams affected by acid mine drainage, and recycling the chemicals removed from the streams into natural, non-toxic dry pigments that could be made into usable paint. They connected with an engineering professor at an Ohio University who was developing technology to clean the iron and other metals out of streams. He in turn connected with an artist and art professor who specializes in using art materials produced in an environmentally conscious manner. Together, they invested in the research and development (intellectual capital) required and developed a manufacturing process that transforms the chemical soup recovered from toxic streams into non-toxic pigments suitable for paint products. They are connecting to markets by making the new technology (built capital) more widely available, creating social capital by collaborating with others around the world; and adding a new product line to an established business while using the pigment itself to raise awareness of water pollution. A portion of the proceeds from marketing the pigment (financial capital) will go back into cleaning up streams in Ohio.

William McDonough and Michael Braungart (authors of *Cradle to Cradle*) envision a world in which materials last forever through continuous reuse and there is no "away." Every product is intentionally designed for its current use *and* its next use and the one after that. Values are designed right into production systems so that work environments promote human health, replacements are found for toxic ingredients, natural resources used in production emerge more pure than when they went in. In this world, instead of knowing that the very ways we live and work are injurious to people and the planet, and being forced to compartmentalize our guilt, live in denial and/or "give back" in other ways, our production and consumption activities themselves could be making the world a better place. McDonough and Braungart aren't just imagining these possibilities; they are working with real companies on real production every day, identifying and addressing gaps, barriers, and opportunities for re-design that makes sense socially, environmentally, and economically.[3]

106 *Technology in Wealth Creation Value Chains*

The approach advocated by McDonough and Braungart is powerful yet nowhere in their work is there any explicit recognition of the real world opportunities to use this approach to create an inclusive economy by engaging economically marginalized people and places in new types of production, co-production, and consumption. Their work tends to be applied in large corporations and is often found to reduce production costs overall. Building relationships with people and companies in marginalized places appears to be outside their wheelhouse. It is time to explore opportunities to bring similar thinking into value chains comprised of multiple smaller transactional players. Could there be multiple scales at which this approach makes sense? What would it look like to embed this approach in a distributed and inclusive economic system that builds multiple forms of wealth including, but not limited to, natural, intellectual, and built capital?

Biomimicry is also a source for technological innovation that is receiving greater attention today. Biomimicry refers to the design and production of materials, systems, and models based on close examination of how nature works. Biomimicry was the basis for Velcro which was invented after observing the power of burrs to stick together. Close observation of termite mounds has led to design of self-regulating building ventilation that does not require additional heating or air conditioning systems. New, painless hypodermic needles have been developed based on close observation of how mosquitos bite. As fascinating as these examples are (and there are many more), the people attracted to biomimicry are often natural scientists or engineers, and not social scientists or social change agents. WealthWorks encourages economic and community development practitioners to reach outside their comfort zones and connect with technologists grappling with how to address human wants and needs in more sustainable ways.

One WealthWorks value chain built around technological innovation and coordinated by Communities Unlimited, Inc. (formerly alt.Consulting), a regional nonprofit development organization and value chain coordinator, is the Arkansas Green Energy Network (AGEN). AGEN's focus has been to build a value chain that would allow rural communities in the Delta to become producers as well as consumers of energy in a closed loop or circular economy, where inputs are supplied locally, energy is used locally, and all waste from the production process is converted to resource. The value chain focused on increasing community and regional energy self-sufficiency through biofuels made from a locally grown cover crop utilizing rich farmland otherwise fallow during the winter while sequestering CO_2 (natural and built capital). The new market-driven opportunities were intentionally extended to minority and disadvantaged farmers as well as other family-owned farms, and to provide the local municipality and consumers with greater energy price stability.

The first aspect of technological innovation in the value chain began with the need to identify an oil-rich crop that could potentially be grown in the Delta in the winter months without competing with existing cash crops.

Exploration into biofuel production systems and related technologies led to the discovery of research conducted at the University of Montana, where camelina, traditionally used for brushes and herbal oils, was being successfully made into biofuel. Camelina was not an instant success in the Delta; bad weather, varieties imperfectly suited to local conditions, and inexperience with the new crop led to disappointing yields two years in a row. Yet persistence has paid off and camelina yields are improving. Camelina seeds are tiny, so farm machinery had to be refined to handle them. The value chain includes 11 farmers plus experimental plots at Arkansas State University and Phillips Community College, DeWitt Campus, as well as Cooperative Extension and others providing technical support in seed variety selection, seed stock, environmental impact assessment, and Communities Unlimited's work in GIS field mapping with weather pattern overlays.

The second aspect of technological innovation was in locating the appropriate equipment that could refine both camelina and waste vegetable oil into biofuel while producing a byproduct suitable for animal feed and glycerin suitable for use in soap. Through local and national networks, CU was able to locate, purchase, and lease a micro-refinery to a local entrepreneur. The entrepreneur took over an abandoned fuel transfer station in the City of DeWitt, cleaned it up, and turned it into Arkansas' first community-based biofuel refinery. Two years later, the entrepreneur purchased an additional refinery to increase his production capacity as well as equipment to extract and reuse excess methane from the refining process. In the meantime, the City of DeWitt designed and built a waste oil collection truck and began using it to pick up waste vegetable oil from more than 15 local restaurants, convenience stores, the DeWitt schools and the Arkansas County Jail cafeteria. During the proof-of-concept phase, all the fuel produced was used locally in city and farm equipment with the intention of selling fuel directly to consumers and other companies as the supply grew.

The Arkansas biofuels value chain has created many new relationships (social and political capital) in the region by bringing a diverse set of stakeholders together to identify and address the many gaps and bottlenecks required when inventing a new value chain from the ground up. The grand opening of the refinery drew 200 visitors, most of whom had never been to DeWitt. The vision of the biofuels value chain has not yet been realized at scale; low prices for fossil fuels and a change in fuel blending requirements over the past few years have cut into the sense of urgency related to energy self-sufficiency. However, the relationships built among and between for-profit businesses, municipalities, technologists, policy-makers, public and private investors, and the new ways of thinking (intellectual capital) about a shared model for economic development based on a circular economy that is intentionally inclusive and builds on and enhances a wide range of local and regional resources remains. The diverse set of stakeholders who had all invested time, relationships and resources into the value chain decided to form Arkansas' first multi-stakeholder cooperative, Delta BioEnergy, to ensure that all would benefit as the refinery became profitable.

108 *Technology in Wealth Creation Value Chains*

Consumers as Co-producers

Our lived experience of what it means to be a consumer is changing. We are living in an era where consumers are often co-producers, for better or for worse. (Those of us who remember when service station employees actually provided the services of gas pumping, windshield washing, and oil checking have had to adjust to the new reality.) When you pump your own gas, check out your own groceries, or download your own bank statements online (instead of having them sent to you), you are essentially co-producing a service. When you purchase a piece of furniture or equipment that requires assembly, you are co-producing a product. Today's technologies offer many opportunities to co-produce through customizing goods and services to meet consumer demand. For example, Custom Ink allows customers to design their own T-shirts using their own logos and select the material and design of the shirt they want to have printed. Uber and Airbnb allow consumers of housing and vehicles to become producers of lodging and transport services by making use of excess capacity. We are only beginning to understand how these changes in the relationships between consuming and producing are going to reshape our economy and the opportunities for inclusive engagement in production as well as consumption.

These and related new ways of thinking about how we satisfy our material wants and needs have the potential to unleash astonishing inventiveness in every sector of the economy. This restructuring in how we produce and consume goods and services offers great potential for increasing inclusivity among economically marginalized people and places while increasing community wealth, but only if it is intentionally designed to do so. This means expanding the technical design of production to embrace its social and economic design as well. Otherwise, co-production will become just another venue for exploitation.

The choice of technology also affects demand because it determines who gets to be a consumer. If the only way to obtain a good or service is over the internet and you lack access to internet services, you cannot participate. Likewise, if you must be literate in a written language or mathematics to consume and you are not, you are excluded. If you have allergies to something contained in a product, you are also not able to consume it safely. Generally, we consider consumers to be those that have the financial means to purchase goods and services in the market. However, consumption also occurs informally outside market channels through barter and exchange. In these instances, if you do not have access to a good or talent that someone else wants, you are excluded.

Our economy also includes considerable unmet demand for goods and services, including basic goods and services. Economists refer to unmet demand as ineffective demand; it is ineffective because those who would like to purchase or otherwise acquire goods and services lack the means to do so. *A wealth creation approach focuses, in part, on turning ineffective demand into effective demand, not by the trickle-down approach of raising wages in the hopes of creating more disposable income that will be spend on consumables, but by changing systems to: a) create goods and services that people with minimal financial resources can afford; b) alter the structure of transactions by changing risk profiles or removing barriers to access to promote market participation; and c) valuing time and expertise as currency in formal and informal market channels.* Raising wages is a relatively short-term solution that increases effective demand; however, in the absence of systems change it will not necessarily result in increases in the stocks of wealth, particularly for those who are economically marginalized.

Technology has an important role to play in unlocking demand. Fahe's energy efficient affordable housing value chain was able to unlock unmet demand by researching and documenting a replicable, cost-effective approach to constructing energy efficient housing. When work began on the value chain, Fahe's many member builders each had their own process for designing and building affordable housing. Fahe brought them together and they led a study that resulted a replicable process for building homes that achieve a Home Energy Rating System (HERS) rating of 55 or lower (the lower the score, the more energy efficient the home). The proper use of high-quality caulk proved to be one of the most cost-effective methods for lowering the HERS rating, but was not the only factor.

Internationally, there are many companies focused on unlocking demand at the so-called bottom of the pyramid, a concept first introduced by C. K. Prahlad in 2004.[4] The bottom of the pyramid refers to the 4.5 billion people in the world who live on less than $8 a day, are at the bottom of the pyramids representing global wealth and income distributions, and have unmet demand across many sectors estimated by the World Bank at $5 trillion. These people are generally excluded from the mainstream economy as entrepreneurs, producers, and consumers. Bottom of the pyramid business and economic development strategies seek to serve this unserved market by addressing the barriers that prevent market participation that include entrenched consumer behaviors and resistance to new products as well as the need to rethink the way products are made and delivered. Many companies are adapting existing technologies and/or creating new ones to enable success with high-quality products that have low prices and small margins per item but can generate a high volume of sales. Many of these strategies actively engage consumers as co-producers.

For example, LaFarge, a Paris-based cement manufacturer, is pioneering a new approach to cement sales in India that involves delivering 15-liter bags of high-quality, ready-mixed concrete to the doorsteps of slum residents seeking to build homes. By delivering pre-mixed product, LaFarge saves consumers' time and reduces concrete waste. Packages of concrete have been redesigned to withstand transportation in three-wheelers. LaFarge has designed mini-plants that can be located near slums so it can make good on its promise of delivery within 50 minutes of ordering. If this value chain proves profitable, it will be sustainable and more slum dwellers will have access to high quality building materials.

110 *Technology in Wealth Creation Value Chains*

Another example that relies on innovative technology to cut the price of the product and its operation is a portable refrigerator for the rural Indian market, where one-third of all food is lost to spoilage. The refrigerator runs on a battery, weighs less than 10 pounds, and keeps food fresh and cool. It relies on a solid state cooling chip and has no compressor. Multiple versions of the product called Chotukool are available in retail channels to consumers across the socio-economic spectrum.[5]

Opportunities for market-driven approaches to wealth creation-based economic development are growing as market participation expands worldwide. In an overview of a global business summit on business solutions at the base of the pyramid, Harvard Business School writes:

> The 4.5 billion people in the world at "the base of the pyramid" (who live on $5 per day or less) represent a $15 trillion economy—a huge under-tapped opportunity and one poised to expand as these people join global markets as consumers and producers. Capitalizing on this opportunity requires bringing basic services to poor communities in developing economies.[6]

There are also many opportunities to convert ineffective demand into effective demand in the United States and in other developed countries where the increasingly uneven distribution of wealth has squeezed more people into the economic margins. For example, banking by cell phone is a well-established process that has benefited millions of heretofore unbanked people in developing countries and is just now beginning to be implemented in the United States. Opportunities Credit Union in Vermont, the only development credit union in New England targeting low-income and unbanked people, is in the forefront of extending this technology to economically marginalized people and places, allowing them to participate in the mainstream financial system and avoid pawn brokers, payday lenders and other financially exploitative relationships.

McDonough and Braungart emphasize the importance of companies basing their production designs on their social and moral values. However, it's difficult to do this unless consumers appreciate and share at least some of the same values. Fortunately, there is increasing evidence that consumers do want to support a better world through their market choices. The Nielsen Global Survey on Corporate Social Responsibility polled 30,000 consumers with online access in 60 countries in early 2014 to understand how and whether consumer passion about sustainability actually translates into purchasing decisions. They found that 52% of consumers say their purchase decisions are partly dependent on labeling that indicates a commitment to positive social and environmental impact. Interestingly, the percentage of consumers whose purchasing decisions are tied to information about sustainability is higher in Asia-Pacific (63%), Latin America (62%), and Middle East/Africa (62%) than in Europe (36%) and North America (32%). Nielsen's research found that responses were correlated with average annual sales increases in nine countries from 2013 to 2014 of 2% for products with sustainability claims on the packaging and a rise of 5% for products that promoted sustainability through marketing programs, compared with a 1% rise in sales of brands without sustainability claims or related marketing.[7]

The Nielsen survey was conducted at a time when existing internet users in developing markets may be younger and more affluent than the population in general. However, online access in developing countries is no longer limited to affluent consumers and the rate of adoption is rapid. Over 46% of the world's population was internet users as of November 2015, ranging from a low of 28.6% in Africa to a high of 87.9% in North America.[8] Predictions are for 75–85% worldwide penetration by 2020.[9] This will certainly impact the way consumers make choices as well as the choices that they make. Trusted sources with verifiable claims to sustainable practices will likely become more valued as scams and rip-offs continue apace.

In both the developed and the developing world, consumers are increasingly beginning to understand that everything is connected and the way they eat, get around, learn, and even die have implications for the health of the environment, their communities as well as their pocketbooks. It is also becoming ever more apparent that the choices of each generation affect the opportunities and experiences available to the next. Notably, Nielsen found that the Millennials (aged 21–34) appear most responsive to sustainable products, though responsiveness exists in all age brackets.[10]

There is exciting work underway in many fields that offer new opportunities to rethink the ways we go about meeting our wants and needs and the very nature of the goods and services we create. There is movement to redesign manufacturing to reduce or eliminate the use of toxic substances, improve algorithms to reduce intellectual isolation through social media, develop new cures for diseases using innovative approaches, bring banking and insurance to the unbanked and uninsured through distributed technologies, provide non-fossil-fuel-based energy through distributed systems, and much more. A few of these efforts are already intentionally connected to an inclusive approach to economic development. Many more may aspire to be, but the connections are not necessarily being made on the ground.

Integrating Technological Innovation into Wealth Creation Value Chains

How can we link our efforts to create wealth that sticks in impoverished areas to state of the art technologies? How do we bring the intellectual capital residing in think tanks, universities, individual inventors, and others to bear on reducing poverty? Trickle-down theory will not get us there; we need to be intentional and deliberate about building bridges between those who create new technologies, those who apply them, and poor people and places that can incorporate them as producers as well as consumers. Building these bridges can enable wealth creation value chains to differentiate

112 *Technology in Wealth Creation Value Chains*

themselves in the market, establish and maintain competitive advantage, and set new standards for inclusivity. Integrating innovative technology into value chains can serve as a catalyst to help "leapfrog" marginalized people and places into productive connection with the mainstream economy, but only if economic and community development practitioners are savvy enough to pay attention to it and aggressive enough to find the right partners to help them identify and integrate those technologies in ways that are economically sustainable and not reliant on ongoing subsidies.

In the next chapter, we will address measuring the impact of wealth creation value chains and the innovative technologies they use on multiple forms of wealth. Effective measurement allows value chains to: 1) tell compelling stories about their work that attract investors; 2) pay attention to anticipated and unanticipated positive and negative consequences in real time so that we can all learn more about what it takes to build multiple forms of wealth without undermining some to build others.

Notes

1 Professional communication between Nick Mitchell-Bennett, Community Development Corporation of Brownsville and Shanna Ratner, Yellow Wood Associates, Inc., 2014.
2 Amin, K. (2017). Strategies to grow a circular economy with Dell, Aquifil and Horsehead Corporation. Ethical Corporation. Retrieved from: http://1.ethica lcorp.com/LP=15742?utm_campaign=4795+11JAN16+TA_US+%26+Asia& utm_medium=email&utm_source=Eloqua&elqTrackId= f283192565e446b5908298c992a20352&elq=dcdbcb484b2c4a75bbada f5dc228d2d7&elqaid=24649&elqat=1&elqCampaignId=11248
3 McDonough, W. and Braungart, M. (2013). *The Upcycle: Beyond Sustainability—Designing for Abundance*. New York: Macmillan.
4 Prahalad, C. K. (2009). *The Fortune at the Bottom of the Pyramid: Eradicating Poverty through Profits*. Revised and updated 5th anniversary edition. Upper Saddle River, NJ: FT Press.
5 Simanis, E. and Duke, D. (2014). Profits at the bottom of the pyramid. *Harvard Business Review*, 92(10), 86–93.
6 Harvard Business School, *Business Solutions at the Base of the Pyramid*, Summit Report 2008. Retrieved from: https://docplayer.net/169462-Business-solutions-a t-the-base-of-the-pyramid.html
7 https://www.nielsen.com/us/en/press-releases/2014/global-consumers-are-willing-to-put-their-money-where-their-heart-is/
8 For updated statistics on worldwide internet usage, see: http://www.inter networldstats.com/stats.htm
9 Internet Users in 2020. (2013). *Internet Stats Today*, April 15. Retrieved from: http://internetstatstoday.com/internet-users-in-2020/
10 https://www.nielsen.com/us/en/press-releases/2014/global-consumers-are-willing-to-put-their-money-where-their-heart-is/

8 Rethinking Measures of Economic Impact

What We Measure Matters

We get what we measure, because measurement focuses our attention and influences our choices. What we choose to measure, individually and as a society, is a reflection of what we consider to be important. Think of something you measure or monitor in your everyday life, like the weather or the money in your bank account, or the amount of gas in your tank or your child's school performance. Why do you choose to pay attention to those things? Generally, it is because you have an unstated goal or condition that you are trying to achieve such as, "I want to be comfortable; not over-dressed or underdressed," or "I want to be able to pay my bills without borrowing." In each case, you have decided, often without thinking too much about it, to measure the thing that you assume is the most important indicator of progress toward your goal.

As a society, we appear to have determined that the "goal" of economic development is the number of jobs created. This is not a goal; it is an activity, i. e. creating jobs. If the goal is, "We have a sustainable and inclusive economy with equitable outcomes," then history has shown that measuring and focusing on jobs alone will not get us there. Measures of spending that are then trans-lated into jobs are equally ineffective. Pick up almost any study of economic impact, whether of a development project, a government program, or anything else, and what you will see is a report that estimates direct spending and uses one of several well-established models to calculate indirect and induced spend-ing. Direct spending refers to the dollars that will be spent implementing a particular business or project, paying for materials, labor, permits, etc. Indirect spending refers to spending by firms and employees on inputs required for them to contribute to the business or project, such as training or supplies. Induced spending refers to spending by households of a portion of the income earned as a result of the business or project. All this spending is then translated into some number of jobs it is assumed to support.

This interpretation of economic impacts reduces our focus to financial impacts (i.e. the impacts of spending), and even more specifically, to finan-cial flows. It does not even address the fundamental questions of who

114 *Rethinking Measures of Economic Impact*

controls the flows and who benefits from them. The use of financial frameworks to measure "economic impact" has only contributed to tunnel vision and overemphasis on flows of income and jobs without respect to underlying stocks. It has also caused us to become blind to the negative impacts of some flow-generating activities on underlying stocks. Economists call these negative impacts that are not counted in the market "externalities." Externalities are consequences for third parties that are not paid for by the person or entity that causes them. Some actors are well aware that they are creating externalities; think for example, of the tobacco companies who knew of the harmful impacts of tobacco but continued to promote it nonetheless. Externalities can also be unanticipated consequences; think urban planners who believed that more spacious roadways would reduce traffic congestion only to learn that the opposite was the case. Both externalities and unanticipated consequences can be positive as well as negative. If I clean out my closet and donate the clothes to a charity, third parties who are not involved in my closet cleaning activity will benefit from it. On a larger scale, vaccination drives not only benefit the individual children who are protected against infectious diseases, but also reduce the risk of infection for those who are not vaccinated. Both positive and negative externalities are easy to miss if you are not looking at an entire system, including stocks as well as flows. *The actual condition and health of our economy is based on the condition and functioning of the stocks of all eight forms of wealth; none of which, including the stocks of financial wealth, are included in the analytic frameworks relied upon by conventional economic development professionals today.*

The economy is about much more than flows of money. The study of economics is the study of how people choose to use resources to satisfy human wants and needs.[1], [2] We shape the economy every time we use resources, individually and collectively. What are the resources available to be used? They are the eight capitals that are the building blocks of survival. The traditional tool of cost–benefit analysis, widely used by government, business, and nonprofits to determine the desirability of specific investments attempts to quantify the costs and benefits on any particular decision or project by reducing all costs and benefits to monetary terms. Focusing on money alone results in an extremely myopic and distorted view of both how and why people make decisions and what really goes into crafting sustainable livelihoods and communities. It also disguises and devalues the non-monetary resources available to improve well-being.

Financial wealth is not the same as the flows of earning and spending. The "economic impact" studies (really financial impact studies) on which we rely to determine the merit or lack thereof of various development proposals, say nothing about underlying stocks of financial capital. Spending is a flow, whether it is direct spending or indirect spending or induced spending. Knowing which project generates the strongest flows tells us nothing about which project creates the greatest financial wealth, let alone how that wealth is distributed. To know that, our "economic impact" studies would have to look at the impact of projects on savings and reinvestment; in other words, they would have to go the next step and actually document what happens to underlying financial stocks when flows increase (or decrease), whose financial stocks are affected and to what extent. In too many instances, the lion's share of flows go from taxpayers to developers and/or shareholders and result in an increase in the stocks of financial capital for owners and lenders, while providing limited opportunity for financial wealth creation for anyone else.

One of the many positive outcomes of adopting a wealth creation approach occurs as people recognize the multiple forms of wealth they already have at their disposal. People learn to focus on the assets that already exist in a community and region instead of a long list of deficiencies or needs. These are assets they can build on without waiting for outside intervention. People and communities often have different names for the various forms of wealth, but our work in the US and internationally suggest that many people in marginalized communities recognize and relate to all the forms of wealth when their attention is drawn to them. A truly sustainable economy must be one that nurtures and improves all the stocks of wealth over time without undermining some to build others, and in which ownership and access to those stocks is widely distributed.

In order to measure the true financial impact of development activities, we would have to begin with baseline data on the status of stocks of financial capital (savings and unencumbered financial resources available for investment in other forms of wealth) before any intervention. Some of the data exists, but because this is not the focus of our attention, it is not brought into discussions of "economic impact" of development projects. Instead, increasing the financial assets of the poor, particularly through independent development accounts (IDAs) has become its own activity that relies on subsidies at least as much as market drivers. We simply assume that increased flows into financial savings accounts will lead to increased stocks over time. However, without fundamental changes in who gets to produce, consume, and own assets we will continue to witness increasing inequality in financial wealth. What would it look like if we structured every economic development intervention so that it intentionally contributed to financial capital for marginalized people and places? Instead, we tend to assume that jobs lead to income and income leads to savings.

The fact is that increased income does not necessarily lead to increased financial wealth. The reasons behind this are many, and include the need to increase spending when income is too low for survival, the role of unproductive debt, lack of financial literacy, discipline and planning, and more. One example stands out for me. Several years ago, IBM, then the largest single employer in the state of Vermont, laid a number of people off right before Thanksgiving. IBM paid some of the best wages of any employer in the state at that time. Yet, food banks in the Chittenden County area (where IBM was located) noted an influx of people from IBM seeking assistance over the holidays. Clearly, some IBM employees had failed to build stocks of financial wealth despite their relatively ample incomes.

116 *Rethinking Measures of Economic Impact*

Another example of misalignment between desired goals and measures comes from work I did many years ago in the State of Maine with seasoned professionals who had spent their entire working lives trying to reduce poverty. We began our session working together to define what they meant by "poverty" and how they knew it when they saw it. The one word that never came up was "income." Yet if you look at the way poverty reduction programs are targeted in the United States it is almost exclusively on the basis of income. If, according to professional who have worked in the field their entire lives, income is not even a meaningful part of the definition of poverty, how can these programs hope to eradicate poverty? They can't, they haven't, and they won't. Using income and income levels to target anti-poverty resources has led to increased isolation for those without and increased disparities between those dependent on social services and those able to contribute to the mainstream economy. Poverty is not a function of income; it is a function of isolation.

People of very limited means do not tend to have formal (or even informal) savings accounts; in fact, many are entirely unbanked. Also, those of limited means often choose to spend any extra inflow on consumables. This is why our economic pundits talk about the value of putting more money into the hands of the poor; they are more likely to spend it quickly, thus greasing the economic skids for the more fortunate. Spending on consumption, generally speaking, does not lead to wealth accumulation. Savings and investment leads to wealth accumulation. When is the last time you heard a talking head suggest that Americans need to invest more to strengthen our economy?

Some of the things that we label as consumables are just that; items that do not last and do not generate additional "income." Others can plausibly be seen as investments. For example, when money is spent on education or health care or improved diet or weatherization or events that strengthen social ties and commitments each of these produce and/or contribute to various forms of enduring wealth; individual, intellectual, built and social capital that are not the same as one-time consumables. This is the true economic impact of spending and we don't measure it at all. Since you get what you measure, what we measure matters. Our measures need to more accurately reflect the difference between spending on consumables and investing in various forms of wealth. Our measures need to help us capture the impacts of our choices and learn more about when and how existing systems lead to exploitation of one form of wealth to create another.

Why Measure?

Measuring is a powerful tool for learning. Simply deciding what to measure requires us to think about what it is we are trying to achieve and how we would know if we were actually making progress. The feedback we get from ongoing measurement lets us know if our assumptions about the way the world works are correct, or whether we need to rethink our approaches in order to have a lasting impact. The process of measuring provides information on whether the interventions we have chosen are positively impacting various forms of wealth or whether they are having negative consequences on specific stocks of wealth that we had not anticipated. If we are serious about implementing the principle of growing all stocks of wealth without exploiting or harming some to grow others we much pay attention to the effects of our interventions over time. A commitment to ongoing measurement or monitoring of the stocks of wealth most impacted by any given value chain is a first step toward learning what we need to know to create a more sustainably and inclusive economy.

Without measures, we are flying blind. We do that a lot. Most decisions are made on the basis of anecdotal information and personal preferences rather than actual data on likely and desired outcomes. In fact, most of the time we do not define our work in terms of desired outcomes, but rather in terms of the activities we pursue. We keep on doing what we're doing and getting what we've got without asking what it is we really want. What is the condition we are trying to achieve?

Activities versus Goals

Many organizations state their mission in terms of what they do, not what they hope to achieve. For example, a food bank might say, "We provide food for those who do not have enough to eat," not "Everyone in our community has enough to eat." If the focus were on the goal, it would soon become clear that providing food is only one way, and possibly not the most powerful way, to reach the goal. It would also become clear that in order to reach the goal, more than one type of expertise is needed and more than one organization must be engaged. In fact, to achieve the goal, we must understand the system as it exists, the leverage points for changing the system, and all the partners who would need to be engaged in a value chain to make it happen (including, for example, technologists and investors as well as transactional partners).

If the goal is defined as an activity, as in, "We provide food for those who do not have enough to eat," where the measures become the amount of food provided and the number of people who received it. This does not answer the question of how close or far away the community is to achieving the outcome that everyone has enough to eat. Outcome measurement is powerful because it keeps practitioners focused on what they are trying to achieve, instead of getting lost in the details of what they are currently doing to try to achieve it. Outcome measurement requires us to learn about what is before we try to change it. We often think we know what is, but as we get involved we find out that we had many misconceptions. Rather than design and carry out an entire plan of work based on misconceptions, the discipline of embedding measurement requires us to learn about baseline conditions before we start to act. What we learn, initially and along the way, helps us redesign our activities to be more effective as we go. It also helps us recognize who we need to partner with to make a difference at scale.

Attribution versus Contribution

Conceptualizing and using measurement in this way gets us away from trying to prove that what a single organization did made all the difference and toward sharing the credit. In other words, it lets us make claims about our contribution to the outcome rather than attributing the entire outcome to a single intervention. Given the complexity of social change, and the difficulty of controlled experimentation, this is often the most beneficial and realistic approach and one that offers all contributors a sense of accomplishment. Funders who are at least as concerned about outcomes as they are about attribution should embrace this approach.

The type of measurement embedded in WealthWorks is not primarily about being accountable to funders. It is about being accountable for outcomes. Here's an illustration of the difference, as explained by Jason Saul of Mission Measurement at a WealthWorks cross-regional meeting. Let's say you are a teenage basketball player who needs a new set of sneakers. You ask your mother for money and she gives it to you. You go to the store to shop for sneakers. When you get home, your mother will ask you "Show me the sneakers. How much did they cost? Where's my change?" These are the types of questions funders typically ask. They amount to, "Did you do what you said you were going to do?" You, on the other hand, will ask the salesperson questions related to performance, questions like, "How well do they fit me? What are the features that will affect my playing the most? How will they hold up over time? How do I take care of them?" These questions relate to the outcome or conditions you are trying to create for yourself with a new pair of sneakers. You want to be a more effective basketball player. WealthWorks measures are geared to understanding performance, generally in the form of behavioral change. It is possible to measure your performance before and after new sneakers to see if it is reasonable to conclude that they did contribute to improved performance. If they didn't, that might lead to the next question, which could be, "What else do I need to do to improve my performance?"

Measuring Different Forms of Wealth

A description of the desired impact of a value chain on a given form of wealth is not a measure. Every impact must be defined in behavioral terms in the context of the specific value chain before it is measureable. Behavioral change is observable, either directly or indirectly and is therefore measureable once the desired behavioral change is carefully defined. There are no universal measures of the forms of wealth; however there are some commonalities in the types of gaps, bottlenecks, and underutilized resources identified by value chain coordinators across sectors. Remember, one of the principles of the WealthWorks framework is that it is place-based and context-driven. Another principle is that it is flexible in implementation. This means that it is unlikely that measures will be the same for any two value

Rethinking Measures of Economic Impact 119

chains, even if they are in the same sectors. However, by using the wealth matrix as a framework, value chain coordinators and partners can learn a great deal from each other about different approaches to improving the stocks of each type of wealth. Measures and measurement processes can also improve over time.

Once the intended and desired impact on each form of wealth is defined for a specific value chain, it becomes possible to measure baseline conditions of the stock of each type of wealth. Measuring baseline conditions serves two important functions that are too often overlooked. The first is the importance of actually understanding current conditions and not simply proceeding based on a set of untested assumptions. The excitement of this work begins when we gain greater understanding of the situation as it is today from the perspectives of multiple value chain partners, including demand partners. What we learn is likely to change the nature of the interventions we undertake.

The second function served by measuring baseline conditions is that of helping us remember where we began. If we do not take the time to measure baseline conditions with respect to the stocks of wealth we are trying to impact, we will not be able to demonstrate the impact we have had. Measuring baseline conditions helps us tell a compelling story about impacts. Here are examples of some of the measures WealthWorks practitioners have used to measure each form of wealth with some discussion of commonalities by types of interventions needed related to each form of wealth.

Individual Capital—Skills and Mental and Physical Health

All the value chains we have worked with have required investments in skill development for transactional and sometimes support and demand partners as well. For example, a transactional partner may need to develop new skills to produce to specific standards, while a support partner may need to develop new skills to provide transactional partners with the type of support they actually need and demand partners may need new skills to communicate and deliver the value of the value chain's goods and services to its customers.

If lack of skills is a significant barrier to some aspect of the effective functioning of the value chain, one way to tell if skills are improving is by the outcomes produced. For example, selling into wholesale markets often requires a different set of skills than selling directly to end users. If a value chain is based on sales into wholesale markets and intentionally invests in helping producers that have never sold into wholesale markets develop the required skills, one way to measure progress is through increased wholesale sales by trained producers over time. For example, the Central Appalachian Network (CAN) measured the involvement of producers with wholesale markets in terms of the size of the farm business, value of sales, number and types of buyers, and the number of years of repeat business with specific wholesale buyers. CAN established baselines during the exploration phase and then re-measured on an annual basis. Each year they delivered research-

120 *Rethinking Measures of Economic Impact*

driven training and technical assistance to producers to improve their skills. Between 2009 and 2014, the number of producers in the value chain increased from 96 to 286 and the gross revenue from wholesale sales went from approximately $3,500,000 to $10,703,690.

Instead of measuring the amount of training received or the dollars spent on training, WealthWorks focuses on the desired outcome, which, in this case, would be increased wholesale sales with repeat business. If this isn't happening, it's important to figure out why not. What are the factors affecting sales, including, but not necessarily limited to, training?

It turns out that a focus on outcomes actually strengthens the training process itself. When value chain coordinators and partners agree and are clear about the desired outcomes, it will affect who they choose to conduct training and who they choose to participate in training. By making the desired outcomes clear to training participants, along with requirements for measuring their own progress toward those outcomes and reporting that progress on a regular basis, rigor and accountability are built in the invest-ment in training from the start. Regular reporting helps identify strengths and weaknesses in the training as well as other factors that the value chain needs to address to succeed.

WealthWorks value chains can impact mental and physical health in a number of ways, depending on their sector and focus. For example, introdu-cing producers to more effective technologies and risk-mitigation strategies can lower the stress involved in maintaining their livelihoods. Reducing or eliminating the use of toxic substances in production and distribution can also have a positive impact on health. Investing in restoring natural resources through the activities of the value chain also contributes to human health. For example, Rural Action's focus on restoring the health of waterways in Cen-tral Appalachia led to a new use for the toxic metals removed from streams. The value chain transforms the toxic waste recovered from streams into non-toxic pigments for artists. The value chain improves the health of the streams and the health of artists. Producing and distributing healthy products, whe-ther fresh nutritious food or toxic-free housing or recreational options to consumers that would otherwise lack access can all have measurable impacts on human health. Wealth creation value chains that connect marginal pro-ducers to new markets and consumers to new goods and services that improve their bottom lines can also reduce stress and improve mental health.

Social Capital—Networking, Trust, and Collaboration

Building social capital is all about creating connections; strengthening social capital is all about building trust. The social capital literature refers to two basic types of connections: bonding and bridging. Bonding connections are those between individuals or groups that are similar to one another and bridging social capital is between those that are not similar. The process of creating WealthWorks value chains requires investments in both types of social capital. Bonding is often critical to allow multiple producers or buyers or support providers to work together effectively. For example, when Fahe began their work on a WealthWorks energy efficient affordable housing value chain, only 14 of their 50 members agreed to sign a green performance contract. At the end of a year, 24 members were active in developing the roles and responsibilities associated with participation in Fahe's Energy Efficiency Performance Contract.

Bridging social capital can create a pathway out of poverty. The poverty-alleviation power of WealthWorks comes from intentionally building non-exploitative bridging social capital between those who are connected to the mainstream economy and those who are not. This can take many forms, depending on how the value chain is implementing the principle of inclusivity. The focus may be on inclusivity among business owners, employees, service providers, investors, technologists, and/or consumers, as well as bridging among and between value chain partners that are and are not economically marginalized.

For example, the CAN food system value chain tracks three tiers of producers, those with annual wholesale farm revenue of less than $10,000, those with $10,000–$100,000, and those with over $100,000. Producers earning less than $100,000 in wholesale revenue are likely to be dependent on multiple sources of income for their livelihoods. There are a total of about 40 mid and larger tier producers participating. CAN recognizes the need to balance the scale of production with wealth creation objectives. Growth in number of value chain producers in CAN's value chains is due to the participation of smaller farms, while overall growth in producer sales across the region is driven by a core group of established producers who are strong partners in the value chains. These larger producers have benefited greatly from the support structure of the value chain and now return the favor by acting as "gazelles" for other producers, exploring new markets and pulling buyers into the chain.

One of the distinguishing features of WealthWorks that differentiates it from many development efforts is the idea that inclusivity works both ways; not only is it crucial to intentionally include economically marginalized people and places in the design and realization of value chains, it is equally crucial to engage non-marginalized people and places to allow value chains to get to scale.

All WealthWorks value chains require interventions to build social capital that creates relationships where none existed before or productively reframes existing relationships to overcome cultural and/or other types of barriers. Baselines can be established by documenting the strength of relationships between partners at the beginning of a value chain exploration and re-measuring periodically. One way to do this is to use a collaboration continuum to define the strength of relationships. The continuum goes from networking to coordination, cooperation, and collaboration, where each step in the continuum builds on the one before. Networking includes exchanging information and ideas for mutual benefit. Coordinating includes networking plus recognizing and/or developing and implementing activities that achieve a common purpose. Cooperating adds sharing resources to the first two behaviors.

122 *Rethinking Measures of Economic Impact*

Collaborating goes even further and includes working together to enhance the capacity of another to achieve a shared purpose.[3] Collaboration can be described as "putting your money on the table and your hands back in your pockets."[4] True collaborators don't fight over resources; they focus on outcomes. The strength of a relationship along the collaboration continuum is one indicator of the level of trust in the relationship.

Value chain maps can be used to indicate the presence or absence of connections among and between partners and changes in the strength of those connections over time. A visual representation of social capital helps identify gaps and opportunities, as well as remind participants of the value of the connections they have established through the value chain. Here are two value chain maps of an agricultural value chain (Figures 8.1 and 8.2), one drawn at the beginning of value chain exploration and the other two years later when proof of concept has begun. Each map is backed by a spreadsheet that contains the names, contact information, and other relevant information about the specific participants in the chain. The line weight illustrates the relative strength of the connection. No line means there is no connection, no relationship, no social capital. Rectangular shapes designate transactional partners and demand partners and oval shapes represent support partners. The map itself is a quick reference tool and visual record of development.

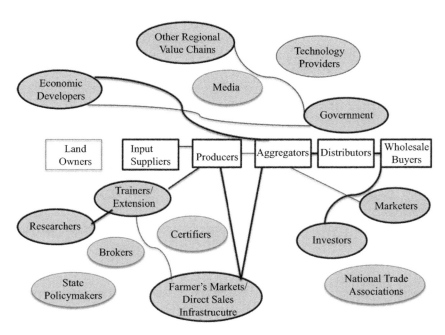

Figure 8.1 Baseline Illustration of Social Capital in a Generic Wealth Creation Value Chain in the Agricultural Sector
Source: Yellow Wood Associates, Inc.

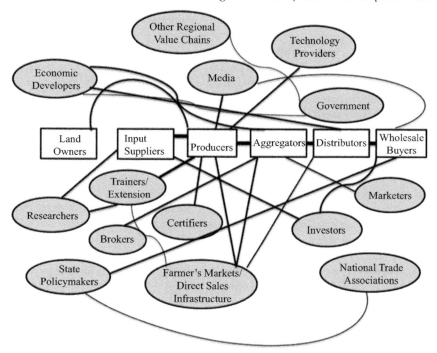

Figure 8.2 Illustration of Social Capital Development in a Generic Wealth Creation Value Chain in the Agricultural Sector
Source: Yellow Wood Associates, Inc.

The first diagram shows weak connections among many of the transactional partners in the chain and limited, if any, connections between transactional partners and support partners. Some potential support partners, like media, techology providers, certifiers, national trade associations, and state policy-makers are not yet connected at all. Some connections exist among support partners, like those between economic developers and government, but have not been connected to the value chain. Producers and aggregators are more strongly connected to the direct market infrastructure than they are to each other.

The second diagram is very different as a result of intentional relationship building activities. Now there are no partners that have not been connected with the value chain in some way. The connections between the transactional partners are much stronger and key support partners like certifiers, investors, and technology providers are working directly with producers. Researchers have been connected directly with input suppliers and national trade associations have been connected with state policy-makers. Although it is not evident from the diagrams themselves, the value chain is also more robust because, where there were once partner categories with only a single person or organization inside them, now there is at least two of every type of partner. Having more than one partner in the

124 *Rethinking Measures of Economic Impact*

value chain related to each function creates redundancy, a key characteristic of resilience.

Most effective interventions that build the stock of social capital are based on experiences of reciprocity and accountability. Rubbing shoulders by being in the same space and breaking bread together are often good first steps in breaking down barriers and relationship building, but our experience suggests that more structured interventions are often required to induce changes in behaviors required for value chain success. This is particularly true wherever society has reinforced deep seated assumptions about people in one group or another that inhibit communication and discovery of shared interests.

Fortunately, social capital building interventions can be designed to deepen relationships and establish positive interdependencies over time. For example, if each partner in a value chain exploration takes on responsibilities to conduct research into various aspects of the proposed value chain and regular meetings are held to share the results, it soon becomes clear which partners are following through and which are not. Similarly, if value chain proof of concept requires that partners share equipment and pass it along in working condition, partners that do not comply are readily identified.

Ideally, a WealthWorks value chain creates a culture of shared problem-solving and mutual aid. This does not happen all at once and it will not happen at all unless there is a willingness to cull partners that do not show good faith. Not every partner is the "right" partner. We have witnessed the need to cull partners who put their own interests over those of the value chain as a whole, who lack the commitment to persevere, and/or who are unwilling to take the steps required to meet the demands of the market and other value chain partners. Value chains that succeed over time are those that engage enough partners related to each key function of the chain so that if one does not perform, there are others who can step in. Mapping connections helps identify areas where redundancy exists and areas where developing it should be a priority. Since working in a wealth creation value chain is a new experience for most partners, it takes time to determine who is and is not a good fit. Designing social capital building interventions that demand reciprocity and accountability helps identify the right partners as the work progresses.

Intellectual Capital—Ideas and Creativity

The absence of models to learn from and a general lack of awareness of what is possible based on what has been achieved elsewhere is a common intellectual capital deficit in economically marginalized places. Intellectual capital deficits can create barriers among different types of partners in a WealthWorks value chain. For example, the lack of financial literacy among potential home owners becomes a barrier to securing mortgages for affordable energy efficient housing and a lack of understanding of business management among entrepreneurs and business owners becomes a barrier to effective value chain participation. The exploration

Rethinking Measures of Economic Impact   125

phase is the first step in addressing this deficit, but the need for exposure to new ways of thinking and doing is ongoing in the life of a value chain.

Every WealthWorks value chain has intellectual capital components or areas where new ideas, imagination and new understandings are critical to success. Sometimes the ideas already exist and need to be introduced in a new place or context. This was the case with MACED's introduction of on-bill financing to Kentucky utilities and with Communities Unlimited's discovery of the University of Montana's research into camelina.

In other circumstances, intellectual capital needs to be created to meet a need. This was the case in the work Fahe did to identify which components of affordable housing construction contributed most to energy efficiency. MACED and the Kentucky Sustainable Energy Alliance outsourced research into the economic impacts on average electric bills and the state's economy of renewable and energy efficient portfolio standards for Kentucky as the basis for influencing the thinking of key decision-makers, including legislators about the possible impacts of reduced dependence on coal. Often, introducing the concepts and potential of WealthWorks value chains is, in itself, an exercise in building intellectual capital. As with all other aspects of this work, it is important to identify areas in which intellectual capital must be introduced, created, or strengthened to ensure the success of the value chain. Once the "what" is clear, there will be many choices as to how the intellectual capital building functions of the value chain are realized.

New ways of thinking and new skills to implement new thinking can be designed into the value chain through intentional investments in intellectual capital, such as learning journeys in which value chain participants meet their counterparts in other parts of the country or the world who have already made progress in the areas that remain challenging to value chain partners. The exploration phase of WealthWorks value chains often includes one or more learning journeys to places that have achieved some of the goals of any given value chain. Learning journeys can be real or virtual (through webinars, virtual "tours" etc.). Learning journeys are most effective when each person on the journey has the opportunity to meet and engage directly with their counterpart (e.g. farmer to farmer and distributor to distributor) and when those on the journey are responsible for sharing what they have learned with all the other prospective value chain partners. There are many ways to introduce new ideas and often the most powerful involve learning from one's peers. Sometimes "seeing is believing"; exposure to new ideas and other realities can be life-changing.

Measures of intellectual capital are specific to the type(s) of capital targeted by value chain interventions and are, like all WealthWorks measures, focused on outcomes. For example, if the focus is to build the stock of financial literacy among potential mortgage applicants, the measure is not the number of financial literacy interventions or participants, but rather the numbers of participants that succeed in obtaining affordable mortgages, and ultimately the number that are able to maintain their mortgage payments over time. One intellectual capital gap in Central Appalachia stemmed from the fact that many buyers approached by

126   *Rethinking Measures of Economic Impact*

CAN's value chains had not previously recognized the opportunity to buy local and organic products, although buyers elsewhere in the country were already doing so. The work CAN did to help buyers understand the value to them of buying local and organic products resulted in an increase of 37% in the number of wholesale buyers involved in the value chains and an increase of over 160% (from $1,794,000 to $4,667,321) in the value of annual sales between 2009 and 2011, a period of economic recession in the US.

Measuring changes in intellectual capital is a matter of: 1) identifying whose mindsets need to change and how they need to change to make the value chain successful; 2) experimenting with interventions that will help people change their mindsets; and 3) identifying the behaviors that will result from the desired changes in mindsets. This is the basis for measuring baseline conditions and changes in outcomes over time.

Built Capital—Infrastructure of All Kinds

Built capital refers to any human-made infrastructure required to carry out the functions of a WealthWorks value chain. The location, ownership and control of built capital have a direct impact on who does and does not benefit from market-driven opportunities. For example, when canals were first built and expanded in the early 1800s to move anthracite coal from the hills of Pennsylvania to cities along the eastern seaboard, those cities gained comparative advantage in heavy industrial development. Without the built infrastructure of the canals, it would not have been possible to develop markets for anthracite coal. Unfortunately for the rural areas from which the coal was extracted, ownership and control of the canals was in the hands of relatively few and the benefits were not widely shared although the costs, in terms of environmental destruction and human health, were. In this instance, as in many others, the built capital investment expedited removal of a valuable resource without corollary investment in protecting the rural environment from which it was extracted and the people doing the extraction.[5]

Built capital gaps in a value chain such as the absence of a processing facility or an aggregation facility or effective communications system become evident when a value chain is mapped out by the functions it must serve to create a good or service that meets market demand. However, as we have just seen, a wealth creation approach to filling a built capital gap is not the same as a conventional approach.

The art of WealthWorks is in designing interventions that build the stock of fully functional built capital while contributing positively to stocks of other forms of wealth as well. For example, if a warehouse is needed, how can it be built in such a way as to increase the skills of workers, contribute to natural resource conservation and restoration, generate clean energy, provide proper ventilation and lighting to enhance worker health and reduce transportation requirements throughout the value chain? If a distribution channel is developed, how can it serve the needs of multiple businesses of different sizes while providing access to a wide range of demand partners?

Measures of built capital may be about the infrastructure itself, e.g. we did not have a warehouse and now we do, but they may also be about the functions that are served by the built capital, e.g. the new warehouse has allowed the value chain to increase throughput or productivity by X, has generated Y amount of clean energy, and reduced accidents associated with packing and transport by Z. For example, MACED's value chain led to an increase in the number of energy efficient homes and commercial establishments in Central Appalachia. This means lower utility bills for owners and occupants as well as livelihoods for building retrofitters and reductions in emissions from using less energy to accomplish the same (or better) ends.

Natural Capital—Ecosystem Services, Renewable and Non-renewable Resources

All WealthWorks value chains have some impact on stocks of natural capital and for some the ways in which natural capital stocks are impacted is primary among their value chain goals. One, though certainly not the only, lens through which to consider natural resource impacts of value chains is in terms of reducing material waste and turning waste into resource. Waste may be generated at many points along the value chain include inputs, production, processing, aggregation, distribution, and consumption. Value chains designed to reduce waste and/or transform waste into resource can contribute to wealth creation.

For example, Rural Action, a WealthWorks value chain coordinator, has been working with Ohio University Civil Engineering Professor, Dr. Guy Riefler, to find ways to treat the acidic, metal-laden water seeping into streams from abandoned mines in Ohio so that it becomes an asset, not a liability. Dr. Riefler has developed techniques to remove pollutants, including iron, from the water and is working with Ohio University Art Professor John Sabraw to develop a high-quality paint pigment from the residue. The group has plans for a pilot plant to test the treatment technique and pigment creation on a larger scale. This pilot plant will be built on the banks of Sunday Creek in Corning at a significant mine discharge site. Rural Action has coordinated with the Village of Corning, which owns the site where the plant will be built and with Rendville Art Works, to ensure that community involvement is a key part of the treatment project. Rendville Art Works supports a small group of artists with disabilities to create and freely express themselves and find their voice through art.

This project represents a potential turning point in the treatment of large acid mine drainage seeps in watersheds across Appalachia. "If this pilot project proves successful at the Corning site and we learn how to scale the technology up, this process could be replicated at discharge sites across the region, cleaning up sites that have had no easy solution."[6] The "project" is a

128　*Rethinking Measures of Economic Impact*

nascent WealthWorks value chain that is designed to connect with market demand while building multiple forms of wealth that stick in rural areas.

Political Capital—The Ability to Influence Resource Allocation Decisions

Political capital is required to change systems at scale. As value chain coordinators and participants learn more about the opportunities and constraints related to the specific value chain they are working on, the most influential changes that can be brought about through the exercise of political capital become apparent. Often it requires a combination of the reallocation of local and/or state and/or federal resources to solve problems and strengthen value chains. It may also require a mix of changes in public and private sector policies. Sometimes, it is not the policy itself that needs to change, but the manner in which it is, or is not, enforced.

One of several political capital targets CAN identified for its WealthWorks food systems value chains was more flexible purchasing policies of local institutions, including hospitals and schools, that support the use of locally produced foods and food products. When they began their work, there were very few such policies in place. They have targeted specific activities to influence relevant policies. Changes in resource allocation decisions related to specific value chain interventions can be documented as evidence of political capital.

Once the most important resource allocation decisions needed to strengthen the value chain are identified, research is often needed to understand who is responsible for those decisions, how and when they are made, and which avenues are available to influence them. Political capital happens by communicating a clear message to decision-makers at the right time, but it is only effective if it comes from a diverse group of people with enough collective clout that they are hard to ignore. Social capital is created through the act of building the alliances that translate into effective political capital. WealthWorks value chains may need to build certain types of social capital intentionally to create effective political capital with respect to the issues of greatest import to the value chain. Change may not happen quickly, but persistence often pays off. As with other aspects of WealthWorks , it is useful to think about the value of the requested change to the decision-makers as well as to the value chain. What are the problems that the desired change in policy will help them solve? Why is it in their self-interest to make the change?

Sometimes it is not worth trying to change the well-established criteria used by key decision-makers; it's better to simply figure out how to meet them. When Fahe thought that they needed the ability to sell mortgages on the secondary market to be able to go to scale, they began working with the Federal Home Loan Board (FHLB) to expand the loan to value ratio, which is a financial term used by lenders to express the ratio of a loan to the value of the asset purchased. The FHLB encouraged Fahe to continue with their work, but did not accept the mortgages until Fahe was able to get appraisers to accept training and to value energy efficient affordable homes appropriately. Once this happened, Fahe was able to meet not only the criteria of the FHLB, but of every established part of the mortgage industry, including national bank chains and the United States Department of Agriculture. Access to the secondary market frees up a larger pool of resources to plow back into the value chain. Measuring political capital is about measuring changes in resource allocation decisions as well as the system-wide impacts of those changes. The key element to changing the system of financing for energy efficient affordable housing that enables Fahe's value chain to be market-driven instead of dependent on subsidies is the change in the nature of the appraisal system. It is possible to measure the number of trained appraisers and the number of appraisals they complete. The system-wide impacts are broader since appropriate appraisals open up the mortgage market to private as well as public and nonprofit builders and investors.

Cultural Capital

All WealthWorks value chains are actively working to establish new norms of doing business in their places and regions. Sometimes, baseline cultural conditions are obstacles to progress. For example, if the cultural norm is pervasive lack of trust, poor communications, lack of self-respect, dependency and/or disrespect for difference, a WealthWorks value chain may need to address these issues and the behaviors that stem from them head-on. Changing culture is often one component of WealthWorks value chain development that unfolds over time. As with all other forms of wealth, careful analysis of the value chain itself will reveal which existing behavioral norms are positive and which need to be changed to enable the value chain to succeed. This will lead to specific interventions to support and/or change behavioral norms. The success of these interventions can be measured in terms of behavioral change and related outcomes once a baseline is established.

Regardless of behavioral norms specific to any given value chain every WealthWorks value chain has addressed creating new norms by publicizing their work. Many WealthWorks value chains have received coverage in local and state news media as well as through word of mouth, field days, videos, newsletters, conference presentations, the WealthWorks website, and other outreach efforts. Normalizing the principles and practices of WealthWorks value chains requires an intentional approach to public relations that demonstrates to partners and skeptics alike what is possible. Every WealthWorks value chain can benefit by considering the key audiences for outreach efforts and gearing those efforts toward the changes they wish to see.

Some WealthWorks value chains may be built to promote certain aspects of culture such as language, arts, foods, or history unique to certain places and/or peoples. These value chains may approach measuring cultural capital as a combination of impacts on the stocks of other forms of capital such as intellectual, individual, and social.

130 *Rethinking Measures of Economic Impact*

Financial Capital

One objective and measure of progress in a wealth creation approach to development is the ability to redirect investment back to geographic areas that are under-served by financial markets by identifying real market-driven value chain opportunities. The other is to activate place-based wealth related to multiple capitals to build and support effective value chains. People with financial wealth exist even in the poorest communities. (See Chapter 5 for more about connecting with investors.)

WealthWorks measures of financial capital are typically measures of savings, including avoided cost, and/or investment. For example, starting from a baseline of zero, MACED measured annual home owner savings due to energy retrofits of $4,554 for the eight houses built in 2010–2011 during proof of concept. CAN measured the level of investment by producers in their farm enterprises before and after engaging the in value chain, distinguishing between subsidized investment and direct investment. Before the value chain, approximately 7% of producer investment was direct and 93% was subsidized. After one year of proof of concept, direct investment grew to 25% of the total, a significant step away from reliance on subsidies.

Financial capital may also include contributions to public revenues, a kind of collective investment. For example, Fahe measured an increase in local tax revenue in fees due to construction of energy efficient affordable housing from $6,750 per unit before the value chain was developed to $8,320 per unit during proof of concept.

Comparing Measures

While specific measures differ by value chain, as they should, the categories of measurement (i.e. the forms of wealth) are the same. This provides the structure required to "aggregate" within categories while maintaining the flexibility that is essential to designing and implementing effective value chains in many places across many sectors. If, for example, one were trying to compare impacts on multiple forms of wealth across many different WealthWorks value chains, it would be possible to come up with a simple color-coded or numeric rubric that shows the extent of impact of each chain on each form of wealth. A matrix could point observers toward those value chains that have had the greatest positive impacts by forms of wealth. The value becomes the ability to go beyond the surface and dig into what they did, i.e. the activities they engaged in that resulted in measurable impacts (and how they were measured).

We embed measurement into WealthWorks for many important reasons. In order to measure anything, we must first define what we are trying to measure precisely enough so that we would know it if we saw it. Most often, when groups and individuals are confused about what to measure, it is because they have not defined their desired outcomes concretely in terms of behavioral or observable change. Once they do so, they not only gain clarity and a sense of shared purpose, but they begin to understand how to know if they are actually getting what they want. Defining outcomes in behavioral or observable terms helps us understand whose behavior matters. This, in turn, helps us understand who needs to be engaged in the Wealth-Works value chain to make a real difference. It also helps focus actions or interventions more effectively by revealing the barriers, gaps, and systems forces that prevent desired behaviors from occurring.

If a participatory process like You Get What You Measure®[7] is used to create the vision of the value chain, define desired changes, and identify measures, the process itself can do much to help value chain partners figure out how to align their competencies and resources most effectively.[8] It can also help identify a measurement plan that is *participatory* and not *extractive*. Extractive measurement refers to requesting or requiring data that is not relevant to the entity from which it required for use by a third party. Participatory measurement means helping partners identify the information they themselves need to improve and succeed and, where necessary, helping them create the systems that will work for them to capture that information for their own benefit. Once those systems are in place, sharing the information with the value chain as a whole is a reciprocal process that benefits the entire chain.

Measures of progress are powerful tools to help the various partners in the value chain see the big picture and to keep the entire value chain focused on outcomes. Reviewing data on a regular basis helps build in the discipline of reflection and facilitates shared learning. The value chain gains importance to its participants in part in relationship to the information it makes available to them that they would not otherwise have access to. Today's technologies provide many new cost-effective options for measuring and monitoring that can create either useful or useless information. Helping value chain participants identify and implement the most effective technologies to capture and report the information that matters to them and to the value chain as a whole in a timely manner is one important role of a value chain coordinator.

Measurement also has the potential to overcome resistance to change. Resistance to change is often fueled by fear. When the nature of the fear is identified in behavioral or observable terms, it becomes possible to measure or monitor over time to determine whether or not it is justified. For example, if a canoe trail is being proposed through a previously untraveled area, people may be concerned that it will lead to environmental degradation in the form of littering. If the proposers partner with objectors to monitor the extent of littering during the first season of operation, they can determine together whether or not the fear is justified and, if so, how best to address it. Including a measurement or monitoring component in any change-based scenario can help raise the comfort level of those who are initially opposed. Ongoing measurement may also help reduce conflict by providing data that can replace misleading assumptions.

Often addressing barriers, gaps, and systems forces requires building new partnerships and relationships with others that would benefit from the

132 *Rethinking Measures of Economic Impact*

desired changes. These are not ideological alliances; they are alliances designed to achieve very specific ends and solve very specific problems. The process of coming up with measures is a powerful way to get diverse interests on the same page. In keeping with the principles of WealthWorks, practitioners generally engage staff and value chain partners in the measurement process.

Measurement is never a simple quantitative process. Numbers arise in context; interpreting them properly requires understanding that context. That's why WealthWorks value chains report numbers associated with each form of wealth along with a narrative explaining what they mean and what they do not mean. Any measurement report is incomplete without a narrative explanation. Sometimes measures move in what seems like a desirable direction, but the underlying change is not happening. For example, in the first year of the affordable energy efficient housing chain, Fahe members built more houses than they had previously, but the gaps and barriers in the value chain had not been fixed. Simply building more houses was not a sign of success. So, rather than congratulate itself on positive progress, Fahe doubled down on efforts to fix the value chain so that it could become driven by market forces and not subsidies.

Linking Interventions to Wealth Creation Outcomes

Measurement allows WealthWorks value chains to tell compelling stories that have beginnings (baselines), middles (results over time based on re-measurement) and ends (impacts at scale resulting from systems changes). Some impacts may occur surprisingly rapidly, while others take more time. Keeping the big picture in mind provides continuity and direction. Wealth-Works measures, unlike measures drawn only from common secondary data sources, are crafted to specific market-driven WealthWorks value chain impacts rooted in specific places.

Instead of starting with either existing data or a catalog of possible measures, the WealthWorks approach to measurement starts with defining how the activities or interventions required to explore, prove, implement, and institutionalize a WealthWorks value chain will positively impact each of the eight forms of wealth without undermining any of them to improve the others.

The Wealth Matrix provides a structure for identifying desired outcomes from value chain development for each form of wealth. (See Chapter 2 for an illustration of the Wealth Matrix.) Each desired outcome is closely tied to one or more specific interventions implemented to allow a specific wealth creation value chain to form and operate successfully. The version of the wealth matrix (Table 8.1) comes from the Arkansas Green Energy Network (AGEN), coordinated by Communities Unlimited (formerly alt.Consulting), a regional nonprofit development organization based in Arkansas. AGEN's value chain involves providing biofuel from locally grown camelina plus waste vegetable oil to municipal and other local and regional buyers.

Rethinking Measures of Economic Impact 133

Table 8.1 AGEN's Wealth Matrix for Planning and Evaluation

Form of capital	Impact
Intellectual	Mindset shift from exporting outputs to creating more local opportunities
Individual	Online agri-entrepreneurship training through two-year colleges
Social	Creating deep collaboration between city government, entrepreneurs, nonprofits, colleges, university
Built	Turning environmental hazard into viable business
Political	Four state legislators actively supporting AGEN through GIF funds
Natural	Regional waste vegetable oil recycling, clean fuel used by farmers and city
Financial	Securing private investment for local entrepreneurs, creating new opportunities for other entrepreneurs
Cultural	Lifting up agricultural and entrepreneurial culture as agents for local change

Source: Courtesy of Communities Unlimited, Inc.

During the exploration phase, many gaps, bottlenecks, and underutilized resources relevant to the value chain were identified. Putting these together with a vision for a fully operational value chain at scale led to specific interventions intentionally tied to wealth creation. For example, it became clear that deep collaboration would be needed between municipalities with an interest in increased energy self-sufficiency and universities and colleges with research and development capabilities related to crop research and biofuel production technologies. This led to interventions specifically designed to build the needed social capital. Also, farming and non-farming entrepreneurs need to be identified to actually grow the crops, crush the seeds, process the oil and byproducts, collect the waste oil, etc. The value chain coordinator provided feasibility studies for each business to justify investment and ensure a smoother start-up. This led to other interventions with politician and local and regional investors and training institutions.

Once the value chain was operational, the impacts would include turning an environmental hazard (waste vegetable oil) into a viable business using innovative technologies, and substituting clean fuels for fossil fuels in the local economy (with other impacts like improved air quality around schools as buses converted to biofuels). The underlying mindset shift from exporting agricultural outputs to creating opportunities through local processing in order to meet market demand led to the creation of new businesses not even related directly to the value chain. The value chain resulted in increased cultural awareness of the power of an entrepreneurial approach to agriculture and business development in general.

Designing Interventions Based on Desired Outcomes

The Wealth Matrix is a tool for planning, designing interventions, and guiding ongoing measurement. The Wealth Matrix captures desired outcomes for each form of wealth at the beginning of value chain exploration. During the initial exploration phase, the gaps, barriers, and underutilized resources related to the value chain are identified and the baseline status of specific stocks of wealth is measured and characterized. Desired outcomes are often adjusted based on new information gained during exploration. Moving from exploration to proof of concept involves identifying key interventions that will contribute to desired outcomes for the stocks of wealth as well as for the value chain as a market-driven business model.

The principles of WealthWorks come into play in the way interventions are designed. Designs themselves need to be inclusive and focused on building wealths that stick in place. For example, if you are designing a Wealth-Works value chain in affordable energy efficient housing, one gap you may identify is the lack of understanding by home purchasers of how to live in a home that is built to be energy efficient. If home purchasers do not understand this, they risk losing the benefits of the home's energy efficient features and functions and the value chain will fail. This may lead you to design the value chain with a home owner education component that helps home owners understand the energy efficiency components of their house and how to get the most energy savings out of them (individual and intellectual capital). Rather than measure the knowledge home owners gain by some sort of quiz, you and they can document energy savings as an indicator of knowledge gained *and applied* over time. It is relatively difficult to measure changes in thinking but relatively easy to measure changes in behavior. In this example, if the utility bills go down after home owner education that is a good indication of behavioral change, particularly if home owners remain comfortable in their homes.

As you explore the value chain, you may discover there are other forms of wealth that also must be built for the value chain to succeed. For example, financial literacy may be needed in helping prospective home owners qualify for mortgages and/or appraisers may need to have a new understanding of how to appraise energy efficient homes differently than energy inefficient homes to unlock market-driven demand. Notice that the target of each of these activities is different: actual home owners, prospective home owners, and appraisers. You may not address them all at the same time or with equal intensity, so you will need to decide where to focus your measurement efforts. Once you have decided, that will help guide you in designing the activities that will move the measures you have identified in a positive direction. Your measures may change over time as you learn more about what it takes to make your value chain successful.

Measuring Systems Change

Since the goal of WealthWorks goes beyond building multiple wealths on a one-time basis and is all about changing systems to support building multiple wealths into the future, it is important to measure or monitor systems change as well as changes in the stocks of the different forms of wealth. In progressing through the four stages of exploration, proof of concept, implementation, and institutionalization, WealthWorks aspires to change the way in which products and services are produced to meet market demand from one that is exclusive and exploitative to one that is inclusive and sustainable. Through the process of building specific WealthWorks value chains we learn which systems constraints and incentives are creating undesirable outcomes and we work to address them directly. As we succeed, systems begin to change and a "new normal" emerges. We know we are succeeding when WealthWorks value chains are operating the way they were envisioned and producing and maintaining multiple forms of wealth over time, and when the nature of the system has changed so that it supports, rather than undermines, WealthWorks principles. We seek to create virtuous cycles in which positive outcomes beget more positive outcomes.

The baseline for measuring systems change is rarely apparent at the beginning of the exploration stage. It takes time to develop enough knowledge about the sector and region within which the value chain is taking shape to have a basis for an accurate analysis of systems constraints and incentives. What we can see at the start are behaviors that are antithetical to the goals of WealthWorks. The work is in understanding the regulatory and power structures, incentive systems, and mindsets that drive those behaviors. We can also begin to identify incorrect assumptions that may be driving behaviors. Assumptions may take the form of "We can't do this because ... " or "This will cost us too much." In our experience, both of these common responses are often based on inaccurate information. Sometimes value chain partners can provide the information needed to counter inaccuracies and false assumptions. In other instances, additional research may be required.

Systems analysis is an ongoing process, not a one-time event. The same value chain maps that help demonstrate changes in social capital over time can also help demonstrate systems changes. For example, the introduction of new technologies that allow producers to sell into wholesale markets appears on a map as new connections between technologists, trainers, and producers. Likewise, a change in policy that supports purchases of locally or regionally grown produce may appear as a new link between government and wholesale buyers.

There can be many drivers of systems change including policies, rules, and regulations that change incentives at various levels of the system. Systems change as new partners are brought into relationship with one another in unprecedented ways. As systems changes occur, new beneficiaries and investors may also emerge. For example, as a food value chain develops

136 *Rethinking Measures of Economic Impact*

relationships with state policy-makers, it may become evident that state college systems would benefit as partners in the value chain. Insights into the systems that shape behaviors related to a specific value chain and changes in the systems that illustrate progress toward a new more inclusive and sustainable market-driven "normal" are best described in an annual narrative. Framing measures help provide context for the narrative.

Framing Measures

Too often, when economic development work is conceived of as a "project" and not systems change, the measures of impact are never contextualized. For example, it is common to see regional food value chains report on the number of pounds of food they have moved without considering how this compares to the total number of pounds of food consumed by people in their region. Or they report on the number of low-income (or other targeted) consumers and producers that have benefited without taking into account the total number of low-income consumers and producers in the region as a whole. In either case, measurements are limited to the activity of the "project" and there is no effort made to look at the accomplishments of similar efforts with comparable challenges. In other words, accomplishments are taken entirely out of context.

This is a good example of using measurement to convince one's self and others that impacts are occurring rather than using measurement to learn how to change systems to achieve scale. This tendency to avoid context in itself reflects the failure of our political and philanthropic institutions to embrace and insist on systems thinking and accountability. One way to change that aspect of the systems we have that are not serving us well is to insist on placing measures in context, even if it makes impacts seem less impressive in the short run. Having the courage to place impacts in context is critical if we are to build a truly sustainable economy. One term for measures that place accomplishments in context is *framing measures*. When they began their value chain exploration, Rural Action used framing measures to determine the percentage of forest land that was under certified forest management by type of certification for each of five states in the Central Appalachian region (Ohio, West Virginia, Kentucky, Tennessee, and Virginia). They determined that only 39 landowners had forested lands that were certified by the Forest Stewardship Council (FSC) in 2010. FSC is a more demanding standard than the other forms of forest management certification in areas including, but not limited to, biological diversity, endangered species, forests of high conservation value, indigenous peoples' and workers' rights, and local communities. FSC does not permit forest owners to change forest management auditing standards.[9]

This framing measure provided context for what it would mean to have an impact on forest management practices by improving market opportunities for products made from FSC-certified wood products. It also allowed Rural Action and its value chain partners to set realistic goals. By 2015,

Through their work on the value chain that resulted, in part, in a Center for Wood and Forest Certification at the University of Kentucky, there were an additional ten individually certified forest landowners and 60 landowners certified under the Center's group certificate. The significance of these numbers is lost without context. Fixing the weak certification link in the value chain has allowed limited resource landowners to participate in markets for certified wood products.

Measurement and the attention it requires to what is actually going on versus what we may think or assume is happening, is a powerful tool for understanding the world around us, but only when it is used properly with that intent. When measurements are imposed by funders or other outside forces they rarely result in true learning on the ground. WealthWorks promotes a bottom-up approach to measurement that begins by understanding context and works toward systems change at scale by carefully defining what needs to change, how it needs to change, and how we will know if it is changing.

Measurement is baked into the process of developing WealthWorks value chains from the beginning. All partners have a role to play in measurement, not as an afterthought, but as a way of determining whether their participation in the value chain is meeting their own goals. Working with value chain partners to create measures that do not represent an added burden but actually help partners by providing information they need to make progress toward their own goals is one of the responsibilities of the value chain coordinator.

Notes

1 What is economics? American Economic Association. Retrieved from: https://www.aeaweb.org/students/WhatIsEconomics.php
2 For a more expansive definition of the economy, see: https://core-econ.org/the-economy/book/text/01.html#111-economics-and-the-economy
3 Modified from Himmelman, A. (2002). *Collaboration for a Change: Definitions, Decision-Making Models, Roles, and Collaboration Process Guide.* Retrieved from: https://depts.washington.edu/ccph/pdf_files/4achange.pdf
4 Thanks to Rich Pirog, Director of the Center for Regional Food Systems at Michigan State University for this quote.
5 Jones, C. F. (2014). *Routes of Power.* Cambridge. MA: Harvard University Press.
6 Turning Toxins into Art. Great Big Story. Retrieved from: http://www.greatbigstory.com/stories/toxic-art-that-s-amazing
7 You Get What You Measure® is a participatory approach to measurement developed and trademarked by Yellow Wood Associates, Inc. More information is available at: https://www.yellowwood.org/you-get-what-you-measure.html
8 Ibid., see also: https://www.youtube.com/watch?v=VNCd2pCtdgI and https://www.youtube.com/watch?v=DCQA6XcBp6o
9 Comparison of Certification Systems. Forests for All Forever. Retrieved from: https://ca.fsc.org/en-ca/marketplace/business-resources/comparison-of-certification-systems

9 The Critical Roles of Wealth Creation Value Chain Coordinators and Coaches

Coordination is Key

The building blocks for WealthWorks value chains exist in many places, including those that have a long history of being economically marginalized. Yet rarely, if ever, do these value chains emerge spontaneously. In today's world of silos and polarization where few are trained or encouraged to think systemically, making the real world connections required for social change is not anyone's job. In any given community or region, there are often many institutions running multiple programs that are related in one way or another to trying to improve the quality of life in a given place, but many are under-resourced and narrowly focused by topic or geography. Many are also often highly dependent on soft money and continuously reinventing themselves to stay afloat. This makes it difficult to provide stable leadership even for more conventional approaches, let alone a systems change approach like WealthWorks, since organizations and their programs are often constrained by eligibility criteria that do not permit uses of funds that would transform systems by, for example, bringing marginalized and non-marginalized partners together in the same value chain.

Creating a WealthWorks value chain requires building relationships between what are viewed as separate sectors (private, nonprofit, government, investor), separate functions (demand, supply and support), and separate geographies (rural, urban, suburban). It also requires building mutually beneficial relationships between marginalized and non-marginalized economic actors and between people and organizations with expertise in and control over various forms of wealth. It requires many unprecedented conversations and a willingness to disrupt dysfunctional systems, policies, and organizations as needed. This can be uncomfortable but necessary. It also means positioning the value chain to retain the independence needed choose the right partners and reject the wrong partners, whether because they cannot deliver or because they are in it to exploit and not contribute to the value chain as a whole. Implementing WealthWorks value chains is an inherently creative process that, when successful, results in systems change from an old normal way of doing business to a new normal.

Coordinating and Coaching Wealth Creation   139

Successful implementation of WealthWorks on the ground depends on the commitment and capacity of one or more organizations to taking on the role of value chain coordinator. The more trained and effective coordinators, the more economic transformation driven from the ground up we will see. A Wealth-Works value chain coordinator is the organization that instigates and supports the four phases of WealthWorks value chain development on the ground. It can be a nonprofit organization, a governmental or quasi-governmental organization, or a for-profit enterprise. Whatever the type of organization, it must have leadership and staff that are open to thinking and working differently than they have in the past. Adopting WealthWorks inevitably means stepping outside one's comfort zone and engaging with partners with which one never expected to engage (and sometimes disengaging with ineffective partners). It means developing deep knowledge of one or more sectors of the regional economy. It means being intentional about building wealths that benefit and stick with economically marginalized people and places. It means remaining focused on outcomes informed by ongoing measurement.

WealthWorks coordinators need to accept the long-term, inclusive, and systems-changing focus of this alternative approach to economic development and they need to be prepared to reframe their work accordingly. WealthWorks is decidedly not "business and usual;" nor is it the version of collective impact that simply looks like parallel play where no one actually changes what they are doing or how they are doing it, but rather simply takes credit for business as usual.

Creating and maintaining a market-drive value chain means being responsive to ongoing market developments. Change is inevitable; new opportunities and challenges continually emerge. WealthWorks requires a different set of expectations with respect to inclusion and accountability; one that is market-driven, transformative, and not limited as so many support oriented community development/social service agencies are to providing services to low income people.

Roles of a WealthWorks Coordinator

Lyons and Wyckoff identified seven major roles of a WealthWorks coordinator (organization).[1] The first is as a *holder of values*. The WealthWorks coordinator not only helps partners understand each other's values and interests, but it must also uphold three foundational values of the WealthWorks approach, namely inclusivity, focus on building eight forms of wealth, and consideration of shared ownership and/or control to root wealth in place. WealthWorks coordinators are also *connectors*. They aggregate resources within and outside the value chain to fill gaps, overcome barriers, and capture opportunities and they convene and build relationships among all participants in and supporters of the value chain and help them build relationships among each other. They may also connect value chains in similar or complementary sectors with one another. In addition, they are responsible for promoting visibility and buy-in for the chain from the communities and region in which it is located.

140   *Coordinating and Coaching Wealth Creation*

WealthWorks Coordinators *hold the big picture*. They understand all the dimensions of the value chain including gaps, barriers, and underutilized resources, the self-interest and shared interests of all of its members and supporters, and the social, political, and cultural context in which it operates. They also grow to understand the sector and the larger systems in which the value chain is embedded, including those elements of the system that need to change for the value chain to flourish. They keep a picture of the entire value chain map in their heads and on the wall and help participants recognize their own roles in the larger picture. They think about and help the value chain address risk including financial risks, production risks, and risks posed by changes in market demand. Addressing risks is a key to creating investable opportunities. They also help identify opportunities for market diversification, shared infrastructure, and shared ownership as the value chain develops. They recognize areas where capacity building is needed and they seek support partners that can provide it.

WealthWorks Value Chain Coordinators are *visionaries*. They hold the vision of what the chain can become as it evolves from exploration through proof of concept to implementation and institutionalization. The vision is often displayed as a value chain map that evolves as new information comes to light. The value chain map provides a way for partners to see themselves and their roles in the value chain and to understand the big picture to which they are contributing.

WealthWorks Value Chain Coordinators are always looking for ways to continue the evolution of the value chain. As any given value chain develops, new functions are identified that need to be filled for the value chain to flourish. Often those new functions can become the foundation for another value chain or "chainlet." For example, an agricultural value chain could identify a need for regionally produced biodegradable packaging that has potential to serve many sectors including but not limited to agriculture and could develop into its own value chain.

As *visionaries*, WealthWorks Coordinators help participants envision and define their own self-interest as well as the shared interests among participants. Self-interest is the glue that holds WealthWorks value chains together. It is the answer to the "what's in it for me?" question. Partners are most likely to stay engaged in WealthWorks value chains when they understand their self-interest in doing so and that interest is being well served. Self-interest is not always obvious. For example, if a small producer does not understand how to account for his or her labor, it may not be clear that he or she is currently losing money and that changing his or her production practices could change that. Likewise, buyers may not recognize at the outset the market potential of associating with a value chain that builds multiple forms of wealth. WealthWorks Coordinators use skilled listening combined with research to help define, illustrate, and educate partners about self-interests that may not be immediately self-evident.

Value chain partners discover shared interests as they recognize their interdependency in effectively meeting market demand. All participants in the value chain have a shared interest in its success, which means that it is in their self-interest to support one another. Sometimes WealthWorks value chain participants also share common interests or values with respect to the kind of impacts on society at large, such as carbon reduction or improved human health, local ownership or a stronger regional economy overall, to which the value chain can contribute. However, to require common interests or to use support for common interests as a litmus test for participation is to undermine the potential for transformative engagement.

The WealthWorks Value Chain Coordinator helps value chain partners use the Wealth Matrix for planning, designing interventions, and measuring outcomes. The Value Chain Coordinator *develops a plan for data collection* on the eight forms of wealth and systems change, beginning with framing data to put the value chain in context and define scale and moving onto baseline data related to the specific forms of wealth the value chain will impact. A good measurement plan decentralizes data collection so that every partner in the value chain is collecting the data relevant to their own goals and contributions and providing that to the entire chain on a regular basis. It is the Value Chain Coordinator's job to guarantee that the information is consistent, comparable, and sufficient to determine changes in stocks of wealth and in the overall system over time. Often Value Chain Coordinators provide (or identify other partners to provide) technical assistance to value chain partners so that they can develop the information systems they need to improve while also providing information to the value chain as a whole. A measurement plan includes periodic re-measurement, reporting, and reflection by value chain participants.

Building a WealthWorks value chain on the ground is not a simple exercise. It requires persistence, resilience to setbacks, an entrepreneurial mindset, and the capacity to maintain focus on the big picture while attending to the many details required for forward motion. It requires the WealthWorks Value Chain Coordinator to be an effective communicator between and among value chain stakeholders, and a *facilitator* and sometimes *mediator* of misunderstandings and even disputes that may arise. The WealthWorks Value Chain Coordinator helps build and maintain transparency, trust, and appropriate governance for each value chain. Trust is based on accountability and reciprocity. Did the partners do what they committed to doing? If not, why not? If some partners are not the right partners (based on their behavior, capacity, attitude, or other factors), what changes need to be made and how will that happen?

As a *facilitator*, the WealthWorks Value Chain Coordinator may also be responsible for convening the value chain and engaging the value chain as a whole in problem-solving. The Coordinator often facilitates networking with external providers of information and research and translates results back to value chain participants. The WealthWorks Value Chain Coordinator may also connect value chain participants with other types of expertise for technical assistance in production processes, marketing, risk management, business planning, and more.

WealthWorks Value Chain Coordinators may also serve as the *spokesperson* for the value chain or, at minimum, the entity that plans and helps to

142   *Coordinating and Coaching Wealth Creation*

execute relationships with the media and the general public. The *spokesperson* role often extends to sharing lessons learned with the larger practitioner communities to which the Coordinator belongs. Often Coordinators engage value chain partners in sharing lessons at professional conferences, through webinars, and at meetings of regional decision-makers.

The WealthWorks Value Chain Coordinator may also *engage additional research expertise* to identify value propositions (self-interests), test the feasibility of alternative approaches, learn about related efforts around the country and the world, develop business plans for the value chain as a whole, compare alternative technologies, and identify demand-driven trends as needed.

During the Ford experiment it became evident that value chain coordinators tended to move beyond the role of coordinator to become participants in the value chain itself. Coordinators that were also participants in the chain had a function to perform as a transactional player. For example, Fahe-financed housing and MACED created the data and inspection system required to implement on-bill financing. Rural Action and Appalachian Sustainable Development started a business together to take on value chain functions. alt.Consulting purchased a biofuels processing unit that it then leased out to an entrepreneur. Appalachian Sustainable Development not only coordinated a regional food value chain, but provided the chain with warehousing and distribution services. Whenever a Coordinator is also a participant in the chain, it is important to maintain transparency and divide roles related to coordination from those related to participation to minimize the likelihood of conflicts of interest. It is important that all participants in the value chain recognize the whole of which they are a part.

Coordinators were able to wear two hats—coordinator and transactional partner—by: 1) staffing to separate the coordination function from the transactional function; 2) maintaining strong in-house communications; and 3) maintaining transparent communications with all value chain partners. The commitment of coordinators as transactional players meant that the value chain became part of the way their organization did business in contrast to a time-limited project dependent on external resources. Having "skin in the game" put the coordinator on a par with the other transactional partners and demonstrated their commitment to value chain success.

Before any organization decides to become a WealthWorks value chain coordinator, its leaders should become familiar with the WealthWorks framework, principles, and practices. We have seen WealthWorks introduced into organizations from the bottom up and from the top down. Generally speaking, it is most effective when there is buy-in from the top based on some understanding of the framework and what it entails. While a single individual may provide the spark that results in an organization being willing to learn about WealthWorks, the work of WealthWorks value chain coordination is more than one individual can support over time.

There are several ways to become familiar with WealthWorks. The WealthWorks website maintained by The Aspen Institute's Community

Coordinating and Coaching Wealth Creation   143

Strategies Group—http://www.WealthWorks.org—provides useful background materials and guides. WealthWorks regional hubs and experienced consultants can provide training.[2] National organizations such as NADO also provide educational opportunities for their members.

Coaching for Coordinators

We are all creatures of habit and the same is true for our organizations. Even though many of us would like to see progress toward a more equitable and sustainable world, risking the relative security of business as usual for a new approach takes courage and willingness to try something different. The WealthWorks framework is powerful and it is also complicated. There are many moving parts and it is easy to lose focus and perspective and become stuck. Even though the principles may seem self-evident, in our experience it takes time for even highly experienced community and economic development practitioners to recognize how to implement them in practice. It is easy to miss the opportunity for progress if you are looking backwards at what was and not forward toward what could be and how to make it so.

We have found that organizations that choose to become WealthWorks value chain coordinators benefit from a relationship with a WealthWorks coach. WealthWorks coaches are individuals that have worked with multiple WealthWorks value chains and are steeped in the WealthWorks principles and framework. Coaches help coordinators learn to apply WealthWorks in their own communities and regions, answer questions, and provide opportunities for reflection, sharing, and trouble-shooting. Coaches hold the big picture for Coordinators in the same way that Coordinators hold the big picture for WealthWorks value chains. Coaches can also help WealthWorks Coordinators steer through new aspects their own role as it evolves over time.

Coordinators bring many different types of concerns to their coaches ranging from, "How do we go about engaging marginalized people and places in our value chain?" to "How do we help our nonprofit partners understand an economic development and business mindset?" to "How do we most effectively communicate the WealthWorks approach and value chain concisely and in a way that excites folks?" to "How do we reach out to demand partners and identify their value propositions?" and "How do we build trust among value chain partners?" This is a small subset of the questions that emerge as coordinators begin to explore and implement a proof of concept for their value chain. Regular communications between coordinators and coaches helped coordinators test their ideas, gain confidence, and stay focused on the forest as well as the trees. Coaches are also able to point out where progress is being made and where old ways of thinking and doing business are still presenting obstacles.

WealthWorks coaches can also be helpful in connecting WealthWorks Coordinators with deep content expertise as needed. For example, WealthWorks coaches brought in expertise in finance to assist Jessica Norwood of Emerging Changemakers in learning what she needed to know to build an

144 *Coordinating and Coaching Wealth Creation*

effective investment value chain in the Deep South. Other Coordinators found their own content experts. In general, we observed that content experts were able to most useful when they gained an understanding of the specific value chain they were advising about and the overall WealthWorks framework and approach.

In addition to coaching coordinators of individual value chains, Wealth-Works coaches can also provide the connective tissue for networks of value chains in the same sector. For example, McIntosh SEED provides coaching for five agricultural value chains in the Deep South that share market opportunities, training, employment, and other related supports for trans-actional partners. McIntosh SEED provides convening support, coaching for individual value chain coordinators and value chain partners, measurement assistance, and learning journeys. Yellow Wood Associates, Community Roots, and Dynamic Consulting also provide coaching for WealthWorks Coordinators. Additional coaches are emerging through the Regional Hubs (see Chapter 10). Yellow Wood Associates developed a training curriculum for WealthWorks Coordinators and a separate training curriculum for Coaches that is available to WealthWorks Regional Hubs.[3] WealthWorks Coaches can be located through the WealthWorks Regional Hubs listed at http://www.WealthWorks.org

Identifying and Enabling Wealth Creation Value Chain Coordinators

We know much of what it takes to apply the WealthWorks framework and we know that one of the key ingredients is coordination. The type of coordi-nation we are talking about that crosses sectors, areas of expertise, and type of organization tends to be no one's job so it doesn't get done. In today's communities and regions, many community and/or economic development organizations are perceived as too parochial and closed-minded, limited in scope or mission, too narrowly focused or closely identified with a single program, too competitive and at odds with other organizations in the area, not trustworthy, ineffective with a poor track record of accomplishment, lacking in capacity to fill the coordinator role, or simply not interested. As a results, people that want to implement the framework often have a difficult time identifying an organization that could be an effective coordinator.

We need to get creative in identifying, training, and enabling more orga-nizations to take on the coordinator role while holding them accountable for measurable outcomes. Sometimes the coordination gap can be filled by having an external partner like the Rural Community Assistance Partnership work with local organizations, boosting local capacity with external sup-port. Other times, existing nonprofit economic or community development organizations are ready to try a new approach to fulfilling their mission either with or without funders' incentives. Sometimes local government is prepared to lead and sometimes a community foundation may take on the coordination role. Sometimes two organizations, like Rural Action and

Coordinating and Coaching Wealth Creation 145

Appalachian Sustainable Development, team up to provide coordination functions. For-profit organizations can also decide to become coordinators. The point is that there is no single type of entity best suited to be a WealthWorks coordinator; it depends on the dynamics in a given region. With training, coaching, and support, many kinds of organizations can be effective coordinators.

For-profit organizations may be able to finance the coordinator role through their own retained earnings or regular business borrowing. Governments may be able to allocate funds from annual budgets for community and/or economic development. The USDA, for example, has begun to fund value chain coordination for food systems having recognized its potential through exposure to WealthWorks value chains in the agricultural sector. We encourage nonprofit organizations to think about how they can reallocate existing funds to support a new approach to their work. These are all ideal scenarios; however, it is often necessary to jump start WealthWorks value chain exploration with philanthropic dollars sourced from government, foundations, community foundations, private firms, and/or individual investors (see more on how to engage investors in Chapter 5).[4]

WealthWorks value chains are intended to be market-driven and not reliant on subsidies once they have achieved scale. If the value chain coordinator is also a transactional partner in the value chain, as the value chain becomes profitable, their role should be supported by a combination of the share of profits they earn as a transactional partner and a fee for coordination services paid by other partners in the value chain. If the value chain coordinator is not a transactional partner, they may be able to work themselves out of a job with key coordination functions being taken over by one or more transactional partners over time. This requires carefully identifying key functions and matching functions with partner self-interests and capabilities. Prior to that, value chain partners should cover a portion of coordination costs. This establishes the value of the coordination function among partners and makes it easier to demonstrate the value to other investors. It is also in keeping with the market-based approach that stresses minimal reliance on "free money" and "free services."

Here is how Jim King, CEO of the Federation of Housing Enterprises, described Fahe's role in the value chain and the transition he envisioned to a relatively self-sustaining, institutionalized, new normal (words in brackets added for clarification):

> Fahe's role in the value chain is both as an intermediary [coordinator] and a direct actor [transactional partner]—we are the lender, and it is incumbent upon us to provide the VC linkage to capital providers. We support interventions across the VC, even when we are not the "provider" of a good or service. As an organizer and intermediary, we often serve as a bridge between actors, a provider of resources, or a catalyst for information exchange and networking (as with the Green Summit).

146 *Coordinating and Coaching Wealth Creation*

Additional examples of this can be found in our role of supporting the development of the Green HBE module, training for BPI/Resnet certifiers, and implementation of the new appraisal methodology. In all cases, we provided resources and/or oversight needed to ensure that interventions are in place and important benchmarks are being made. We coordinate access to other actors on the supply chain, but expect that role to become less important as the VC matures. If our VC work is successful, then the ability of the market to deliver EE housing will be established, functional, replicable, scalable, and relatively self-sustaining.[5]

Philanthropic investment in value chain coordination through the exploration and proof of concept phases such as was provided by the Ford Foundation can make a real difference not only in the success of a specific value chain, but in a region's and even a sector's entire orientation to community and economic development.

The Transformative Power of WealthWorks: Bet You Can't Start Just One

The experience of exploring and proving a wealth creation value chain tends to permanently change the culture of coordinator organizations because it produces real and tangible results for marginalized people and places; not by segregating them from the mainstream economy, but by engaging them in it in response to market demand. Exploring a value chain and taking it through proof of concept reveals numerous gaps, bottlenecks, and underutilized resources that were not previously recognized or understood. Addressing the gaps and bottlenecks and making best use of underutilized resources results in new economic opportunities.

Gaps may be related to any one of the eight forms of wealth—or all of them. Gaps refer to functions that are missing in the value chain such as the lack of demand partners, the lack of connection and information flow among transactional partners, the lack of product standards, the lack of understanding of how to incorporate improved technology, the lack of ownership structures to protect and build local wealth for marginalized people and places, the lack of training opportunities, the lack of appropriate insurance products, the lack of aggregation, etc.

Bottlenecks refer to inefficient functions in the chain, which, if addressed, would allow it to be more effectively market-driven. For example, in Fahe's value chain, the fact that appraisers did not account for energy efficiency in their appraisals was a bottleneck. In agricultural value chains like CAN, the lack of a cost-effective system for product aggregation and distribution is often a bottleneck.

The examples above refer mostly to transactional bottlenecks, but gaps and bottlenecks in support services can be every bit as problematic. For example, the lack of appropriate financing and insurance mechanisms is often a gap, as is the lack of targeted and effective training for transactional

Coordinating and Coaching Wealth Creation   147

partners. The lack of relationship with demand partners is a primary gap that must be filled early in development of any value chain and becomes essential in determining the structure of the chain itself.

Once coordinators unshackle themselves from the constraints of past approaches and realize they have the freedom to reach out across sectors, roles, and geographies, and address all forms of wealth all kinds of things become possible. It is a freeing process. It becomes possible to aggregate resources from a much larger pool of potential partners and beneficiaries than previously imagined. As the value chain progresses, obstacles and constraints take on tangible form and can be tackled not by a single firm, but by the entire chain including transactional, support, investor, technologist, and other partners. As value chains begin to solve problems together, systems begin to change and more becomes possible.

Effective value chain coordinators can and do acquire the knowledge and skills they need to address all kinds of gaps and bottlenecks as they move through the phases of value chain development (exploration, proof of concept, implementation, institutionalization). Identifying gaps and bottlenecks is learning process; coordinator organizations are often surprised by the gaps and bottlenecks that emerge as well as by the underutilized resources available to address them.

Figuring out how to address gaps and bottlenecks requires creativity. Ongoing learning and applied creativity focused on a specific value chain transforms coordinator organizations' capacity and approach to development going forward. We have yet to see any organization that adopts and implements the WealthWorks framework through proof of concept that does not go to apply the framework and principles to future endeavors. Even if specific value chains do not pan out as expected, the lessons learned are put to good use in new value chains.

New Opportunities for Support Partners

It is not enough to change the behavior of value chain coordinators. If we are going to transform our economy into one that is inclusive and sustainable, we need to change behavior of existing institutions. Simply creating new institutions on top of the dysfunctional patterns we already have is like putting a Band-Aid over an infected wound; if left untreated, the wound will continue to eat away at anything healthy around it.

Support partner organizations that become involved with wealth creation value chains may experience the need to change the way they do business if they are going to actually make a real contribution to the success of the chain. In our experience, the majority of support organizations in workforce training, education, food and nutrition, community and economic development and social services are not, themselves, market-driven. They are accustomed to relying on subsidies and grants to fund their work. They often lack staff with strong private-sector experience. Their models for service delivery are often transactional, i.e. based on giving things away, and

148 *Coordinating and Coaching Wealth Creation*

not transformational, i.e. based on helping clients change behaviors so that they can get things for themselves. As a society we have many systems in place that reinforce dependency and economic isolation for marginalized people and places and our institutions often reflect that.

WealthWorks provides a leverage point for systems change from the ground up. It starts with demand and transactional partners, *not* support partners. Coordinators and partners identify real-world gaps and bottlenecks and the targeted interventions needed to address them. Coordinators and partners decide which support organizations are best suited to deliver the specific support they need. The value chain decides whether or not the support provided is working and is in a position to educate support providers about what they would need to do differently to be effective in helping the value chain succeed.

For example, we've seen community colleges such as Mid-State Technical College in Wisconsin transform the way they staff and schedule classes once it was recognized that the existing system was not meeting the needs of manufacturers (transactional partners). The system changed from one where the community colleges selected instructors, approved curricula, and set course times to one where instructors were selected by the employers whose workers required the training, the selected instructor developed curricula tailored to the needs of employers, and employers worked with students to develop a schedule that made sense. Instead of being stuck with the bottleneck of ineffective training and the complaint that there were no local options for providing the training companies needed for their employees, the system changed to be responsive to market-demand. This systems change was not only beneficial to the employers that instigated it with the help of their coordinator it opened up new possibilities in other sectors as well. It allows the administrative and built resources of the community college to be put to use more effectively as a support partner for economic development.

By making discoveries in a value chain context, where goals and returns on investment are clearly articulated, implementing the WealthWorks framework can help change systems of service delivery on the ground by filling gaps, removing bottlenecks, and encouraging organizations to focus on the things they do best while allowing others to address remaining issues. Through its foundation as a market-driven framework that incorporates measurement, WealthWorks provides leverage for systems change from the ground up for coordinators, value chain partners and many kinds of support organizations, with ripples beyond any specific value chain.

Beginning with demand, being intentionally inclusive, learning how to grow multiple forms of wealth simultaneously, creating ownership and control of forms of wealth in heretofore marginalized areas, and creating the social and political capital to create systems change starting with demand and transactional partners profoundly impacts the way practitioners perceive the possibilities for the work they do and the work they *can* do. The more coordinators we have the more wealth creation value chains will be created and the more opportunities for transformation there will be.

Notes

1 Lyons, T. S. and Wyckoff, B. (2014). Facilitating community wealth building: Understanding the roles played and capacities needed by coordinating institutions. *Community Development*, 45(5), 443–457.

2 Community Roots serves ME, VT, NH, NY, MA, RI; the Central Appalachian Network serves OH, KY, TN, VA, WVA, NC; Communities Unlimited serves AL, LA, MO, OK, TX; Region Five Development Commission serves MN; the Rural Community Assistance Corporation (RCAC) serves NM, AZ, CO, UT, NV, WY, MT, and Rural Development Initiatives (RDI) serves ID, WA, OR, CA in cooperation with RCAC.

3 For more information, see: https://www.yellowwood.org/wealthworks.html

4 More information on WealthWorks financing can be found in "Financing the Evolving Role of the Value Chain Coordinator" (January 2014), "Enterprise Financing for WealthWorks Value Chains: Overview and Guide" (April 2014), and "Guide to Crowdfunding for WealthWorks Value Chains" (January 2014). All these publications are available at http://www.wealthworks.org

5 Fahe Wealth Creation Proposal Narrative, November 2013 (unpublished internal document, used with permission).

10 Taking a Wealth Creation Approach to Scale

Building on the Past

The Ford Foundation experiment lasted eight years (2008–2015) and market-driven revenues were generated through investments in stocks of multiple forms of wealth benefiting marginalized people and places even during a period of severe economic recession. The approximately $25 million invested by Ford is the equivalent of roughly 0.01% of our $20.658 trillion economy.[1] The lessons learned continue to inform a relatively small number of economic development and community development practitioners around the country and around the world. What would it look like if a wealth creation framework and approach were in widespread use?

Today, there are five regional hubs in the United States supporting WeatlhWorks value chain coordinators. Training is being offered by the National Association of Development Organizations (NADO), Community Roots, Dynamica Consulting and others. The Aspen Institute's Community Strategies Group maintains the WealthWorks website (http://www.wealthwork.org). USDA in cooperation with the Rural Community Assistance Partnership (RCAP) is funding value chain coordinators and regional hubs. Community foundations like the Tillitson Fund in New Hampshire, the Fremont Area Community Foundation in Michigan, and the Greater Kanawha Valley Community Foundation in West Virginia have incorporated the framework into their work with grantees, thereby re-shaping the role of their community foundations in economic development. There are also organizations like Rural Development Initiatives in Oregon and the Region 5 Development Commission in Minnesota that became wealth creation value chain coordinators or providers of support to value chains without funding from the Ford Foundation.

The WealthWorks framework is now being used in about half a dozen countries thanks to ActionAid International. ActionAid was drawn to the WealthWorks framework because it complements and expands on ActionAid's rights-based work.

In the introduction to *Gender Sensitive Access to Markets: A Training Handbook* prepared for ActionAid based on the WealthWorks framework, ActionAid describes the methodology as follows:

Taking a Wealth Creation Approach to Scale 151

Women's access to markets remains a significant challenge for many of the groups that ActionAid works with. Women face multiple barriers and inequalities to accessing markets, which are often seen as the domain of men. Along with the challenge of climate change, these factors can make it difficult for women to make sustainable livelihoods. Many groups lack a deep understanding about what markets are, how they operate, what the buyers in the market are really looking for and how to establish win-win relationships with buyers. Some producers' groups do not know if the economic activities that they engage in are truly profitable or what it would take to make them profitable. In many cases, groups just need simple adjustments for becoming more sustainable and profitable. In other cases, however, a group may need more complex interventions.

Most frameworks on market access depend on market assessments made by external consultants and are focused on income generation alone. ActionAid's approach is different. This framework empowers women to undertake and act on the assessment themselves. It emphasizes the importance of analyzing markets from a gender perspective, examines the economic, social and environmental sustainability of initiatives, and ensures that all actors in the market can share the value equitably, creating wealth for all.

This handbook uses a range of participatory tools to explore how women and local communities can identify the challenges and potential to access markets. We hope that local groups will be able to use this methodology with support from ActionAid and its partners to improve the way they understand, access and benefit from markets. Our objective is for local groups to follow the steps proposed here to increase their self-understanding about their weaknesses, challenges, potentialities and market opportunities. The aim is to help local groups to be more self-sufficient and independent, able to take control of their initiatives to access to markets, and capable of identifying their own demands related to knowledge, infrastructure, market relations and technologies.[2]

As the adoption by ActionAid illustrates, the value of WealthWorks is not as a brand; it is as a way of providing a shared language for a new approach to community and economic development that creates the building blocks for a sustainable, inclusive economy by bringing best practices in production and consumption into market-driven value chains built from the ground up.

Envisioning the Future

The WealthWorks practitioners that were part of the Ford experiment began to realize the potential power of developing wealth creation value chains in multiple sectors within regions, particularly if those value chains were connected with one another. If wealth creation value chains were

152 *Taking a Wealth Creation Approach to Scale*

operating in multiple sectors, e.g. housing, energy, manufacturing, tourism, agriculture, transportation, health care, etc., opportunities would almost inevitably emerge for cross-sectoral cooperation. It would be possible to develop an "ecosystem" of wealth creation with synergistic benefits. Early signs of cross-collaboration were in evidence, for example, in Central Appalachia in the interplay between MACED's energy retrofit value chain and Fahe's energy efficiency affordable housing chain. For example, some of Fahe's member contractors were able to provide energy retrofit services through MACED's on-bill financing value chain and MACED's work on the economic benefits of energy efficiency helped inform the value proposition of Fahe's value chain. It is plausible to imagine, for example, a transportation value chain that could serve multiple value chains within a region including, but not limited to, value chains in manufacturing, health care, and tourism. Likewise, an agricultural value chain can serve value chains in multiple sectors. Energy-related value chains can also touch multiple sectors as MACED's value chain showed. On-bill financing led to retrofits for homes and also for commercial establishments, in particular rural grocery stores with outdated structures and equipment. This is a small example of how value chains can grow and develop to serve multiple types of demand.

Early practitioners also recognized the power of connecting regions together through sector-based wealth creation value chains. For example, in August of 2013 the Red Mantra group brought value chain partners in the Central Appalachian Network and the Deep South Community Agriculture Network together with representatives of private sector companies on the demand side including Walmart, Nestlé Global, C. H. Robinson, and Eastern Carolina Organics, among others, to explore opportunities for building a thriving regional agricultural economy in Central Appalachia and the rural South. The convening explored gaps and bottlenecks common to both regions in the areas of farmer readiness to engage with the formal marketplace, logistics and the efficient sourcing and distribution of product, and finance including accessing the right forms of capital to grow a sustainable value chain.

The main finding was the extent to which hobbling information gaps exist at all levels. Large participants on the demand side recognize their self-interest in being able to procure regionally grown products, but they do not work effectively together, nor do they understand how to tie into locally available resources. Large demand partners find working with individual small growers too costly compared with continuing to purchase from large producers. This has made it even harder for small and marginalized farmers to benefit from increased consumer demand for regional products. The value chain approach can help address this problem; however, demand partners do not know how to find value chain coordinators to do the necessary work of putting a value chain together. Marginalized farmers lack an understanding of the opportunities available to them as well as access to the technical assistance required to take advantage of those opportunities. Older farmers, in particular, may feel overwhelmed by the need to meet a new set

Taking a Wealth Creation Approach to Scale 153

of standards. Support partners in the value chain, including insurers, investors, technical assistance providers, packagers, and others may not have sufficient understanding of the requirements of the market as expressed by demand partners to provide support that is appropriate, effective, and affordable.

A wealth creation framework provides a structure within which solutions to these gaps can be envisioned and implemented. For example, demand partners can begin to understand the value of the coordination function, not as an externality that someone else should pay for, but as a cost of doing business that to which they can contribute individually and collectively. Likewise, the demand partners can begin to understand the value of transparency in pricing, the use of long- term contracts instead of one-off annual agreements, and investment in forms of wealth such as individual capital (skills and health) and social capital (relationships among and between value chain partners) to enhance the likelihood that inclusive value chains will provide acceptable (if not superior) products in volumes that matter. On the other side, personal relationships with demand partners can help farmers, support partners, and coordinators develop the trust needed to risk new ways of producing.

Transforming market relationships cannot happen without building actual relationships between people. As relationships between demand and transactional and support partners develop within regions, opportunities for cross-regional cooperation are likely to emerge. These will look different depending on the nature of the value chain and its sector, but the principles are the same. In the beginning it may simply be an opportunity to aggregate production to meet market demand for volume. Over time, however, the value chains in any given region have the chance to specialize in their areas of comparative advantage, i.e. do better at what they do best, and then share their specializations across regions. In agriculture, this can mean sharing crops that grow best in one zone and not another; in manufacturing it can mean sharing expertise in building and repairing particular types of machinery.

There is nothing new about the concept of comparative advantage, used in economic theory to mean the ability of an individual or group to carry out a particular economic activity (such as making a specific product and/or delivering a specific service) more efficiently than another activity. What's new is the idea of intentionally building comparative advantage through inclusive wealth creation value chains that measure efficiency by taking into account impacts on all forms of wealth, instead of letting it be defined by conventional efficiency measures that typically undermine some forms of wealth to create others. The wealth creation concept of comparative advantage brings all forms of wealth into consideration, recognizing that comparative advantage can arise from more than just natural resource endowments.

Comparative advantage in wealth creation within sectors extends beyond product or service specialization and includes specialized knowledge (intellectual capital) pertaining to how to produce any given good or service in ways that build multiple stocks of capital without undermining others. One

154 *Taking a Wealth Creation Approach to Scale*

can imagine a host of beneficial synergies emerging as the density of wealth creation value chains operating within and between regions increases. The prevalence of more wealth creation value chains would broaden the scope of knowledge regarding opportunities in specific sectors. For example, what works in housing in one part of the country might need to be adapted in other regions, but some lessons are likely to be transferrable. With a critical mass of wealth creation value chains in exploration, proof of concept, implementation and institutionalization, new systems will begin to emerge that encourage investment in multiple forms of wealth to meet market demand. This in turn, could give rise to a pool of support partners at the local, regional and national levels with needed (often sector-specific) expertise as legal counsel, insurers, investors, inventors, technologists, businesspeople, researchers, ecologists, economists, and more who understand the wealth creation framework and know how to and are willing to think and act creatively to prototype systems changes to enable specific value chains to succeed.

If the language and vision of a wealth creation approach to development were widely embraced within a mutually supportive covenant similar to that to which the cooperative movement subscribes where cooperatives support other cooperatives, such that wealth creation value chains work together to learn from, support, and benefit each other, the underpinnings of a new economy could evolve from current conditions without waiting for a revolution. Multiple wealth creation value chains would uncover many opportunities to unlock market-driven change by encouraging targeted investments in multiple forms of wealth in specific places that are tied to measurable outcomes. The social capital created among partners in multiple wealth creation value chains could translate into powerful multi-partisan political capital. Wealth creation is not a Democratic, Republican, or Independent cause. It has been adopted and promoted by coordinators and partners across the political spectrum because it provides solutions valued by parties across the political spectrum.

If a wealth creation framework and approach were adopted more broadly, we could also expect to see some changes in the relationship between rural, urban, and suburban areas within regions. This would come about as more coordinators forged relationships between urban, suburban, and rural producers, consumers, demand, transactional, and support partners and identified opportunities for shared investments in forms of wealth that produce shared benefits. Lessons learned about how to increase awareness of the value of these investments, and how they can be structured to keep wealth in place and provide inclusive benefit could be broadly shared.

With denser networks of intentional, market-driven relationships, we would also expect to see increasing political capital that includes urban, rural, and suburban partners, because the conditions and policies that reinforce economic isolation are quite similar across geographies and have led to shared experiences. For example, economically marginalized communities wherever they are share limited access to high-quality health care, relatively ineffective public education, weak political capital, limited access to jobs, limited transportation options, subpar financial literacy, limited access to state of the art information technologies and more.[3] Regionally based collaborations designed within the WealthWorks framework to be market-driven rather than subsidy-dependent can identify and implement specific policy changes to strengthen specific wealth creation value chains even without major changes in federal policies. It is time for local and state development practitioners to experiment with a more inclusive sense of place in which value chain connections based on self- and shared interests are not restricted by political boundaries. By focusing on the region, instead of the community, as the unit of analysis, wealth creation value chains become another vehicle to heighten awareness of interdependencies between rural and urban and engender direct investments to strengthen underlying stocks of wealth for shared benefits.

Each wealth creation value chain is unique since it draws on relationships that are rooted in place. Each wealth creation value chain uncovers multiple gaps, bottlenecks, and underutilized resources often constrained in one way or another by unhelpful public and/or private policies. Such policies may concern product standards, purchasing specifications, labor practices, lending criteria, resource targeting, and much more. There is never a one-size-fits-all solution to policy. However, the deep work of learning what it takes to make a wealth creation value chain work in a given sector in a given place yields insights into high-leverage policy changes that have a greater chance of being addressed when coordinators can help bring the diverse social capital created in the value chain to bear on policy decision-makers. Many wealth creation value chains would result in many seemingly small but often high-leverage changes in existing policy to support inclusive investments in multiple forms of wealth driven by market demand. Over time, these changes add up to systems change. The more wealth creation value chains there are; the more visible the need for policy changes becomes and the greater the extent of social capital that can be brought to bear to bring them about.

A wealth creation framework could also become the basis for developing new public and private policies that contribute to greater sustainability. Imagine the change in perspective and policy development outcomes if politicians were pressured to use something like the Wealth Matrix to plan, develop and evaluate policies with the caveat that no policy can undermine one form of wealth to create another! The pressure would come not from partisan lobbyists, but from demand partners, transactional partners, and support partners responding to consumer demand for goods and services that make them and the world we all live in more, not less, sustainable. The Region 5 Development Commission, which receives part of its funding from the State of Minnesota, has already experimented with using the forms of wealth to frame its annual reports to the legislature. The framework has been well received and is helping to create a common language related to desired outcomes of public investment. This approach can provide a way to think systematically about new policies as well as existing policies.

156 *Taking a Wealth Creation Approach to Scale*

If wealth creation value chains knew about and supported other wealth creation value chains in their region and/or sector or as cross-sector partners, they could share everything from insights into how to engage investors to strategies for changing policies that are counterproductive and enforcing policies that would make a real difference. Networks of value chains within sectors and regions could emerge and greater creativity could be generated by forging relationships among value chain partners in different sectors and regions. The Ford experiment included structured opportunities for communication and sharing among value chains in each of the three targeted regions: Central Appalachia, the Deep South, and the Lower Rio Grande Valley, which led to recognition of some opportunities for cooperation within each region. However, the Ford Foundation only supported a small number of value chains in each region and these value chains crossed multiple sectors.[4]

As more wealth creation value chains emerge and tangible measured benefits ensue, the demand for organizations to fill the coordinator role will also grow. Ideally, market-driven opportunities will emerge to grow the cadre of experienced value chain coordinators and coaches available to support new coordinators and coaches. As part of the Ford experiment, Yellow Wood facilitated what we called Cross-Regional Convenings that brought participants in all the value chains across the country together face to face. These convenings offered participants and coaches a chance to kick the tires and determine what was working, what wasn't, what issues were shared and what issues were context-specific, thus clarifying and refining the framework. The convenings helped to speed participants along what were often steep learning curves by finding the analogies across different regions, sectors, and value chain dynamics. Convenings helped practitioners identify opportunities to share resources, techniques, and expertise.

Theses convenings were powerful precisely because all the participants were working within the same framework. Each value chain was unique, but as all the participants came to understand the basic principles and functions of a value chain and the characteristics of the different forms of wealth they could begin to compare notes. Coordinators were able to learn from each other across regions and across sectors. However, there was still a lingering concern that each Ford grantee would be judged not on the basis of their contribution to shared learning, but strictly on the basis of their individual results. Both are important. There is no substitute for learning that is developed through face-to-face interactions. It is "expensive" in terms of time and resources but a bargain compared with the resources it takes to continuously re-invent the wheel instead of learning from one's peers.

As more organizations adopt this approach and commit to the principles on which it is based, opportunities to share what is being learned, and thus speed up the learning curve related to applied sustainability can also accelerate based on demand by the value chains themselves. As long as the principles are followed, self-interest can lead to shared interest and ultimately the common interest that is a more equitable and sustainable economy derived from ongoing investment in multiple forms of wealth can result.

Conclusion

WealthWorks is an economic development framework that offers a systematic approach to creating market-driven opportunities in communities and regions by intentionally engaging a wide range of relevant partners in turning those opportunities into results that both build and capture wealth that sticks. WealthWorks is not a silver bullet; it is hard work without guarantees. But we know that it can work right now to improve the livelihoods of economically marginalized people and places. The world we live in is filled with unrealized opportunities for connection that breaks down isolation and brings underutilized resources into productive use. By beginning with self-interest we can find shared interests tied directly to economic activity and we can create systems of production and consumption that allow ongoing reinvestment in the multiple stocks of wealth required for true sustainability.

At this historical moment when so much is uncertain and the pendulum has swung so far in the direction of inequality in ownership of and access to financial wealth in particular, it is imperative to experiment with a variety of ways to integrate the power of market forces for good. We do not yet know how to manage an economy that does no harm and we will not learn how without being willing to try and without learning from the mistakes we make along the way and taking corrective action. Now is the time to harness new ways of thinking, new technologies, and new relationships to build a more inclusive economy from the ground up, with faith that there are enough people in enough sectors, businesses and institutions that want to find win–win–win solutions for themselves, their partners, and the planet so that together we can make progress.

This work does not require broad changes in federal or state policy to begin; it requires digging deeply into the potential of place and sector, reaching out to those we never expected to be in relationship with, and learning the specifics of what needs to change and how it needs to change to conceptualize, pilot, implement, and institutionalize wealth creation value chains that connect economically marginalized people and places to the economic mainstream through investment-driven relationships with demand partners.

There are many groups in the United States and around the globe working to achieve outcomes similar to those advanced by WealthWorks, but they lack a shared framework, language, and approach that would elevate and connect their efforts across time and space. The framework and principles that is WealthWorks can provide a shared language and tools such as value chain mapping, the Wealth Matrix, and outcome measurement of multiple forms of wealth to enhance and accelerate learning.

What we call the approach doesn't matter; what matters is a commitment to all of its principles. We must enhance and accelerate our learning in applied sustainability if we want to create a healthy world for those of here now and future generations all over the world. Instead of wishing for changes that will not spontaneously arise, we have the opportunity to push

158 *Taking a Wealth Creation Approach to Scale*

changes one wealth creation value chain at a time with confidence that the system shifts we will engender will add up and, as they do, our collective resilience will increase.

Notes

1 Estimate of nominal US GDP in the third quarter of 2018 provided by US Bureau of Economic Analysis.
2 Ratner, S. E. and Wyckoff, B. (2015). *Gender Sensitive Access to Markets: A Training Handbook*. ActionAid. Retrieved from: http://actionaid.org/sites/default/files/gender_sensitive_access_to_market_2_e-book_final.pdf
3 Kubisch, A. C., Topolsky, J., Gray, J., Pennekamp, P., and Gutierrez, M. (2008). *Our Shared Fate: Bridging the Rural–Urban Divide Creates New Opportunities for Prosperity and Equity*. University of Missouri. Retrieved from: http://exten sion.missouri.edu/exceed/documents/BridgingUrbanRuralDivide2008.pdf
4 For more information about the Ford Experiment, visit http://www.yellowwood. org and search for "Formulating a Sustainable Economic Development Process." There you will find four interim reports and a final report on the Ford experiment.

Index

ActionAid 76, 150
Appalachian Regional Commission 43
Appalachian Sustainable Development 35, 142, 145
Arkansas Green Energy Network (AGEN) 106, 132–33
Aspen Institute 77: Community Strategies Group 142, 150

Banfield, Edward C. 12
Black Belt Treasures 95
Blackwell, Angela Glover 3, 5
Bourdieu, Pierre 12, 13
Braungart, Michael 105–106, 110
built capital 12–13, 16, 84, 105–106, 126–127

capitalism 26n16, 45, 71
Carolina Textile District 71–72
Center for Disease Control 84
Central Appalachian Network (CAN) 119, 152,
circular economy 104–107
coaches n18, 143–144, 156: coaching 143–144
collaborative investing 96–98
common interest 141, 156
common resources 60
Communities Unlimited 40, 64, 106–107, 125, 132–133
community benefits agreements 59
community covenants and easements 58–59
community currencies 60
community development 1–2, 34, 46–47: practitioners 106, 112
community endowments 59
community fees and taxes 58

Community Foundation of South Central New York 98
community land trusts 54–55
Community Reinvestment Act 92
Community Roots 144, 150
community wealth 10, 16, 25, 41, 51, 55, 58, 84, 99
comparative advantage 39, 42, 126, 153
consumption 7, 18–19, 42–43, 84, 102, 105–106, 108, 114, 127: consumers as co-producers 106, 108–111; exploitation 21–26, 32
control 7, 32, 48–53: structures of 53–62
cooperatives 53–54, 80, 154
coordinators 33, 70, 75, 85, 87, 92–93, 97, 100, 118–119: as transactional partners 142; identifying and enabling 144–146; roles of 139–143;
Costco 76–77
Craft3 24
Cross-Regional Convenings 156
crowdfunding 15, 91, 94–95
cultural capital 13, 129
Custom Ink 108

Dabson, Brian 43
Deep South Community Agriculture Network (DSCAN) 5, 21, 45, 103, 152
Dell Corporation 104
demand 6, 29–31, 33–35, 46, 64, 70, 75–79, 89, 108–110, 148, 152: demand-driven 64; demand partner(s) 6, 30, 66, 82, 86, 93, 119, 147–148, 152–153; effective demand 60, 66–67, 108–110; ineffective demand 60, 67–68, 81,108; nascent demand 68–69
Development Corporation of Brownsville, Texas (CDCB) 40

160 *Index*

ecological footprint 42
economically marginalized 4–7, 34–35, 48, 69, 81, 86, 96, 102, 106, 108, 110, 121, 124, 138, 154, 157
Economic Development Administration 43
Edwards-Orr, Laura 79
Emergent Media Center at Champlain College 31
Emerging Changemakers Network 89, 143
employee ownership 54
externalities 2, 31, 76, 114

Fahe 37–39, 52, 73, 109, 121, 125, 128–129, 132, 145, 152
Fair Food Network 94
Fair Trade 69
Federal Reserve Bank of Atlanta 56
Federal Home Loan Board 128
financial assets 7, 9, 13–14, 115 *see also* financial capital
financial capital 13–15, 89, 114–115, 130
Flora, Cornelia and Jan 9
flows 15–17, 23–24, 42, 43–44, 53, 58, 114–115
Ford Foundation 88, 89, 146, 150, 156
Fremont Area Community Foundation 32, 85, 99, 150

Galbraith, John Kenneth 10
Greater Kanawha Community Foundation 9, 150
governance 49, 55, 60, 61–62, 141

Hanifan, Lyda Judson 11
Harvard Business School 110
Heineken Mexico 75
horizontal integration 31–32, 48

ImpactAlpha 84
import substitution 69
inclusivity 39–41, 68, 70, 86–87, 92, 102, 106–108, 125, 134, 153, 157: inclusive business 79–82; inclusive value chains 98
income 3, 5, 7, 14, 19, 23, 25, 44, 52, 56–57, 84, 109, 113–116, 121, 151: "income" 13, 17, 19, 21–22, 25, 30, 49
individual capital 10, 16, 50–51, 79, 119, 153
inequality 3, 7, 10, 14, 61, 115, 157
iIntellectual capital 9–10, 11, 22, 39, 52, 85, 89, 124–126

interventions **20**, 25, 41, 72, 76, 117, 119, 121, 124, 125–126, 128, 132–134, 145–46: designing 126, 134
intrapreneur 77
investing 11, 12, 13–15, 55, 85–88, 105, 116, 120: investment partner 30–31, 36; philanthropic investment 87, 146; private investment 14, 89, 96, 107; public investment 15, 58, 155; *see also* collaborative investing
isolation 15–16, 32, 41, 43, 64, 111, 116, 148, 154, 157

Jacobs, Jane 11
jobs 2, 5–6, 15–17, 19, 29, 40, 51, 113, 115: job creation 4–5, 19, 74

Kentucky Sustainable Energy Alliance 125
King, Jim 92, 145

LaFarge Corporation 109
Leadership in Energy and Environmental Design (LEED) 70
local ownership 4, 56–57, 141
Lyons, Tom 139

MacArthur Foundation 98
market driven 19, 38, 43, 45–46, 78, 87, 94, 98, 106, 110, 129, 132, 139, 146, 147, 148, 154–157: *see also* demand driven
McDonough, William 105–106, 110
McIntosh SEED 6, 103, 144
Meadows, Donella 23, 71
measurement 7: activities versus goals 117–118; aggregation 130; attribution versus contribution 46, 118; baseline conditions 25, 117, 119, 121, 135; extractive versus participatory 131: framing measures 136–137; ongoing 116, 131; narrative 132, 136; systems change 135–136
Michigan State University Extension 32, 85
Mid-State Technical College, Wisconsin 148
Mission controlled ownership 57–58
Mountain Association for Community Economic Development (MACED) 11, 67–68, 125, 127, 130, 142, 152
multi-solving 7, 24, 25, 97
municipally owned enterprises 55

Index   161

National Association of Development Organizations (NADO) 143, 150
National Cooperative Business Association 36
National Wildlife Federation 11
natural capital 12, 21, 50, 105, 127
New Economics Foundation 22
new normal 36, 46, 135, 138, 145
New River Center for Energy Research and Training 38
Nielson Global 77
Norwood, Jessica 89, 91. 143

Opportunities Credit Union 110
Organically Grown Company 58: Perpetual Purpose Driven Trust 58
Ostrom, Elinor 60–61
ownership 7, 49: and place 50–53; structures of 53–58; shared 53; transitions 62

Passeron, Jean-Claude 13
perfect information 70–71, 74
phases of Implementation 33: exploration 33–35, 61, 65, 73, 76, 87, 89, 93, 99, 103, 107, 121–122, 124–125, 133, 134–136, 145, 146; implementation 36 *see also* scale; institutionalization 36, 46 *see also* new normal; proof of concept 35–36, 46, 87, 92–94, 99, 107, 122, 124, 130, 134, 143, 146, 147
philanthropic 57, 87–88, 104, 136, 145, 146
place-based 7, 15, 41–42, 48, 50–52, 56, 58, 59, 89, 91, 96, 118, 130
political capital 11–12, 25, 36, 49, 60, 85, 91, 100, 128, 154, policy 11, 22, 49, 72–73, 91, 128, 130, 135, 155, 157; policy-makers 107, 123, 136
Popova, Maria 77
positive deviance 40
poverty 3–5, 12, 23–41, 43, 56–57, 64–65, 77, 81, 111, 116, 121
private Sector 70, 81, 147
profitability 62, 73–74, 88–89, 104: profit maximizing behavior 74–75
public ownership 55–56

Red Tomato 78–79
regional economies 1, 5, 7, 42, 152,154: Cross-Regional Convenings 156; cross-regional cooperation 153, 156; regional development 43–46; regional hubs 150

Region 5 Development Commission, Minnesota 150, 155
Rendville Art Works 127
resilience 36, 71, 78–79
Rensselearville Institute 87
Riefler, Dr. Guy 12
risk 35, 80, 81, 94, 95, 97, 100, 109, 134, 140: risk mitigation 74, 93, 100, 120
Robert Putnam 11
Rural Action 35, 105, 120, 127, 136, 142, 144,
Rural Community Assistance Partnership (RCAP) 144, 150
Rural Development Initiatives 97, 150
rural peripheries 43–44
Rural Policy Research Institute 43

Sabraw, John 127
Sacramento Area Council of Governments 44–45
savings 13–14, 84, 89, 130 *see also* investment
scale ix, 7, 24, 30, 35–36, 45–47, 52, 64, 77, 88–89, 93–95, 106, 117, 121, 128, 133, 141, 145
Schumacher, E.F. 12
self-interest 8, 13, 31, 32, 48, 56, 61, 68, 69, 71, 75, 78, 79, 85, 86, 88, 92, 99, 140, 145, 156,
shared interest 71, 73, 78, 82, 124, 140–141, 155, 156. 157
social capital 10–11, 41, 49, 120–124, 128
Social Impact Bonds 95–96
social impact investing 88
Social Justice Bonds 96
South Texas Adult Resource and Training Center 65
Sterman, John 24
stocks 15–16, 135, 157
supply chain 28–29, 76–77
Sustainable Food Lab 76
sustainable livelihoods 3, 7, 29, 40, 114, 151
systems change 7, 33, 52, 88, 109, 148: systems thinking 23–24; with investors 94–100; *see also* measurement, *see also* scale

Tellus Institute 95
Tillitson Fund 150

underutilized resources 5, 33, 61, 91, 118, 134, 157
University of Michigan Health System 16
USDA Rural Development 39

162 *Index*

value chain 29

Wake Forest University School of Community Law and Business Clinic 62, 89
wealth: people-based and place-based 50–51, 52, 59, 86, 92; *see also* built capital, cultural capital, financial capital, individual capital, intellectual capital, natural capital, political capital, social capital
wealth creation value chains 29–33: beneficiaries 32, 86–87, 135; bottlenecks 146–147; chainlets 43, 152; demand partners 6, 82, 86, 93, 147, 30, 152–153; gaps 126, 146–147, 153; investment partners 30, 93–94; maps 122–123, 135; relationships 6, 31–33, 52, 71, 87, 121, 138, 153 *see also* social capital; sectors 32, 34, 81, 152, 156; supporting partners 30, 34, 49, 64, 66; transactional partners 30, 34, 41, 65, 66, 71, 119, 148;
wealth matrix 19–21, 88, 119, 132–134, 141, 155, 157: as tool for planning 134
WealthWorks framework and approach 4–5, 9, 11, 25, 34, 41–42, 44, 46, 50, 51, 67, 69, 70, 71, 81, 92, 97, 118, 135, 137, 139, 142, 148, 150, 151, 155: as bridge between economic and community development 40; assumptions 5; guiding principles 6–7; *see also* phases of implementation
WealthWorks value chain 11, 35, 36, 71, 81, 85, 95, 105, 106, 120, 121, 124–130, 132, 135, 137, 138–139, 141, 145
World Bank 22, 109
World Economic Forum 85
Wyckoff, Barbara 139

Yellow Wood Associates 144
You Get What You Measure® 131